W. B. YEATS AND TRADITION

THE MACMILLAN COMPANY
NEW YORK · CHICAGO
DALLAS · ATLANTA · SAN FRANCISCO
LONDON · MANILA
BRETT-MACMILLAN LTD.
TORONTO

W. B. YEATS AND TRADITION

by

F. A. C. WILSON

New York
The Macmillan Company
1958

FOR JOANNA
Perch' io non spero di tornar già mai

CONTENTS

PREFACE

THIS BOOK IS centrally a study of the last five plays Yeats wrote: *The King of the Great Clock Tower, A Full Moon in March, The Herne's Egg, Purgatory* and *The Death of Cuchulain*. These are, of course, very obscure works, and they cannot be approached without full understanding of Yeats's theories both of symbolism and of the drama. An introductory essay therefore explains these theories, or as much of them as is to the purpose, and I then proceed to a detailed study of the plays themselves. A third section considers those lyrics which are related; among other poems such difficult works as 'Byzantium', 'The Black Tower', and 'Cuchulain Comforted'.

An ulterior function of the book is to examine the rationale of Yeats's philosophy. The last plays, and the lyrics which connect with them, are eminently philosophical. Almost the whole of Yeats's thought is relevant and is therefore reconstructed in my essays: they go, indeed, beyond the mere statement of fact into a very thorough investigation of his authorities. My attitude has been frankly sympathetic, in that I have found it less difficult than most writers to accept Yeats's cardinal beliefs, and this, I think, differentiates my book from much previous Yeats criticism.

If the last plays have been misunderstood in the past, this is largely because of the difficulties presented by their symbolism. Most of Yeats's mature symbols are used in the course of their composition, and I have tried to relate each to its literary or philosophical 'source'. Yeats's symbolism is not, as has been thought, fluid, but it is for the most part fixed and constant, so that the interpretation of any given image has an ulterior value. The reader who understands the symbol in one context should be able to understand it in all contexts, and to demonstrate that this is so is part of the purpose of my book.

These essays, it will by now be clear, are interpretative; and my attempts at evaluation are no more than casual. I have usually given my own estimate, as for example of *The Herne's Egg*, but I have done so in full awareness that I may have overpraised the work. A result of the New Criticism, or so it seems to me, is that Yeats's stature as a poet has been too rashly guessed at; his poetry has been evaluated before it has been perfectly understood. The present essays may be a first step in the reversal of this process: I have tried, at all events, to give a definitive statement of meaning, in the hope that another critic, who will be concerned with evaluation, may use my work as a foundation upon which to build.

The shaping of my arguments has involved a certain number of omissions. Chief among these, I think, is the absence of any sufficient reference to Nietzsche, whose early work was of considerable importance to Yeats's developing thought. The play which owes most to Nietzsche is, however, beyond doubt *Calvary*, and only faint traces of his philosophy survive in the later verse. I have therefore decided to postpone this whole issue to a book which I contemplate writing, and which should be concerned with the earlier dance-plays and the poetry of the middle period. I have also postponed to that book a study of G. R. S. Mead's work on the Sacred Dances of Jesus, whose relevance to Yeats's poetry was very kindly pointed out to me by Mr. Iain Fletcher. This material, if I had used it here, would have confirmed my interpretation of *A Full Moon In March*.

While I do not think that my terminology is in any way ambiguous, some of Yeats's own terms may require a preliminary definition. He speaks of himself as a student of 'heterodox mysticism', and both these words are liable to misinterpretation. By 'heterodox' Yeats did not at all mean 'eccentric': he felt that his philosophy was quite orthodox when viewed *sub specie aeternitatis*, and he implied merely that it *seemed* heterodox—in the sense of being unfashionable—by the disintegrating standards of the present day. By 'mysticism' Yeats could and did mean either of two things. He might mean the individual mystic's quite personal insight into the nature of things, or he might mean the great 'subjective' tradition of mystical philosophy, based as it is upon the correspondence of many of these insights. In this book I have used the word 'heterodox' of Yeats in his own sense, and I have used the word 'mysticism'—for want of an alternative—in each of the two senses he does himself. I think that my meaning, in any particular context, will be quite clear.

Some clarification will be needed of my system of quotation. I have quoted usually the translation of an author which Yeats himself had read. In the case of Plotinus, however, he knew both Taylor's and MacKenna's translations; he clearly preferred MacKenna as a stylist, but Taylor's elaborate commentaries made his versions also useful. My quotations may be from either Taylor or MacKenna, and I have used, in any given context, the version I think it most probable that Yeats had in mind. Where there is nothing to choose, I have preferred Mac-Kenna. In the case of the pre-Socratics, on the other hand, I do not know what translations Yeats will have read—he often differs from Burnet—and here, in one place, the translation is my own.

Yeats is an eclectic poet, and any attempt to survey his sources will involve a number of notes. I have tried, as far as possible, not to distract the reader's eye. Matter of first importance is given in the form of footnotes, while all supplementary material is relegated to the back of the book. Arabic numerals are used to indicate the location of these notes. The last section of the book contains also an index and a bibliography, where will be found listed, together with the books, the several unpublished theses I have used.

I do not suppose that I should have written this book without the advice and encouragement of two people, Kathleen Raine and Mr. T. R. Henn. When I first came to Cambridge I was overjoyed to be able to work with Mr. Henn, whom I knew well enough to be the most distinguished of all Yeats's critics. His wisdom in questions of art, and that ulterior wisdom which made him the first scholar to recognise Yeats's greatness as a thinker, have always been at my disposal, and his courtesy and 'natural kindness' have placed me under a very great debt. Knowing Kathleen Raine has been of equal importance to me. I have been able to read her—as yet unfinished—work on Blake, and I have drawn on her research in the pages which follow. We have also had many talks on the traditional religious symbolism, and I must thank her, both for all she has taught me and for her friendship, based as it is upon that perennial philosophy by which we both live.

I am also most grateful to Dr. M. C. Bradbrook and Dr. D. Daiches, who read, and helped me to improve, the draft of two of my chapters; to Marilyn Denton, who visited Cambridge from America and placed her knowledge of Yeats's prosody at my disposal; to Edward Engleberg, for several very lively discussions of Yeats's theory of poetry; to Rupert and Helen Gleadow, whose knowledge of the subjective tradition did much to reinforce my own; to Hiroko Ishibashi, for all that she has taught me of Zen Buddhism and the Japanese Noh theatre; and of course to Mrs. Yeats, for her kindness, hospitality and assistance to me. With this I am indebted to the editor of *Modern Philology*, in which periodical some of my findings first appeared.

It may seem to the reader that I have rejected some previous Yeats criticism, but I should like to express my indebtedness to those scholars who have been before me in the field. I could not have come to the conclusions I have reached without the benefit of their researches. A scholar whose work was not available until my text was in course of completion and on whom I have drawn in only one place is Sr. Giorgio Melchiori; and I should like to point to his research as corroboration of my own. Sr. Melchiori's expected essay on *The Player Queen* has not yet appeared, or it might have made my own notes on the play super-fluous. As it is, the reader who doubts whether Yeats was really so eclectic a writer as I suggest may be referred to the one full-length study by Sr. Melchiori we so far have, the long essay *Leda And The Swan*.

F. A. C. WILSON,

St. Catharine's College, Cambridge.

April 10th, 1957.

NOTE FOR THE AMERICAN EDITION

Some of my critics have been antagonised by my writing (of 'Byzantium') that 'Yeats did not write mere imagery' and, it being impossible in this edition radically to revise my text, I should at least explain my meaning. I am here drawing a distinction between the 'image' as decoration or local colour and the poetic symbol; and my meaning, which I vehemently reaffirm, is that Yeats seldom if ever used an image for purposes of local colour alone, and that all or almost all his images have symbolic meaning in addition to the literal.

INTRODUCTORY.

PART ONE

INTRODUCTORY

CHAPTER ONE

THE SUBJECTIVE TRADITION

I

YEATS'S LAST PLAYS are difficult but not intractable: there is a sense in which he is always one of the easiest of modern poets to follow, but to be able to follow him we must have the right approach. The 'new criticism', I had better say at the outset, seems to me to impose conditions which make such an approach impossible. It may be desirable in poetry that the words on the page should make their full meaning felt without recourse to any ulterior body of knowledge, and the current tendency in criticism is to apply these presuppositions to Yeats: but Yeats was not a new critic, and he knew nothing of its disciplines, nor (I suspect) would he have been much in sympathy with them if he had known. I hope it may become classical in Yeats criticism that his poetry does require for its full resolution an ulterior body of knowledge, just as Yeats himself felt that Shelley's or that Blake's poems demanded such anterior information; for Yeats, like Shelley and Blake, belonged to the tradition of 'heterodox mysticism' (his own term), and on a knowledge of this convention the full understanding of his poetry depends. I do not mean that this, or any, information is needed for a first, superficial reading: the 'poetry' on the page will no doubt partially communicate of its own accord, and the reader may afterwards guess at the radical meaning; but guesses of course may conflict, or be simply wrong, and Yeats criticism has been much impeded by both these misadventures. Thus it has been possible for Cleanth Brooks[1] to demonstrate, by what I hope to show is a mistaken survey of Yeats's authorities, the 'total meaning' of 'Byzantium', and for John Crowe Ransom[2] to show the technique by which the new criticism could have arrived at the identical (mistaken) reading without recourse to any authorities at all. But if the criticism of poetry is more, as I believe it is, than a mere exercise in taste, ingenuity and what Yeats called 'opinion'; if a poem demands of us, for its total appreciation, that we shall know it totally (its full meaning, for the poet, as much as any other facet of its beauty); and that we shall live, perhaps for years, with the total possession of this work of art before pronouncing on its ultimate value; then Yeats's poems and plays clearly require a definitive statement of meaning, proved up to the hilt, before the final evaluation of his stature as an artist can be thought possible. It is the function of this study to provide such an exegesis for a small part of Yeats's work, and to suggest the analytical process to which the remainder of his poems commend themselves.

I have begun from a reference to the 'heterodox tradition in mysticism' on which Yeats founds himself, and this tradition is central to his poetry: the interested reader may compare Neville Rogers' book on Shelley,[3] or Fränger's on Hieronymus Bosch,[4] as showing how it affected the work of other artists. Like Bosch and Shelley, Yeats systematised his attitude to religion, and he founded himself upon much the same principles as themselves: his knowledge of the convention to which all three subscribe was not in any sense 'fragmentary' (as has been supposed), but broader than theirs, broader perhaps than that of any other English poet. I do not think it could be said that Yeats's position was inimical to the Christian; he accepted the Christian revelation; but, in human sympathy and in sincere conviction, he could not accept it as exclusive: the Upanishads, Buddhism, the religion of Platonism, the Jewish Kabbala and the Neoplatonic tradition of alchemy (of all of which he made himself a student) seemed to him also meaningful and valid; and he finished with a philosophy that would enable him to connect all these traditions, and to concur with Blake's maxim that 'all religions are one'. It is characteristic of the heterodox mystic to make a synthesis of this kind; and it is characteristic of him too (as Blake did) to prefer some aspects of what will seem the universal religion above others: Shelley was content with the Platonic, Bosch preferred the alchemical position, Blake and Yeats a broader complex of the alchemical, the Jewish and the Greek. Now it is the case that there runs (or has seemed to the English poets to run) through Platonic, alchemical and Kabbalist doctrine a certain tendency towards a systematic, even perhaps inflexible symbolism: and this symbolism Yeats found, as the other artists named in this paragraph did also, and used copiously and faithfully throughout his verse. It is not my purpose to try to assess how far this symbolic convention is in fact consistent within any or all of the religions mentioned, or how well Yeats's symbolism correlates with Blake's, or Shelley's, or Hieronymus Bosch's; though I shall touch later on several parallels. But in so far as the convention was believed to exist, and in so far as Yeats faithfully converted it into his own poetry, it is clearly indispensable to the full understanding of his meaning. With it behind us, if he employs it consistently and with fidelity, little in his work can ever be obscure; without it, and especially if Yeats intends us to have it, we are likely to run into uncertainty. Here I should perhaps add that I have no personal doubt that Yeats, especially in his last plays, does presuppose in his more serious readers a knowledge of the convention. He writes at two levels, as other dramatists have done before him: the surface detail is there for the general reader, and the ulterior allusions for the *cognoscenti*. There is a very real sense in which Yeats is a visionary writing for the visionary, or for readers who feel in full sympathy with his beliefs: if we cannot at least inform ourselves as though we shared them, there is a level at which (as with Blake) his poetry is not for us.

These are general considerations; and it may be as well to postpone study of Yeats's symbolism as such until we have understood the impulse which led him to find it: the incentive which made him take up the theological or theosophical studies he did. One cannot suppose that he was motivated by a mere dispassionate interest in comparative religion. Denis Saurat, whose *Literature and Occult Tradition* seems to me to combine the virtues with some of the deficiencies of a pioneering work, suggests several general psychological factors which may predispose a poet in the direction of heterodoxy. Speaking, as of 'one of the most curious phenomena of modern literature', of 'the existence among a certain number of great poets, between whom there is often but a slight direct connection, of a common, non-Christian stock of myths and of ideas—of symbols which seem to have a particular fascination';[5] and listing among these poets (we may think over-zealously) 'Spenser, Milton, Blake, Shelley, Emerson and Whitman in Anglo-Saxon literature; Goethe, Heine, Wagner, Nietzsche in German; Hugo, Vigny, Lamartine and Leconte de Lisle in France';[6] Saurat concludes that they were guided by:

> the community of moral ideas. Nearly all are in revolt against the orthodox conception of God . . . have preached liberty, justified sensuality, and claimed for the individual the right to follow his inclinations, because these inclinations are divine.[7]

This is no doubt a secondary predisposing factor in Yeats's case also, though one would wish to have it clearly said that human sympathy and generosity were the precipitants which led him, and Shelley, and Blake, to wish a more tolerant morality on humanity than the orthodox Christian as they saw it preached in the contemporary pulpit: the denial of the five senses seemed to Yeats, as to Blake, a form of spiritual 'death'. But the primary motive for a poet's looking beyond Christianity to unorthodoxy, and not, say, cultivating atheism, must naturally be a certain visionary susceptibility, and this Saurat allows. He continues, however, with a significant reservation:

> While the mystics are above all sentimentalists and generally mediocre as to intellect, the philosophical poets are intellectuals in their own particular way: great lovers of debate, great masters of logical subtleties, rationalists to the very core.[8]

This again one may feel to be a rash statement in Saurat, and I cannot suppose that Yeats would have stigmatised the mystics—Plotinus, or the architects of the Upanishads, or even St. John of the Cross—as he does here: but the distinction is worth notice. Yeats was a master of logical subtleties, a rationalist to the very core, as well as having a certain visionary susceptibility, and the fact goes far to explain his occasional levity, his *Selbstironie*, his intellectual unsentimentality and toughness; qualities which have led most of his critics to regard his rather remote personal philosophy with suspicion, as if it were insincere. Yeats was an occultist and a Platonist, but his thought was not so transcendental as to have excluded the possibility of the *bon mot*; and his levity is sometimes savage:

> Throw likely couples into bed
> And knock the others down.[9]

The 'philosophical poets' of Yeats's stamp tend to balance their spirituality against a certain compensatory earthiness.

When we think of Yeats himself, however, it may be useful to concentrate in the first place on his visionary sensibility, rather than on his earthbound irony and wit; his vision, which is the constructive side of his talent, has too often been denied him in the past. I may perhaps define my own attitude in saying that I see no trace of charlatanry, or of the *poseur*, in Yeats's successive prose definitions of his religious position, or in his speculative writing; there may perhaps be remote allusion, an Irish habit of parading authority and knowledge, and sometimes an element of levity, or of gaiety simply: but I do not know that gaiety in itself need be inimical to the life of visionary experience, or that a poet's determination to display his often rather exotic learning need make that learning spurious. I shall hope later to demonstrate that

Yeats's authorities, Platonism, the Kabbala, the rest of Saurat's 'occult tradition', are as genuine as one could wish, and that Yeats himself was as genuinely equipped to receive them: his mind, it seems to me, was extraordinarily sensitive to the distant faiths of history, and in his eyes even the most remote religion could seem to live. With this we have to remember that he was in the best possible sense a religious rebel: he saw much virtue in what have conveniently been regarded as the here-sies of the past, and their adherents seemed to him good men, fighting against oppression for the rights to live and believe. Until recently there has been scant tendency to see things as he saw them, but the past few years have brought him a great deal of extra-literary support. The religion of alchemy, once beneath serious literary consideration, has surely taken on a very different complexion with the publication of *Psychology and Alchemy*:[10] and the achievement of men like Cornelius Agrippa, who 'served human liberty' at the dark close of the middle ages and in circumstances so similar to ours, may be more easily under-stood now that we have Wilhelm Fränger's noble defence.[11] When Yeats medievalises, it may thus be more easy for us to see the middle ages as he himself did, as we have to do if we are to understand his drift: and what we shall see will not be the middle ages of convention, for the nature and balance of the contending forces seemed to Yeats some-thing quite other than what has popularly been supposed. Similarly when he Platonises, we have to remember that the Platonic philosophy was for him a living religion, its history a long struggle to defend what he thought of as truth against the pressures of a changing world: he came to it through the scholarship of such enthusiasts as Thomas Taylor and G. R. S. Mead, and the rationale of his beliefs will seem much more obvious if we approach it (as I have done) in the same way. This is not to say that *A Vision* is necessarily a success, or that it says what it has to say in the most lucid symbolic language at Yeats's disposal: but it does mean that it has its own sturdy integrity, and that it cannot conceivably be thought of as a kind of *jeu d'esprit*. Yeats, and his sources, are only fallible, and it is possible that he is terribly mistaken, but we convict ourselves of false bias if we think of him as insincere.

A Vision is for me the product of acquired learning and of the visionary faculty; that is, Yeats's sanguine conviction of the immortality and the perfectibility of the human soul, and perhaps his conception of a divine pattern working itself out through history, seem to me to have this two-fold root; I am not speaking of the claims he makes for his wife's automatic writing, which are after all peripheral. And here perhaps I should define my terms: years of love for the man and his work have left me in the position of believing that what Yeats meant by visionary experience, the greatest sustaining influence on his life and art, was not substantially other than the state described by more orthodox mystics. I would parallel Eliot:

> I can only say, *there* we have been: but I cannot say where.
> And I cannot say, how long, for that is to place it in time.[12]

And Eliot goes on to depict the visionary state:

> The inner freedom from the practical desire,
> The release from action and suffering, release from the inner
> And the outer compulsion, yet surrounded
> By a grace of sense, a white light still and moving.
> *Erhebung* without motion, concentration
> Without elimination, both a new world
> And the old made explicit, understood
> In the completion of its partial ecstasy,
> The resolution of its partial horror . . .[13]

Yeats, like Eliot, would not have claimed any very consistent knowledge of this condition; both poets saw themselves as 'in the middle way', though Yeats would no doubt have agreed with his mentor Von Hügel that even in the most ordinary soul 'there is, there never can fail to be, some, however implicit, however slight, however intermittent, sense and experience of the Infinite'.[14] Yeats's contact with what he came to call 'reality' came largely in waking reverie: under occult discipline, or simply 'between sleeping and waking', symbols floated up in his mind which seemed, while they lasted, to be of immense spiritual significance, and which he frequently used for later poems: the symbol of a man in golden armour was used in the poem 'The Old Stone Cross':[15] a girl who appeared, her hair aflame, may be remembered in the later lines on 'Berenice's burning hair'.[16] Jungian psychology would, I think, tend not to dismiss these visitations, which occurred often in a self-induced condition approximating to trance, and which often resemble so closely image-sequences Jung traces back to the collective unconscious: Yeats himself attributed them to a momentary contact with 'Anima Mundi'.* And beyond this, that Yeats had known

---

*As for their *function*, Yeats thought that they represented the soul's attempt to clarify to itself the perceptions of visionary communication, using the only language available to it.

visionary communication in a more direct form we know from those moving passages in his 1930 diary which deal with his experience of the spiritual world and conclude by quoting Shelley:[17]

> For love, and beauty, and delight,
> There is no death, nor change: their might
> Exceeds our organs, which endure
> No light, being themselves obscure.

With the lines from 'Burnt Norton' I have quoted one might profitably compare Yeats's (which is the Platonic) definition of the visionary world, as it is given in that diary, or as I shall reconstruct it in my essay on *The Death of Cuchulain*. I do not think the two are very different.

Where Yeats and Eliot differ is, essentially, in the type of discipline which they felt the visionary world demanded of them. Eliot, from Yeats's point of view, would be a classic type of the *objective* (or 'primary' personality): that is, he accepted the Christian procedure of purification through renunciation, and sensing human inadequacy and impurity tried to perfect his life by self-denial:

> Emptying the sensual with deprivation,
> Cleansing affection from the temporal.[18]

Yeats thought of himself, however, as what he called a *subjective* (or 'antithetical' personality): that is to say, he preferred the road to visionary experience which leads through the sense of self-sufficiency and joy. For the belief that there was this alternative road, he relied primarily upon the Upanishads, as I shall presently show: a late essay turns on the point that, when the human Self can truly say and know 'I am Brahma', or identify itself, in all its understood purity, with divinity, the way to mystical experience is open to it.[19] It is central to Yeats's thought that he allows these two contrary disciplines, which are not seen as militating against each other in any way; he develops his theory by assigning all human personality to either the objective or the subjective mould; and the two categories, looked at from the Christian point of view, reflect very adequately his distinction between orthodox and heterodox mysticism. In the Christian world, the orthodox mystic would be the objective: in the India of the Upanishads, subjectivity would have been the norm.

It is obvious that Yeats's hypothesis is not invalid in itself; it is founded upon a distinction between two opposite types of mind. One

might say that Eliot senses beatitude as something infinitely far removed from humanity, Yeats as something infinitely near at hand:
Yeats certainly approximates to what psychology would call the
ecstatic condition, as we have work like 'A Prayer For My Daughter'[20]
to show. But mysticism of this kind is not uncommon; and this fact
has to condition our whole attitude to Yeats's thought. Yeats's response
to visionary experience was joyous: it convinced him that the human
mind was 'blesséd', that its origin was heaven, and that it still dimly
retained the memory of its home; man's soul seemed to him a thing of
immense stature, and it seemed to extend its experience over enormous
vistas of time. If we accept his initial response as valid, it is natural for
him to have adopted reincarnation, the pre-natal memory, and most
of the other articles of his personal faith; and if we are not able to
accept that possibility (Yeats would himself have added) we are rejecting all Eastern mysticism and most of the received religions of the
world. For response of this kind may be unEuropean, but we cannot
stigmatise it as erratic: it is the response of Plotinus and the Vedanta,
the Hindu and the Greek, and Yeats's logic is founded upon their logic,
his philosophy upon theirs. Nothing that could be called central to his
thought is ever unconventional, though the conventions he follows may
be unfamiliar to the European; if we attack A Vision at any vital point,
we shall usually be attacking some authority much more powerful than
Yeats himself. A Vision is thus firmly founded upon received belief,
which seems to me what is meant when we say that a poet's thought is
eminently defensible. And I do not think that this argument buys Yeats
respectability at any cost, or that the Eastern religious insight could be
thought less responsible than the European. If Yeats is an ecstatic, then
Eliot might equally well be called a depressive mystic: the categories of
vision are to some extent supplementary, and we may well find room
for either kind.

Such at least are the contentions of modern psychology, which has
done so much to confirm Yeats in all that he supposed. One of the most
remarkable parallels in contemporary religious speculation is that between Yeats's thought and Jung's; it is not merely, as Graham Hough
has noted,[21] that Jung has lent Yeats support in his theory of Anima
Mundi, the collective unconscious; but the general effect of his independent researches is to bear Yeats out at every turn. This is especially
true of Yeats's claims for his religious position. Jung's theory of a
mandala symbolism, working through the collective unconscious to
enforce a recurrent imagery upon all the received religions of the
world, has led him to re-examine all Yeats's sources, Platonism, the

Kabbala, the religion of alchemy; and his conclusion is that none of these apparently exotic faiths is beneath our consideration. Their symbolic systems, as he shows at very great length, are in correspondence with one another and with those of more orthodox religion, which is to say that each of them is based upon archetypal religious perception:

> [The symbols of heterodoxy] are all variants of certain central types, and these occur universally. They are the primordial images, from which the religions each draw their universal truth.[22]

When disciplines of this kind can be shown to centre upon man's deepest aspirations and beliefs (to say nothing of a possible influx from outside the individual mind, and so from something quite beyond human comprehension) it is difficult to regard them as spurious. Jung, in fact, has been brought to the belief that 'God has expressed himself in many languages and appeared in many forms, and that all these statements are true'.[23]* But they are not, obviously, equally 'true' to any one intelligence, and this has led him to a distinction which is precisely Yeats's; between the *objective* thinker, who will tend towards Christianity, and the *subjective*, who will tend towards heterodoxy and the religions of the East. Jung is by no means in favour of the orthodox European synthesis: he deprecates the Christian tendency to regard Godhead as something external to humanity, and thus outside the Self:

> The Western attitude, with its emphasis on the object, tends to fix the ideal Christ in its outward aspect and thus to rob it of its mysterious relation to the inner man.[24]

The subjective position, he says, is in many ways the more stable:

> The Eastern attitude (more particularly the Indian) is the other way about: everything, highest and lowest, is in the (transcendental) subject. Accordingly the significance of the Atman, the Self, is heightened beyond all bounds. But with western man the value of the Self falls to zero: hence the universal depreciation of the soul in the west.[25]

---

*Jung anticipates the objection that it 'is impossible for contradictory religious statements to be true':

'The only statements which have psychological validity concerning the God-image are either paradoxes or antinomies. Non-ambiguity and non-contradiction are one-sided and thus unsuited to express the incomprehensible.'

I cannot pursue this argument into more detail—I would refer the reader to the preface to *Psychology and Alchemy*—but perhaps I have done enough to span the deep places in Yeats's thought. The theory of the mandala confirms Yeats in the importance he attached to his authorities, and (incidentally, as we shall see) in his theory of symbolism; and, where Jung goes beyond it, the conclusions of the two men are much the same.

All this, I think, would have been much more obvious if Yeats had restricted himself to a single creed, but the religion of *A Vision* is a compendium from many faiths. Some of Yeats's sources are extremely remote—Egyptian theurgy and the Greek mystery religions are representative examples—and so unlikely a synthesis has naturally been received with suspicion. But if Yeats combines subjectivity with an interest in archaic myth, these are faculties which it is by no means unusual to find in conjunction: I will quote the philosophical scholarship of Maud Bodkin, whose moving statement of her own personal position will be seen to bear Yeats out:

> For those of us who cannot accept the dogmas of any one religion as uniquely revealed by God, faith may be possible that the more universal ideas or patterns underlying these doctrines are God-given, their evolution into greater clarity and relevance to life part of the divine intent for man.[26]

This is the Blakean concept that 'all religions are one'; and Bodkin goes on to remark (as all Yeats's critics should be aware):

> The diversity of form through which different individuals encounter the Divine: the failure of forms significant in one life to make any similar appeal to another.[27]

She quotes classical scholarship to show how much of value there may be, for a given individual, in even the most primitive or obscure religious myth:

> Jane Harrison has indicated the unseen forces present in the manifestations of Greek and more primitive religion: her own conviction that the approach to unseen reality which she studied in so many strange myths and rituals was a thing of immense significance, 'worth a lifetime's devotion'.[28]

And she goes on to suggest, as evidence of their continuing importance to the human psyche, that symbols from the most primitive religions tend to be thrown up from the collective unconscious in our dreams; she speaks, as a fact demonstrable in Jungian psychology, of:

> the spontaneous production of ancient patterns in the dreams and fantasies of individuals who had no discoverable access to the cultural material in which these patterns were embodied.[29]

That Yeats had fantasies of this kind I have already indicated, and that he had the type of mind which is here under consideration I think there can be no question. He synthesised, one feels, because it was a psychological necessity for him to do so, drawing always upon parallel, 'subjective' faiths: the religions to which he turned all answer the mandala test for validity, and the integrity of his synthesis seems to me to be beyond doubt.

This is not to deny that Yeats's philosophy is strange. The modern reader, I suppose, must often feel at odds with the poet who is also a mystic, and who has nothing finally to offer us save the simplicity, which is also the *terribilità*, of affirmation:

> The awful daring of a moment's surrender
> Which an age of prudence can never retract.[30]

It has always seemed prudent to disparage Yeats as a thinker. And indeed there is much in the detail of his philosophy that one feels has appealed to the poet's, rather than to the logician's, eye; whatever in a faith is beautiful, or simply picturesque, is likely to find a place in Yeats's own system; and since beauty is not always consistent with probability, it may sometimes be hard to understand how he could have believed as he did. Here I think we have to consider both Yeats's idea of his function as an artist (which was as a decorative worker) and beyond this the nature of his personal vision. It is a very easy matter for the ecstatic to believe. We need not of course believe with him —in his elaborate angelology, for instance, or in his theory of a transcendental and divine intersexual love in heaven[31]—but I can see no reason why the informed reader should be unsympathetic: a failure to sympathise with Yeats's position is usually a failure to understand. The highroad to proper understanding of Yeats's poetry lies through his symbolism, and this in turn requires a knowledge of the tradition on which it is based. We may begin by seeing what grounding Yeats had in his tradition.

II

Yeats's intentions may have been good, but his early authorities were hardly respectable. This does not affect the fact that they played a considerable part in shaping his thought. He has himself recorded that his latter-day philosophy was largely a process of exploiting 'with the excitement of new discovery, things known in my youth',[32] and it seems clear that his mature ideas, and even the themes of poems and the plots of plays, can be traced back to these somewhat dubious beginnings. Yeats had fine tact and intelligence and his ideas, as they emerge, are usually much purer than those of his early authorities, but there is this connection.

Growing up in the heyday of the French Symbolist movement, which had its roots in unorthodox mysticism, Yeats turned naturally to the occult. Maeterlinck believed in a 'cosmic subconscious';[33] de Nerval's *Le Rêve et la Vie*, found in his pockets after his suicide, was 'interrupted with Kabbalistic signs and a demonstration of the immaculate conception by geometry';[34] of Villiers de l'Isle Adam, Yeats's friend Symons records that 'whether or not he was indeed a Kabbalist, questions of magic began at an early age to preoccupy him'.[35] What is significant in this is less that Yeats's early heroes were occultists than that they were dilettantes in occultism: the emotional climate of their work shows, often, how immature their approach was (I would instance *Axël*); and the nature of their interests, as Yeats followed them up, led him in the first place to alchemy, to Kabbalism and to ceremonial magic: to the medieval inheritance of occultism, that is, rather than to the heterodox philosophy in any radical form. The disciplines he went to are not necessarily unrewarding in themselves—I think I have shown why the religious perceptions on which they are based should be taken as valid—but the fact remains that for Yeats, for Villiers de l'Isle Adam, for Maeterlinck, a knowledge of medieval occultism alone did not suffice to support a mature and major art. It was not until, in later life, Yeats worked backwards to the Platonists, to the Greek mystery religions, and to a systematic study of the Upanishads—all, I would say, providing him with purer and fuller versions of the subjective philosophy—that his art began to proliferate. Literature, it would seem, cannot thrive on the magical writers alone.

If Yeats's early studies did not leave him with a pure philosophy or a deeply communicative art, at least they provided him with the materials for a theory of symbolism. By 1895, Yeats was very widely read in medieval traditions of imagery: he had not, as I have said, any comprehensive knowledge of the Greek religious symbology, but he had read Taylor's translation of Porphyry, which he quotes as early as *The Celtic Twilight*.[36] This, since Porphyry is a mine of information on the Platonic symbolic system, ensured him at least an insight into that convention. Yeats knew enough, I think, to have noted two salient facts: that there was to some extent a received tradition in ancient symbolism, and that there were also remarkable correspondences where evidence of cultural contact was lacking. It is after all fact proven in scholarship that the Greek mystery religions, and through them Greek philosophy, derived a large part of their symbolism from the ancient Egyptians; that even the Bible bears witness to an influence; and that, since the alchemists were the heirs of the Neoplatonists, a great deal of the received symbolism descended to them.[37] And Mohini Chatterjee will have shown Yeats what Jung has shown the modern reader, that the symbolism of Buddhism and Brahmanism compares closely with this European convention, though here there is less likelihood of a direct influence. All this, I think, Yeats will have gleaned from his own knowledge of comparative religion: there were also the critical writings of his authorities, which were specifically devised to point it out.

Yeats received information with considerable urbanity: he saw, and it seems to me avoided, the pitfalls of dogma into which some of his first authorities fell. We see this from his relations with Magregor Mathers, who introduced him to the Kabbala and arranged his reception into the Order of the Golden Dawn. Mathers understood that there was a subjective tradition, in symbolism as in belief, and the preface to his most important book[38] is meant to bring it out: but he was a fanatical Kabbalist, and was gullible enough to found his exposition upon Jewish popular myth. The Jews, he says, were given the 'secret doctrine' by divine favour, and 'emigrated with it to Ancient Egypt', where it became generally known:

> It was in this way that the Egyptians obtained some knowledge of it and the other Eastern nations could introduce it into their systems.[39]

From the Kabbala, we are further told, 'Pythagoras' and his 'numerical symbolic ideas' will have derived,[40] and through his school the tradition passed into the currency of Platonism and thence to the middle ages. Mathers' theory may perhaps be seen in action in the ritual of the Golden Dawn, which is a curious (and I think an exceptionally tasteless) blend of ancient Egyptian, Kabbalist, medieval and even orthodox

Christian imagery,[41] all, one presumes, felt to be working in concert to the one end. Yeats accepted him where one could, as we have concrete evidence to show: what is purest in Mathers is remembered in so late a poem as 'The Statues',[42] where Pythagoras is presented as the fountainhead of all that is best in European culture; but Yeats's verse traces Greek thought back to ancient Egypt, and not to any Kabbalistic source. He quite clearly refused his authority at the point where Mathers became irrational: the tradition itself seemed, at this stage, a real possibility, but much more evidence was needed as to its origins and scope.

Another of Yeats's authorities was Madame Blavatsky. It is not a part of my purpose to ridicule Madame Blavatsky: she was, doubtless, a poor logician, and her works are made almost unreadable for me by her endlessly reiterative method; but I am content to agree with so responsible a scholar as W. Y. Evans-Wentz that she was a learned if a muddled woman;[43] she was certainly a mine of information for Yeats. One does not, perhaps, outgrow such an authority; one reorientates oneself as regards her, but her work retains part-validity, especially when one's own later researches confirm her conclusions—and much that Yeats was to read confirmed hers. Madame Blavatsky wrote a book, The Secret Doctrine, less to demonstrate that all religions are one than that all symbolisms are one (there must have been a good deal of speculation about this in the occult circles of the time); as fanatical an anti-Semite as Mathers had been a Kabbalist, she does not seriously consider his explanation, but postulates a single parent doctrine, 'one primeval, universal wisdom' now lost, from which all world religions and their symbolisms will have sprung; a source which 'was once the one fountainhead at which were fed . . . the later religions of all nations . . . Buddha, Pythagoras, Neoplatonists, gnostics'.[44] Madame Blavatsky on comparative symbolism is quite fascinating: her great erudition does indeed make out a strong case for the identity, or near-identity, of different religious symbolic systems, though her ulterior explanation may be mistaken. If we want to see how powerfully her demonstrations influenced Yeats, we have only to read his three-volume study of Blake.[45] There, he confidently assumes a subjective tradition, and that Blake (as indeed he did) will have drawn on that tradition: even where he does not know Blake's source, he enforces the traditional interpretation upon his work.

The last years of the 'nineties saw Yeats consolidating his position, as is clear from his elaborate notes to The Wind Among The Reeds.[46] By this time he had read Frazer, the patient studies of ancient Welsh and

Irish symbolism in Rhys's *Celtic Heathendom*, and the *Mabinogion*, and had seen that there were correspondences of usage here also, as indeed there are. Thus we find him remarking on parallels between Celtic and Indian, and even ancient Assyrian symbolism,[47] while the poems themselves are a determined amalgam, drawing upon images from the most diverse faiths. For Yeats had by now unequivocally accepted the postulate of 'a tradition ... older than any European church';[48] what he calls his 'search for the tradition'[49] had led him to folklore (in which he thought something of its imagery persisted); the received symbolisms of the world seemed to him to be inter-related, and he thought of them as legacies from one original faith. The verse of *The Wind Among The Reeds* thus marks the end of Yeats's apprenticeship as a symbolist, though it may not be very successful in itself. He had taken his cultural material and made a synthesis: what remained was to purify and refine upon his use.

If we now turn from this subject to the poetic efficacy Yeats may have supposed to reside in his tradition, we shall find him moving away from Madame Blavatsky's thought. Madame Blavatsky was interested in a corrupt form of mysticism and not at all in poetry, and the convention was important to her in the sense of a revealed religion: she saw it as an arcane, God-given body of knowledge, and to deviate from it was quite simply to deviate from the truth. If Yeats agreed with her here, he was too urbane to say so.* When he announces his own theory of symbolism, which he does in *Ideas Of Good And Evil*, we find that his claims are much more moderate, and come in fact very close to those of modern Jungian thought. A symbol is powerful, and a traditional symbol is peculiarly powerful, not so much by divine right as being vouchsafed to Mathers' Jews or Blavatsky's *Ur-menschen*, but because, if it has at one time been associated with man's deepest emotions, it will have acquired an individual life in Anima Mundi, the collective unconscious:

> Whatever the passions of men have gathered about becomes a symbol in the great memory.[50]

For proof of the existence of his 'great memory', Yeats turned to the testimony of visionary experience:

> Anyone who has any experience of any mystical state of the soul knows how there float up in the mind profound symbols.[51]

*He says simply that the tradition can be traced back to remote antiquity, and reflects 'what men then thought'.

These symbols would almost always be traditional, and that they did
not come from the personal memory could easily be shown: Yeats
instances some which were received by friends of his own, and which
could be traced back to a text in the Kabbala and to an alchemical
picture:

> Where did those intricate symbols come from? Neither I nor the
> one or two people present nor the seers had ever seen, I am con-
> vinced, the description in *The Book Of Concealed Mystery* or the
> medieval diagram.[52]

And this, Yeats makes it clear, is in every sense a typical experience:
'mystics of every country and century'[53] could be used to bear him out.
A traditional symbol, then, retained forever an archetypal validity, and
would communicate with a mysterious poignancy and power.

It follows from this that there are two main branches of symbolism,
and Yeats differentiates sharply between the kinds. One could follow
Shakespeare's general method, and use a merely personal imagery, or
one could use a traditional symbolism, accepted with full understanding
of its traditional significance, as Dante and the mythological poets had
tried consistently to do. Yeats calls these methods the *emotional* and the
intellectual respectively: the intellectual, he thought, was always to be
preferred, because it would bring men into contact with Anima Mundi
and so with something probably quite ineffable:

> Shakespeare is content with emotional symbols that he may come
> the nearer to our sympathy, but if one is moved by Dante, or by the
> myth of Demeter, one is mixed into the shadow of God.[54]

As for the purely personal symbolist, his images would always be
relatively shallow, for they would be deficient in archetypal depth.
Even Shelley could be faulted in this respect:

> I am certain that there are many who are not moved as they desire to
> be by the solitary light burning in the tower of Prince Athanase,
> because it has not entered into men's prayers, nor lighted any through
> the sacred dark of religious contemplation.[55]*

Yeats preferred Shelley's poetry where it was more thoroughly conventional, as in *Laon and Cythna*, or *Hellas*:

---

*Later, of course, Yeats remembered that the lamp in the tower was a Rosicrucian
symbol, and as such sufficiently traditional to be converted to his own use.

Shelley's poetry becomes the richer, and loses something of the appearance of idle phantasy, when I remember that its images are ancient symbols, and still come to visionaries in their dreams.[56]

So also, Yeats believed, with all poetry: beside the mystical element in communication I have mentioned, it would gain urgency and even intelligibility from a symbolism which made its meaning felt 'not only to the dark portion of one's own mind, but to the mind of the race'.[57] On these very Jungian premises he advocates traditionalism in imagery: not a merely random synthesis 'picking stories and symbols where it pleased', but an informed process, by which the poet's imagination could be united to the cultural past of his own race, married 'to rock and hill'.[58] And here perhaps I should stress that the process as Yeats saw it would not be in any sense uncreative. An inherited symbolism, for him, was always potentially a living and a personal thing, because it would have passed through the crucible of the poet's own private faith.

Yeats was fully aware that his theory would be unpopular, and by 1918 it must have seemed to him that symbolism was a dying art. Only in the east, I think he felt, was the poet still able to draw on the inherited traditions of his country: this is reflected in his praise of Tagore:

A tradition, where poetry and religion are the same thing, has passed through the centuries, gathering from learned and unlearned alike metaphor and emotion . . . A whole people, a whole civilisation, seems to have been taken up into [Tagore's] imagination.[59]

The western alternative he thought of as an essentially dispossessed poetry, which would send down no roots in imagery, in 'inherited subject matter', or in belief:

Literature dwindles to a mere chronicle of circumstance, or passionless phantasies, and passionless meditations, unless it is constantly flooded with the passions and beliefs of ancient times.[60]

If we understand that the word 'phantasy' meant for Yeats 'uninformed imagination' (Coleridge's fancy) one central function of his argument will become clear: he is contrasting a received symbolism, accepted by the poet at all levels of his being, and the personal, merely intellectually excogitated imagery of the twentieth century, divorced from the main cultural stream. For it was clear to him that the fine arts in Europe

stood at a crossroads: the older schools of literature, and even of painting, had always 'appealed to a tradition' of some sort (sometimes the
Christian simply, sometimes the subjective: we may compare his notes
on the Platonism of Botticelli);[61] but because of 'that slow dying of the
heart which men call the progress of the world',[62] all sense of those
traditions was in process of being lost. Poet and painter had therefore
to be persuaded back to the main current: they had to rediscover those
'images' that had been 'long a part of the imagination of the world'.[63]
Yeats's advice is perfectly unequivocal:

> [I say to the painter]: express personal emotion through ideal form,
> a symbolism handled by the generations.[64]

Yeats's advice was not taken, and the intellectualised symbolism current
today has been deprecated by several critics. We have still, however,
the availability of his example.

I have tried so far to demonstrate two things: that Yeats was consistently attracted to the use of an inherited symbolism, and that he
was aware, from several sources, that there were close correspondences,
which might be thought to constitute a tradition, between the several
streams of his subjective philosophy. An example of the kind of correspondence he detected would be the use of the bird as a symbol for the
soul after death, and of a king among birds as a symbol for God. Yeats
knew as well as Jung that:

> in the Babylonian Hades souls wore a feather dress and in ancient
> Egypt the *ba* or soul was thought of as a bird . . . in Homer the souls
> of the dead 'twitter'.[65]

He would have added that in the Greek mystery religions, in the Kabbala, and in Indian and even Japanese legend, this symbolism persists.[66]
And knowing this, he followed the convention as he knew it, as for
example in each of the following works, later to be discussed in this
study: 'Byzantium', *The King Of The Great Clock Tower*, *The Herne's
Egg*, *The Death of Cuchulain*, and 'Cuchulain Comforted'. It remained
possible for him to use the symbol in some special sense—for the soul
of the lover, for example, since spiritual love seemed to him a form of
visionary experience, taking the lover's soul altogether out of time—
but the special sense would have to be in conformity with the traditional, and he would require precedent within the tradition for its
use. Similarly, Yeats knew that the sea was a traditional symbol for the

malevolence of the natural world,[67] and always used it as such, or in some special sense connected: it would not have been possible for him to speak with Arnold of 'the sea of faith', for this is not a traditional usage. This, then, was his method: and it does not seem to me in any sense eccentric. If Yeats had been a Christian mystic he would no doubt have been content with a Christian symbolism, as Eliot usually is; but being a subjective, he went to his own convention. It is usually quite apparent to the reader at ease in the convention what Yeats's meaning in any given passage must be; and where there is doubt, since Yeats consistently founds himself upon particular passages in his reading, the juxtaposition of his special source is usually all that is required. This may seem a large claim, but the pages which follow will show how consistently effective such a method can be.

Yeats began to write poetry, as I have said, when he was only partly educated in subjective mysticism: his early symbolism has usually a medieval root. The years between 1910 and 1920 mark a turning point in his thought, for in them he made a systematic study of Greek philosophy, on which all this medieval imagery so largely depends. When he had done so, the Platonic symbolism became what I will call a consistent point of reference for his own work: this I will demonstrate from the importance he attaches to Porphyry. Yeats knew Porphyry as early as 1895, but he made little use of him in his early verse, save perhaps for the Platonic symbolism of the sea (meaning life) and the boat (representing the soul of man while in time) on which he bases his play The Shadowy Waters.[68] When he returned to Porphyry in the 'twenties, however, he began to use him copiously: he gives Porphyry as a source for his mature symbols of the zodiac, honey and honey-bees, water ('What's water but the generated soul?') the cave and the nymph:[69] he also interprets both Shelley and Botticelli by an elaborate system of reference to Porphyry,[70] on whose work he believed they drew. What is true of Porphyry is true also of other Platonic philosophers: the images of spool, spindle and (in one sense) the cave have a source in Plato; the sphere in Parmenides and later philosophers; the gyres, as I shall show, beyond Plato in Empedocles.[71] Some of these symbols are of course so typical that one cannot assign to them a single source; for others, it is possible to point to the precise authority and passage Yeats was following, as he himself was always anxious to do when analysing Shelley and Botticelli: one merely adopts his own method. The precise relation between Yeats's symbolism and the Platonic will be found indicated in my first appendix: what I must insist on here is the importance of the system to his work. The Platonists were not only Yeats's most informative source, but they informed most of the other branches he knew of the tradition; if therefore I suggest that this or this should be the interpretation of a given image 'because it is the Platonic', it will be understood that I mean it is the traditional interpretation generally, as is indeed with regularity the case.

Yeats's critics, I should say, have not had the knowledge of the tradition which he himself had: they may have gleaned here and there, and traced a certain symbol to a certain root, but they have not consistently followed him back, or even sensed, sometimes, that there was anything tangible to follow him back towards. And indeed there may well be some reason in their hesitation: Yeats was in some ways a headstrong thinker; the tradition may be less uniform than he imagined, and it may have no justification through the collective unconscious at all. Discrepancies between Kabbalist and Platonic dogma can be pointed out; Yeats's idea of the consistency of the Platonic symbolic system was conditioned by the scholars in whom he read, Taylor and G. R. S. Mead, and dispassionate modern analysis may show that these scholars have over-reached themselves. Taylor, the contemporary of Shelley and friend of Blake, was after all an unconventional scholar, and Mead has the heterodoxy of the enthusiast: Jowett[72] might have been a safer, and a less wilful, prop. All these considerations are however irrelevant to the present study, if only because Yeats himself did not think of them as telling. Convinced that there was a convention which passed by direct descent from Egypt to Agrippa's middle ages, and thence to the occultists and heterodox mystics of his own day, and that this symbolism had a peculiar efficacy through Anima Mundi, he determined to avail himself of it. To do so he needed, for his lyrics, to make a style; and for his plays, with which we are here concerned, a form of drama which could support such a symbolism.

III

Yeats modelled his mature drama on the Japanese Noh theatre. There was nothing wayward in his decision; it was the culmination of a long search. He went to the Noh as a result of his theory of drama, which is an extension of the theory of symbolism my last section sets out; he wanted to create a fully subjective theatre, as religious a form as his lyric medium, and he was willing to accept any model which would help him to bring this about. Precedent, however, was hard to find, for the form Yeats envisaged had not often been attempted:

Shelley and Blake were his models in the sphere of the lyric, but a similarly orientated drama was further to seek. Yeats sought for it widely, and found what he needed in the masked dance-plays of fifteenth-century Japan: that is, in a very unfamiliar *genre* indeed. The pages which follow are an attempt to explain it.

One has to begin with a statement of Yeats's intentions: he is nothing if not a theorist. His dramatic theory had begun to take shape by 1903. It was based, in the first place, on his acceptance of the French symbolist theatre and, negatively, on his repudiation of the naturalistic drama, which had a considerable vogue in London before the war. As a visionary, it was inevitable that Yeats should have reacted away from the 'soullessness' of realism, and he believed for a time that men like Maeterlinck had 'created a new form';[73] but I do not think he was in any lasting sense indebted, or even that the French symbolists had much that was constructive to give. They experimented, but their experiments did not go far enough; I shall show later that they failed Yeats as models. It was therefore not long before he moved away from their influence, and he gives several reasons for having done so: he felt, centrally, that they had capitulated to the popular theatre, which it should have been their business to oppose:

> The rhetoric of d'Annunzio, the melodrama and spectacle of the later Maeterlinck, are the insincerities of subjectives, who being very able men have learned to hold an audience which is not their natural audience. To be intelligible they are compelled to harden, to externalise and deform.[74]

At other times Yeats doubted whether they were really subjectives at all. He detects, and deprecates, a strain of joylessness which runs through all their work:

> Why did they not speak out with louder voices or move with freer gestures? What was it that weighed upon their souls perpetually? Certainly they were all in prison, and yet there was no prison.[75]

It follows from all this that Yeats cannot have owed much to his French counterparts. Their theories of symbolism, as I have shown in my last section, were much less adequate than that he had formulated for himself, and he also had doubts of their integrity, and even of the temper of their minds. As a dramatist, then, he stands as a peculiarly lonely figure, and the principles on which he built are peculiarly his own.

One of these guiding principles has already been indicated. Yeats wanted to base his drama upon 'received imagery'; not the 'vague symbols'[76] he had discerned in Maeterlinck, but the full archetypal convention as he knew it from his own research. He had assimilated the subjective tradition while still a young man, and he tells us in *Autobiographies* that he had fallen in love with it: he wished for a world where he could 'discover the tradition perpetually',[77] in all the fine arts, and in every decorative object that he saw and touched. This ambition may be seen working itself out in his early dramatic poetry, where there is archetypal imagery in almost every play: sun and moon symbolism in *The King's Threshold*; apple, yew and dragon symbolism in *Deirdre*: there is even traditional usage in *The Green Helmet*, which is no more than farce. The function of this symbolism is usually subsidiary, but one feels that this is *faute de mieux*: both *Cathleen Ní Houlihan* and *The Unicorn From The Stars* are experiments in a more fully symbolic form; and there is also the elaborate evidence of *The Shadowy Waters*, which I shall show to use an archetypal situation as the foundation of a plot. It failed, and Yeats did not repeat the attempt until he had the advantage of the Noh formula, but his prose does nothing to suggest that his ambitions had changed. From this we may deduce a first requirement for his mature drama: he had to be able to promote traditional symbolism to a central position within a play.

Another of his requirements will be seen to follow from his religious preoccupations: 'every argument', Yeats writes of his dramatic theory, 'carries us backwards towards some religious conception'.[78] Yeats had a mystique of the theatre, as it is natural that he should have done: he did not abdicate from his position as a visionary when he assumed the responsibilities of the playwright. Part of his interest in the theatre was an interest in mass emotion, and it seemed to him the dramatist's duty to direct emotion to the proper end: the great Indian critic Ananda Coomaraswami, in the manual of eastern stagecraft which was in Yeats's possession, confirmed him in his speculations as to what that end might be:

> The essential characteristic of aesthetic emotion is a timeless delight akin to that of Brahmasvadana (mystical union).[79]

Yeats arrived at his own theory independently of Coomaraswami, but he did so by logic of a very Indian kind: he was a subjective by nature, in harmony with eastern thought, and it can hardly be surprising that his conclusions should have been much the same.

That they were we see from his dramatic criticism, which is nothing if not mystical:

> Tragic art, passionate art, moves us by setting us to reverie, by alluring us almost to the intensity of trance . . . This reverie, this twilight between sleep and waking, is the condition of tragic pleasure.[80]
>
> The arts which interest me, while seeming to separate from the world and us a group of figures, images, symbols, enable us to pass for a few moments into a deep of the mind that had hitherto been too subtle for human habitation.[81]

It follows that what Yeats primarily requires of the theatre is less katharsis than what he calls 'stillness';[82] a single moment of emotional equipoise to which all the 'passionate intensity' of the action will tend, and which will give the audience temporary use of all their most hidden faculties; one might define it as an awareness of stasis, a moment when the mind passes through profound emotion into a condition of absolute calm. His early criticism may pay lip-service to pity and terror, but this sense of stasis, I think, was what he valued in his response to Shakespeare: it was what he felt, and describes for us, on watching a first performance of *Deirdre Of The Sorrows*, by Synge.[83]

Yeats's mystique of the theatre led him to sweeping innovations. The symbolist drama, he believed, was orientated away from the physical world, and this had to be remembered in every detail of a performance. Any attempt at mimesis would consequently be out of place:

> If the real world is not altogether rejected it is but touched here and there, and into the places we have left empty we summon rhythm, balance, pattern, images that remind us of vast passions . . . all the chimeras that haunt the edge of trance.[84]

Suggestiveness thus became the keynote of Yeats's drama, especially in stage arrangement. He felt that representational scenery would inhibit the imagination of an audience:

> We must have a scene where there is no painted light and shade, no realism, no objects represented in mass.[85]

Under the influence of men like Gordon Craig, Yeats conceived the ideal of an almost bare stage. In these austere surroundings the actors

would speak their parts: they would half-chant the words given to
them, in a style which would have as little as possible in common with
natural speech, for modern mimetic acting seemed to Yeats an alien
skill. He thought of it as a device for the expression of character; and,
in a form that aimed at lyrical stasis, there would be little attempt to
individualise:

> It is in the moments of comedy that character is defined; while amid
> the great moments [of tragedy], all is lyricism, unmixed passion, the
> integrity of fire.[86]★

Yeats remade his early theatre to effect the changes he required. His
scenery grows progressively more simple, while the tenor of his verse
grows more formal; character comes to be no more than suggested,
and the representation of emotion—what Yeats called 'the sleep-
walking of passion'[87]—becomes the dramatist's single aim. When performance had thus been made fully suggestive, the collective unconscious could operate; 'stillness' could be achieved, and visionary communication might take place.

If we now look for the confirmation of Yeats's theories in his
practice, it will be obvious that they by no means ensured him of
success: the more ambitious of the early works are usually failures. We
see this well from The Shadowy Waters, which is clearly symbolic as
Deirdre, say, is not. In both plays we have a fertile secondary symbolism: in Deirdre the images I have noticed of apple, yew and dragon;
and in The Shadowy Waters such symbols as the 'morning star', 'white
fawn' and 'silver fish' (all traditional),[88] meant to decorate Yeats's
dialogue and lend it archetypal depth. But in The Shadowy Waters we
have a primary symbolism also; the sea, the boats in which the lovers
sail, and the harp on which Forgael plays to win Dectora; this symbolism is central to the play, and lends it ulterior meaning. I have said
that the sea in Platonism is the symbol for the material world, and that
the boat is the image for the soul of man: Forgael and Dectora, sailing
the sea in their separate ships, represent any man and any woman in
their essential spiritual loneliness. At the climax of the play they are
united by Yeats's Gaelic symbol of the harp, representing the magical
power of poetry: together on Forgael's boat, they sail on towards the
west, traditionally the country of reverie and mystical experience.[89]

★This may seem an extreme statement, but Yeats felt he had precedent in both the
Greek and Indian theatres. The Elizabethan seemed to him a hybrid form; but he felt
that, at the crucial moments of the action, even Shakespeare rejected 'character' in favour
of pure lyricism.

The play, then, is an elaborate study of the relation between love and the visionary world; and it tends always towards archetypal stasis and away from the 'minute particulars' of life. The characters are prototypes for all humanity: they are not individuals.

It is specious to say that Yeats ought not to have wanted to write this kind of play, when it was the only kind that really interested him: if *The Shadowy Waters* fails, as I think it partly does, there must be concrete reasons. I think Yeats fails largely because he was imitating unsafe models. *Axël*, and Maeterlinck's early dramas, combine a facile and sometimes rather cloyingly pretty symbolism with a certain timidity in execution: they try to impose an archetypal imagery on a drama otherwise conventional, in pattern and in general tone. Yeats wrote his own play before he had moved away from them, as we have internal evidence to prove: his rather mannered style can be shown to remember *Axël*,* and the French influence persists in his conservative approach to form. *The Shadowy Waters* is modelled on five-act conventional tragedy: this is enough to damn it. A symbolist play deals always in a sense with vast generalities, but it has to be made dynamic if it is to succeed on the stage; it has therefore to aim at its own special form of intensity, which will be of the kind that follows from immediacy of impact. Much of its urgency will be dissipated if it is cast in the conventional mode, for the orthodox plot unfolds slowly, and is founded on the laws of cause and effect: the symbolist drama cannot afford to move with deliberation, and it is not concerned with cause and effect at all. More than anything else Yeats needed an extreme compression of statement; he had to isolate, in as small a compass as possible, a single sequence of images, which were to communicate mystical emotion, 'stillness', or what the reader will. This problem of concision he does not begin to solve, and the result is the lethargy into which *The Shadowy Waters* falls. The matter does not sort with the mode.

Another early work which was at least intended to be properly symbolic is *On Baile's Strand*.[90] Yeats began work on his text with the intention, which he came later to deprecate, of giving the play a double meaning: the characters would be living men, but they would also serve as counters in an elaborate philosophical game:

I made the fool and blind man, Cuchulain and Conchubar whose shadows they are, all image . . . they meant in some sense those combatants who turn the wheel of life.[91]

*The whole episode of the treasure is a very obvious borrowing.

In work of this nature, which I shall call metaphysical to differentiate it from the kind of thing attempted in *The Shadowy Waters*, the problem before the dramatist is of a slightly more complex kind. Since Yeats was ostensibly engaged in recounting a Gaelic myth, there seems no way for him to have told his story, if not to rob it of its proper individual life, save as plain legend; then, if there were to be ulterior symbolic meaning, this could have been suggested through a chorus by means of commentary on what had taken place. Yeats clearly realised this, for he experiments with a chorus in *On Baile's Strand*, but it is not very successfully integrated into the work as a whole; it slows down the progress of the action, and its effect is largely inhibitive. The chorus, for Yeats, was a meditative instrument, and as such was not easily assimilable into his orthodox 'objective' form: the problem, indeed, ran even deeper than this, for there was very little material on which it could hope to meditate. Where a poet wishes to comment on the symbolism implicit in a given dramatic action, it is important that all the action presented should be susceptible of extended meaning: one does not want a farrago of symbolism and realism combined, with confusion as to what has ulterior significance and what has not. But, as the Shakespearean convention he was following made inevitable, Yeats could not possibly pare down or condense his text: he was committed to a drama of cause and effect, with scenes of preparation and motivation: only a residuum of his content could be fully symbolic, and that not clearly or concisely set out. The chorus could not point the action because they had no sufficiently simple statement on which to comment: the attempt, while the form remained what it was, could not even be made.

These and other experiments made Yeats aware of his needs. He needed a very succinct form, where the vitality could emanate from the concision; he needed a chorus which would not retard the action, and which would have some positive contribution to make to a play's colour and life. He also, I think, needed a plain verse for the dialogue, and to obtain whatever effects of surface brilliance he was to provide by some means other than language: the alternative would be the retarding factor of an ornate style. All this he needed for symbolic and metaphysical dramas alike: and these were the forms to which his mature art turned.

Yeats would never have solved his problems by *avant-garde* experiment, for he was opposed to personal innovation as such: 'in literature, if we would not be parvenus, we must have a model'.[92] To find the model he required, he searched the dramatic poetry of the world: the essays in *Plays and Controversies* show how much he knew.[93] Then in the winter of 1914–15, Ezra Pound introduced him to the Noh, 'a form distinguished, indirect, symbolic . . . an aristocratic form',[94] and he recognised its potentialities at once. The fixed laws of construction it laid down answered almost all his needs. The Noh was extremely concise, compressing the action into a single short scene, or, in the Noh of Ghosts, into two scenes: Yeats's own ghost-plays condense these two scenes into one. A play had to be built round the representation of a single meaningful action, and any preliminary or motivating action had to be expressed by means of reminiscence; the play itself always began *in medias res*. There was also a chorus, who combined this function with that of musicians; they stood apart from the action, which their comments served often to universalise, but they could be used to speak any part which there would otherwise be difficulty in representing: thus they speak as the severed head in Yeats's *A Full Moon In March*. The style of the dialogue was by tradition simple, but colour was lent to the whole by music and choric song, and, by the expression of emotion, at the climax of a play, through the medium of a dance. With all this there was a parallelism of intention: the Noh, or at least that form of the Noh which Yeats most commonly followed, existed to convey the emotion of *yugen*, which is translated both as 'ideal beauty' and as 'mysterious calm'.[95]

The Noh, then, was an essentially religious form of the precise description that Yeats required; and he soon found that he had not much to learn before he could avail himself of it. The laws of construction themselves required his careful study,* but the Noh stagecraft was easily assimilable; it confirmed Yeats in the experiments he had been practising for years. As he had learned to do, the Japanese dramatists rejected naturalistic scenery and all the appurtenances of mimesis; their art was designed to be both lyrical and mysterious, and one of its first principles was 'remoteness from life'.[96] Some location in place was of course necessary, but a landscape could be evoked through the words of the opening song: Yeats naturally welcomed a form which would 'substitute for painted canvas the poetic description of landscape and event', the emotion of the words being deepened by music, 'drum or cymbal, gong and flute'.[97] He was able to use for his backcloths a plain hanging, decorated, often, with a single symbol. Then again, he welcomed the masks, 'forced upon him' (as in his models) by the

---

*The reader who wishes to study these laws in more detail may be referred to *At the Hawk's Well*. In this play, though Yeats simplifies, he follows the Noh rules more closely than elsewhere.

nearness of the audience and the consequent impossibility of using greasepaint, because they would impose the author's will upon the actor's:

> What could be more suitable than that Cuchulain, say, should show to us a face not made before the looking glass by some leading player—there, we have had many quarrels—but moulded by some distinguished artist.[98]

The expression Yeats required on his masks was usually of mysterious calm. And, as for the acting itself, the musicians chanted their songs, and the rest of the cast had to acquire a style formal enough to blend with them: modern mimetic playing became impossible. The Noh dramatists, in fact, specifically advise that it should not be attempted: their subject matter was always legendary, and, in that mythical world of gods and heroes, it was felt that only a 'distanced' performance would serve.[99]

Together with all these concordances of theory, there were many practical advantages in working to the Noh formula. Yeats knew that the subjective theatre would find it hard to pay its way, and the Noh helped him to avoid expense. The chorus-musicians, for instance, took also the place of stagehands, preparing for a performance as they chanted their opening song by 'unrolling a carpet, or marking out a place with a stick, or setting a screen against a wall'.[100] There was, as I have said, no naturalistic scenery, and such properties as were needed were always simple and symbolic, a folded cloth serving Yeats for his Hawk's Well, and a toy donkey, in The Herne's Egg, doing service for a real. As for the players themselves, they would not be very many: the compression of the form ensured that casts would not be large. Then again, the Noh was essentially a private form meant for performance before 'some Shogun and his personal friends'; it was well adapted to the needs of the 'forty or fifty readers of poetry' who were all the audience Yeats could bank on for his plays.[101] For as long as he had remained tied to the public theatre, Yeats had had to align himself to some of its demands: his meaning had had to be patent, and his construction to conform to certain requirements of length. Now, his audience would be the intelligentsia, and a drawing-room performance made brevity as essential as it was desirable. His new technique promised him his freedom.

It promised him, in fact, to break down all the barriers that separated his drama from his lyric verse: we must always remember that Yeats had one central ambition, to introduce the subjective tradition into the theatre. The Noh dramatists had composed for a highly cultivated audience: they were court poets writing for the aristocracy, and, as Yeats notes, the fifteenth-century Japanese aristocracy had the 'traditional language' of Eastern symbolism at their command: it was a part of their inheritance, 'a knowledge learned in leisure and contemplation'.[102] And, even where the performance might be before an audience of peasants, there was no danger that the author's meaning would be misunderstood: the Noh drama grew up in a medieval world, where values were as uniform as in Chaucerian England, and 'learned and simple had in common much allusion and symbol'.[103] In twentieth-century Dublin, of course, nothing of this solidarity obtained, but at least Yeats did not have to rely upon the general support; a private drama implied an invited audience, and the uninitiated, even among the intelligentsia themselves, could easily be kept out. Yeats did not doubt that there would be a sufficient volume of approval:

> In most towns one can find fifty people for whom one need not build all on observation and sympathy, because they read poetry for their pleasure and understand the traditional language of passion.[104]

He wanted 'an unpopular theatre and an audience like a secret society';[105] with such people there would be no need for explanation, and he could compose without misgivings in the traditional mode. Yeats had in mind 'a style like Dante's, distant, musical, metaphorical, moulded by antiquity';[106] he planned to make for himself 'a form Shelley could have composed in without ceasing to be himself, or even Blake in the mood of *Thel*'.[107] If we remember the kind of poem *Thel* is, there can be no doubt of his intention: the *genre* Yeats hoped to create would be a very highly symbolic form indeed.

In cherishing the ambitions that he did, Yeats went further than his originals: we may say, if we wish, that he realised potentialities which are latent in the Noh drama, but we cannot say that he followed its rules as they were handed down to him. The Noh is to some extent symbolic, but it could not be called symbolic in the absolute sense of which I have been speaking; its imagery, which follows the Sino-Japanese convention, is usually kept subsidiary, and is used to decorate and enhance a perfectly straightforward plot.[108] Yeats had, however, good reasons for thinking he could make of it the kind of thing that he required: there were certain special features of the plays which made them susceptible of conversion. It is a peculiar characteristic of the Noh that it manages to combine very great intensity with a high degree of eclecticism in reference: the allusions, which need not be in any way connected with the symbolism, are to classical Chinese literature and to Japanese poetry, legend and myth. Yeats knew that the Noh is extremely allusive, 'self-conscious and reminiscent'[109] as he calls it, and he knew also that the 'few cultivated people' who made up the audience could be expected to understand the 'literary and mythological allusions and the ancient lyrics quoted'.[110] Accordingly, he proposes to adopt a similar principle in his own work: to make his own drama very highly allusive also, and to give his allusions a consistent direction by referring them to subjective convention and to archetypal myth. He would not have done so without precedent, for he had at all costs to preserve the dynamic impact of his form: but the Noh taught him that he could make the attempt without being undramatic. Its eclecticism had, in fact, a curiously haunting effect, 'always reminding those who understand it of dearly loved things'; it led to a style opaque and secret, 'like a memory or a prophecy'.[111] Such usage seemed to Yeats to contribute to the whole texture of a play, and he tried to make his own practice as creative.

I think I have now sufficiently demonstrated the level at which Yeats's dance-plays have to be read. They are allusive because his originals are allusive, and the direction their allusiveness takes will naturally be that of all his verse. The meaning will therefore follow from the subjective tradition, though this is less than obvious from the plays themselves: Yeats makes very little effort to uncover his sources, for he felt that his form precluded him from the attempt. He was working in a *genre* which was both courtly and visionary: the Noh taught him to be at once sophisticated and indirect:

> I desire a mysterious art, doing its work by suggestion, not by direct statement, a complexity of rhythm, colour and gesture.[112]

At first, Yeats tells us, he had intended to make his symbolism as accessible as possible; but the need for concision, together with his desire to preserve the 'opacity' of his original, led him in an opposite direction. He came, in the end, to decide on a system of allusion left unexplained within the play:

> Now I prefer to give [the actor] some mystery or secret. A reader can always solve the mystery or learn the secret by turning to a note.[113]

Dante, he says, had not hesitated to use a parallel technique: he had annotated his odes in precisely this way.[114] And, as for the reader who did not care to turn up the notes, no doubt Yeats thought he could sufficiently enjoy the play without them. There were colour and spectacle, music, song and dance; and there were also the possible operations of the collective unconscious, which might bring the observer to 'emotion of stasis' without his having to look beyond.

Yeats's mature drama has thus a two-fold appeal: he had created a form for initiates which would also be meaningful for the innocent eye. This seems to me the summit of his achievement as a theorist. The chain of reasoning which goes to make the dance-plays the blend of mysticism and spectacle that they are is an eminently logical, one might even say a beautiful one: it is vulnerable, as all theories are, but I think it is vulnerable at two points only. One may, in the first place, deny that any form of drama can or should exist which—to use Yeats's own words—is 'not imitation of something in the outer world, but . . . uses the outer world as a symbolism'[115] only, to express 'subjective', visionary perceptions. Or, ceding this point, one may argue that the Noh technique is alien to the Western mind, and that Yeats was justified in his general theory, but wrong in his determination to 'copy the East'. To the first of these objections there is of course no answer, but my quotations will have indicated already how Yeats would have replied to the second. It is quite clear that Yeats (and Pound with him) saw in medieval Japan a society not unlike that of the Florence of Dante and his circle.[116] The awaré (gentle sympathy) of Japanese love poetry they would have paralleled from the sonnets of Guido Cavalcanti,* and the mysticism, eclecticism and esoteric symbolism of the Noh from the Divina Commedia itself. The Noh, then, adding to these elements the universally accepted techniques of dance and choric song, seemed a form that might have appealed to courtly and visionary Florence at the moment of 'unity of being'; whether it could appeal to modern England 'in its decline and fall' was of course another matter. By restricting his dance plays to an invited audience, Yeats made the issue an academic one.

For those of us who side with him on both premises above—who accept the idea of a visionary 'reality', or simply the dramatic efficacy of the archetypes, and who admit no racial divisions of the human aesthetic sense—the theory of Yeats's dance plays will seem eminently

---

*This quality in Japanese poetry persists in some Noh plays which are love-stories, e.g., Nishikigi. One has only to compare the beginning of Pound's translation of this play with, say, the ballata Perch 'io non spero to see the similarity of temper.

defensible. There remains only one factor which may seem disquieten-
ing: the initial unfamiliarity of his form. As Yeats himself remarked of
Blake, he needed a commentary on his intentions, and, his intentions
having remained obscure, public interest in the dance-plays has largely
fallen away. Yeats's mature drama, however one looks at it, is important, and it is tragic that it should have been lost to sight. I hope I
may have done something to rehabilitate it.

IV

Yeats modified his intentions only slightly in later life: his last plays
are also his most difficult. They present the general reader with a solid
front of obscurity. Three of them, *The King Of The Great Clock Tower*,
A Full Moon In March, and *The Herne's Egg*, are fully archetypal,
symbolic, that is, in the sense of *The Shadowy Waters*; one, *The Death
Of Cuchulain*, is what I have called a metaphysical play; only *Purgatory*
is immediately intelligible, and even here there is a great deal of philosophical allusion beneath the surface of the verse. It is, however, by no
means obvious that the plays communicate in depth at all; Yeats's
critics have been slow to understand them. Largely, one feels, because
his theory of the drama has consistently been misrepresented, it has
generally been supposed that they are manifestations of a failing talent:
Louis MacNeice has examined *The Herne's Egg*, and has concluded that
it is 'nonsense satire';[117] and Peter Ure has been similarly unresponsive
to *The King Of The Great Clock Tower* and *A Full Moon In March*.[118]
In fact, the last plays are an achievement of the utmost subtlety: they
cover, between them, the whole field of human experience, and convey
some of Yeats's acutest criticism of life. They are also technical per-
formances of very considerable interest: Yeats wrote them as the past-
master of his form.

I am concerned with Yeats's meaning, and there should be no doubt
of the level at which his last plays have to be taken. In the preface to
The King Of The Great Clock Tower, he makes their provenance very
clear. Any new plays he might write, we are told, would be 'founded
upon a Japanese model', and would be designed for the *cognoscenti*, or
for readers prepared to study them with care: he would pacify the
uninitiated by means of surface narrative, but his symbolism would
remain as 'secret' as in the past.[119] It was the virtue of the Noh pattern
that it made this kind of writing possible:

> In this form I can be as subtle or metaphysical as I like, without
> endangering the clarity necessary for dramatic effect.[120]

In some ways, in fact, Yeats promises to bring his art closer to his Japanese originals. His earlier dance-plays had been designed for a drawing-room performance, but now he would return to the public boards:

> *Fighting the Waves* and the present play so far emulate the Japanese model that they climax in a dance and substitute suggestion for representation; but, like the Japanese plays themselves, they are stage plays.[121]

Each of the five works with which we are concerned is meant for a small private theatre—a hall where some Shogun and his friends might have passed away an evening—but this is the only way in which they deviate from Yeats's norm. They are as sophisticated, and as mysterious, as anything that had gone before: Yeats has a long passage of advice for the chorus, in which he tells how his 'secret meaning' is to be conveyed.[122] It is therefore quite clear that the plays have occult significance, and the critic will have to read them on the esoteric plane.

A first problem lies in the nature of Yeats's probable sources. He promises to build upon both 'literary and mythological allusions', and it will not always be clear in which of these directions his meaning is to be found. The Salome image, for instance, is central to two of the plays, and it is an image which constantly recurs in nineteenth-century poetry and painting; Yeats himself gives us a list of parallels to his own usage, citing Heine, Ricketts, Mallarmé, Wilde.[123] It remains the case that none of those artists convert the image into *symbol*, or at least that they do not avail themselves of its central traditional meaning: the nineteenth century is notorious for the extent to which it deviates from the tradition, and an eccentric source is a source on which Yeats will not have relied. A symbol, for Yeats, was essentially a learned thing: it was the concrete expression of a philosophical concept. He tells us himself how he tracked such concepts down:

> If some philosophic idea interested me, I tried to trace it back to its earliest source.[124]

Yeats searched, always, for the ultimate rationale of his symbolism; he followed it back to its archetypal origin. He makes it very clear that his sources are not contemporary: the meaning of *The King Of The Great Clock Tower* is to be looked for in 'religion'.[125] The last plays therefore require a metaphysical criticism, and they will not yield to a merely literary search; they may draw on modern poetry for some of their local colour, but the 'heterodox tradition', or some visionary author mediating between Yeats and his tradition, will be their *raison d'être*.

If the provenance of Yeats's imagery is often uncertain, this is because he did not keep to his original intentions. He had meant, in the first place, to explain his allusions in a series of footnotes, and these notes do indeed exist for some of the earlier work: it remains perfectly clear that he found it very difficult to write them, and, by the time he composed the last plays, he had given up the practice in despair. In a letter to Maurice Wollman, Yeats gives reasons for his apparent unco-operativeness:

> I don't want to interpret 'The Death Of The Hare'. If an author interprets a poem of his own, he limits its suggestibility.[126]

This letter implies, of course, much more than a mere romantic tendency to let a poem mean what the reader will; Yeats hoped (though twenty years of misunderstanding may suggest that he hoped unwisely) that the collective unconscious would guide the reader to the correct interpretation. But the letter raises also a perhaps more crucial issue: the impossibility of defining a symbol's meaning in a few lines of print. There is probably only one way to explain a traditional symbol: the commentator has to reconstruct the whole ethos of feeling that underlies it, for to do less than this is to present the symbol as a dead fact. It cannot possibly live if divorced from the tradition that bred it; it has subtle nuances, which are only apparent to the informed reader; and, beyond this, the whole rationale of its meaning will be lost if we go to it in partial ignorance. It is one thing to be told that the nymph is a symbol for the material body;[127] it is quite another thing to know why it is a just and beautiful symbol, and why another image would not serve as well. Yeats could not hope to reconstruct the whole of his subjective tradition: he had other, more creative work to do. For this reason, I think, he distasted the task of annotating his lyric poetry, and left much that he might have written on the later plays unsaid.

The pages which follow are an attempt to do what Yeats could not: to explain his symbolism without falsifying it, which implies its careful relation to the conventions on which it is based. I have tried to find a method which will be creative rather than definitive. One could present the reader with a table of correspondences, and the traditional meaning for each of Yeats's symbols could be read off from this; but a method of this kind would hardly be remunerative; it would leave so much unsaid. I have preferred to relate each symbol to its precise background of feeling, giving, where possible, Yeats's exact authority, and quoting that authority at proper length: I have not allowed myself to generalise from the tradition, for generalities will not help me to make his poetry live. The tradition, however, has been my consistent point of reference. It has a considerable literature, and it follows that this study is an elaborate undertaking; it must necessarily cover a great deal of unfamiliar ground, but I think that it performs an essential service for Yeats's verse. The last plays are in many ways his best, and they shed much light on the meaning of his poetry generally. On this justification I am content to rest.

PART TWO

THE LAST PLAYS

CHAPTER TWO

THE KING OF THE GREAT CLOCK TOWER
AND A FULL MOON IN MARCH

A FIRST POINT WORTH noting with regard to these two works is that they are printed in incorrect order in the Macmillan *Collected Plays*. *The King Of The Great Clock Tower*[1] was in fact written first; the dialogue was originally in prose, and Yeats turned it into verse because he felt his audiences expected it of him; he did so against his own inclination, only to rewrite the play completely as *A Full Moon In March*[2] because he was not satisfied with his plot:

> In 'The King Of The Great Clock Tower' there are three charac-
> ters, King, Queen and Stroller, and that is a character too many;
> reduced to the essentials, to Queen and Stroller, the fable should
> have greater intensity. I started afresh and called the version 'A Full
> Moon In March'.[3]

Yeats was never very fond of his two dance-plays; they were written at a low ebb of poetic inspiration. We see this from a letter to Dorothy Wellesley written some time after their publication, in which he deprecates *A Full Moon In March* as 'a fragment of the past I had to get rid of' and explains that the prose version of *The King Of The Great Clock Tower* was written 'to force myself to write lyrics'.[4] He made, in the end, a superabundance of dramatic lyrics, and could not find a use for 'The Alternative Song for the Severed Head'. *A Full Moon In March* and *The King Of The Great Clock Tower* have really no right to separate existence, but the high standard of his lyrics probably inclined Yeats to publish and preserve both plays.

There is some evidence of a further textual complication. When *The King Of The Great Clock Tower* was first published, the lyric 'He had famished in a wilderness' had already been written, for it is quoted in a note, though it is not made a part of the text itself.[5] Yeats makes it clear that this lyric is salvage, and that it bears witness to a false start: he had attempted to put the Irish legend of Dectira and Aodh 'into a dance-play', only to find that the story he really wanted was

closer to Wilde's *Salome*.[6] I imagine that Yeats had intended a specifically Irish play, and abandoned the project with reluctance in favour of
a more general treatment. This would account for the vein of Irish
allusion which persists even into *A Full Moon In March*.

Yeats stubbornly refused to explain his plays' meaning. 'I did not
explain the poems in *The King Of The Great Clock Tower*, nor will I
explain these,' he says in a note on 'Supernatural Songs'.[7] In a passage
I have discussed he reveals that the plays have a hidden meaning, but
says that a stage performance need not be much concerned with it:

> I say to the musicians: 'Lose my words in patterns of sound as the
> name of God is lost in Arabian arabesques. They are a secret between
> the singers, myself, yourselves. The plain fable, the plain prose of the
> dialogue, Ninette de Valois' dance are there for the audience. They
> can find my words in the book if they are curious, but we will not
> thrust our secret upon them.'[8]

In a later passage he explains for us as much of his symbolism as he was
ever directly to do: 'it is part of the old ritual of the year: the mother
goddess and the slain god'.[9] He also acknowledges a debt to Wilde's
Salome, and we recall that, years before, he had condemned the play:

> Salome is thoroughly bad. The general construction is all right, is
> even powerful, but the dialogue is empty, sluggish and pretentious.
> It has nothing of drama of any kind, never working to any climax
> but always ending as it began.[10]

Yeats really owes little to Wilde beyond the climactic dance, and even
here Wilde is not allowed to be the source. We are told that Wilde
found the idea for his scene in Heine, and Heine, perhaps, in
some ancient Jewish myth now lost.[11] Here again we are asked to
think of the symbolism as traditional, and Wilde is merely a link in
a chain.

I feel that the few hints we have are enough for an exegesis of Yeats's
two plays, and that the task is an essential undertaking if they are ever
to be produced with success. Even if the meaning is to be a secret
among the actors and musicians, future actors and musicians must be
made aware of it. Again, if Yeats's symbolism is here, as he says, a
fragment of his past, we may expect to pick up the threads of that
symbolism in his earlier work. A letter to Olivia Shakespear shows
us in what direction we have to look. In it, Yeats draws an analogy

between the life of an individual and the progress of a culture, using elemental symbolism to make his point:

> The four ages of individual man . . . are also the four ages of civilisation. . . . First age, earth, vegetative functions. Second age, water, blood, sex. Third age, air, breath, intellect. Fourth age, fire, soul, etc. In the first two the moon comes to the full—resurrection of Christ and Dionysus. Man becomes rational, no longer driven from below or above. My two plays . . . both deal with that moment. . . . The slain God, the risen God.[12]

Most of this passage suggests Yeats's lyric 'The Four Ages Of Man' more than anything else,[13] but the last few sentences are to the point. His plays deal with the moment when man 'becomes rational', or enters into the full possession of his faculties, though it is hardly yet made clear when this takes place. Beyond this, the plays are at least connected with the myth of the victim-God, and the legends of Christ and Dionysus.

In the pages that follow I shall use the Dionysus legend as my lever, and proceed from an examination of Yeats's interest in this myth. It will soon appear that the Dionysus legend is an allegory for the descent of spirit into matter, and from there we shall be led some way into Platonic theology, so I will begin by defining my terms. By the union of spirit and matter Yeats's authorities could mean any or all of several things. They could mean by it the act from which spiritual life in the universe originated, and from which the world as we know it began; or they could mean by it the Incarnation; or they could mean merely the descent of the soul into the human body at the time of birth. All these subjects were of course much in Yeats's mind before he had made contact with the Dionysus myth, and I will begin from his own beginnings. No fact so gleaned will be irrelevant to his two plays.

II

When Yeats first joined the Order of the Golden Dawn he took as his motto or name within the order DEMON EST DEUS INVERSUS. This name is in fact the title of an important chapter in *The Secret Doctrine*, by Madame Blavatsky,[14] a connection which the membership of Yeats's order could not fail to make; and it seems therefore clear that in taking the name Yeats wished it to be understood that he subscribed to the teaching contained in the chapter, and found it important in his spiritual life. The chapter in question seems to me an odd fusion of Platonism and Kabbalism; it is Madame Blavatsky's account of the union of spirit with matter, which had for her a pantheistic connotation. In her system, every living thing has its share of 'soul', and this chapter is her explanation of how soul came to be diffused into matter at the beginning of the world.

She begins by denying that the universe contains a principle of evil as distinct from that of good:

> As there is far more evil than good in the world, it follows on logical grounds, that either God must include evil, or stand as the direct cause of it, or else surrender his claims to absoluteness. The ancients understood this so well that their philosophers—now followed by the Kabbalists—defined evil as the lining of God or good, 'Demon est deus inversus' being a very old adage. Indeed, evil is but an antagonising blind force in nature; it is reaction, opposition and contrast,— evil for some, good for others. There is no *malum in se*: only the shadow of light, without which light could have no existence, even in our perceptions.[15]

To confirm this point, she explains the true significance of the fall of Satan, and of the rebellious angels who 'took unto them wives' from 'the daughters of men'. This she interprets to refer to the 'law of descent into materiality and ascent into spirituality', or the entry of spirit into matter and its consequent withdrawal, on the human plane, after death:

> The fall is a universal allegory. It sets forth . . . the Rebellion, i.e. the action of differentiating intellection or consciousness on its various planes, seeking union with matter.[16]

Here the phrase 'differentiating intellection' has a Platonic implication. The Platonic theology distinguished between those Gods which took part in the material union, and those of greater purity and remoteness which did not. Thus, Satan and his angels represent that portion of divinity which descended into the world to endow it with spiritual life, a task from which another portion of the divine mind held back. But this symbolism, she says, has been misrepresented by Christianity:

> The multivocal, profoundly philosophical narrative, under its poetical form of the 'Marriage of Heaven and Hell', the love of nature for

Divine form, and the Heavenly Man enraptured with his own beauty mirrored in nature—i.e. Spirit attracted into matter—has now become, under theological handling, 'the seven rectors disobeying Jehovah, self-admiration generating Satanic pride, followed by their fall, Jehovah permitting no worship to be lost save upon himself.' In short, the beautiful Planet-angels become . . . Demons.[17]

The seven planet-angels and rectors are of course part of Madame Blavatsky's own system, and are here synonyms for the rebel angels. Christianity has mis-stated their case. Their crime is no more than to love the divine beauty mirrored in the physical world. They descend into matter, and merge their identity in it. And for this reason, Madame Blavatsky concludes:

When the Church therefore curses Satan, it curses the cosmic reflection of God; it anathematises God made manifest in matter or the objective; it maledicts God, or the ever-incomprehensible wisdom, revealing itself as light and shadow, good and evil in nature, in the only manner comprehensible to the limited intellect of Man.[18]

The argument here given is central to *The Secret Doctrine*; it is in fact a central premise of Madame Blavatsky's thought.

Madame Blavatsky's contentions were generally inherited rather than her own, and could be paralleled in occult tradition; views similar to those I have given were held, in fact, by Blake. In *The Marriage of Heaven and Hell*, Blake denies that the fall of the angels represents the eviction of evil, Boehme's 'desire', from heaven. He maintains that the principle of Good descended: 'the Messiah fell, and formed a heaven of what he stole from the abyss'.[19] How well Yeats understood what was in question may be gathered from the commentary on this passage in the Yeats-Ellis Blake. The writers distinguish between the 'mobility' of God and his 'eternity', that is, between the angelic powers which descended into matter and those which held aloof. Evil

is mere energy when rightly understood, and a necessary portion of the pair of wedded contraries without which there is no progression.[20]

Blake's argument, the commentary continues, is:

that the mobility of God is distinguished from his eternity, that this mobility is Christ, that it fell, or went out into the void which then became nature, and on returning, that it formed the joys of heaven from what it took from the energy or 'eternal hell' outside.[21]

If the material world needed the infusion of spirit, the heavenly world in its turn needed an infusion of energy, the property of matter: 'eternity is in love with the productions of time'. In this passage, as I shall show, the germinal idea of *A Full Moon In March* was already in Yeats's mind.

III

If the thematic material was there, the classical symbolism was still to seek. Though Yeats read a little Platonism in the 'nineties and Frazer before the turn of the century, there is no mention of the Dionysus myth in his early writings, and the first reference we have suggests that he was not fully informed as to its significance. In the momentous year 1903 Yeats resolved to remake his art, to turn away from the study of the absolute and to celebrate life. The choice before his poetry, he explains, lay between the unqualified pursuit of visionary experience and full acceptance of the world, 'the way of the bird until common eyes have lost us' and 'the market carts', and he suggests that the right course is downwards to 'delight in the whole man'. At the same time 'we must see to it that the soul goes with us, for the bird's song is beautiful'; the 'frenzy' of those capable of direct mystic vision must not be discarded but integrated into 'new unity, simplicity, solidity'.[22] Accordingly, we find him writing to A.E.:

> I am no longer in much sympathy with an essay like 'The Autumn Of The Body', not that I think that essay untrue. But I think that I mistook for a permanent phase of the world what was only a preparation. The close of the last century was full of a strange desire to get out of form, to get to some kind of disembodied beauty, and now it seems to me the contrary impulse has come. I feel about me and in me an impulse to create form, to carry the realisation of beauty as far as possible. The Greeks said that the Dionysiac enthusiasm preceded the Apollonic, and that the Dionysiac was sad and desirous, but that the Apollonic was joyful and self-sufficient.[23]

Here the reference in the last sentence is clearly to Nietzsche's *The Birth Of Tragedy*, which Yeats was reading at about this time and where the distinction he is making is prominent, but Nietzsche's remarks on the Dionysus myth could hardly be called comprehensive. He shows that the Bacchic worshipper thought of the ordinary process of living as misery, while the Apollonian found the Self, and life in general, a source of joy, but he does not go on to interpret the Dionysus myth as symbolism.[24] If Yeats's interest in the legend began from Nietzsche, as I think it did, he could therefore not have informed himself fully from his authority, and an essay on the cult by Arthur Symons, which he probably knew, is hardly full enough to have repaired the lack.[25] On the other hand, Yeats had clearly mastered the symbolism by 1925, for it is used, with consummate skill, both in *A Vision* and in his play *The Resurrection*.

At some time between 1903 and 1925, then, Yeats clearly studied the Dionysiac mysteries in some detail, and I think it virtually certain that he did so through Thomas Taylor's *Dissertation*. Madame Blavatsky had recommended Taylor to her circle,[26] and Yeats had his *De Mysteriis* in his library, and refers familiarly to his *Porphyry* and *Select Works of Plotinus*;[27] I am also convinced that he read Taylor's *Life of Pythagoras* and took from it the allusion in 'Among School Children' to Pythagoras' golden thigh. In Taylor's translation of Iamblichus, Pythagoras shows Abaris the priest this mark of divine favour, and again 'rising up in the Olympic games he showed his golden thigh'.[28] When Yeats knew these works of Taylor, he is not likely to have missed his *Dissertation*, in some ways the centrepiece of Taylor's achievement. Internal evidence goes to confirm that he had read the book. He took from it, I think, the translation of Heraclitus, 'Men and Gods die each other's life, live each other's death,'[29] which is common in his middle period prose, and which appears in the poetry with 'Byzantium':

> I hail the superhuman.
> I call it death-in-life and life-in-death.[30]

He probably took from it also the symbolism of 'mire and blood' in the same poem, for Taylor gives 'mire or mud' as an orthodox Platonic symbol for the material world.[31] More significant still, Yeats tells us, in a note to *The Winding Stair*,[32] that he has employed Dr. Sturm to look up for him a quotation from Macrobius on Scipio's dream; he proceeds to interpret the quotation in a highly esoteric sense, which he will not have done without precedent. He could have learned his interpretation from Taylor's *Dissertation*, where the passage is discussed at length.[33] For these reasons I give Taylor as Yeats's source with some confidence, though I do not suppose it really matters who his immediate authority may have been. What is important is that

Yeats's interpretation of the Dionysus myth corresponds with Taylor's, and this will be demonstrated.

Taylor begins by recounting the story of Dionysus, and I will give the salient details in his narrative only, quoting nothing that is without bearing on Yeats's two plays:

> Dionysus, or Bacchus, while yet a boy, was engaged by the Titans in a variety of sports . . . and among the rest he was particularly captivated with beholding his image in a mirror; during his admiration of which, he was miserably torn in pieces by the Titans.[34]

Minerva, however, snatched away and preserved his heart. Then:

> Jupiter, perceiving the cruelty of the deed, hurled his thunder at the Titans; but committed the members to Apollo that they might be properly interred. And, this being performed, Dionysus by a new regeneration again emerged, and being restored to his pristine life and integrity, he afterwards filled up the number of the Gods.[35]

This myth was of course symbolic, and Taylor continues to explain its meaning in the rites associated with the God. His purpose is to show that Platonic theology derives from the mystery religions, and he therefore makes use of Platonic terms.

Dionysus, he explains, is a symbol for spirit in its descent into matter. In Platonic terminology, he is a principle of the mundane intellect, which corresponds in Yeats's phrase with the 'mobility' of heaven, the angelic powers that fell. Minerva is a principle of the intelligible world, Yeats's 'eternity', or the portion of the divine mind that does not make the descent. In Platonic theology, there is no essential opposition or friction between the two. Minerva is the guardian who presides over the descent, though she does not participate in it:

> By Minerva we must understand that fontal, intellectual, ruling and providential deity, who guards and preserves all middle lives in an immutable condition, through Intelligence and a self-energising life, and by this means sustains them from the depredations of matter.[36]

Jupiter is 'the artificer of the universe', and Apollo 'the source of all union and harmony'. By the Titans the myth implies the Gods associated with matter, decoying the young Dionysus and bringing about his fall.[37]

Dionysus, fascinated by the mirror of the natural world, is captured and dismembered by the Titans; that is, spirit is attracted into matter and diffused into all its parts:

> The ultimate design of the first part of this mystic fable . . . appears to be no other than to represent the manner in which the form of the mundane intellect is distributed into the material universe.[38]

This fall, Taylor goes on, is very properly represented as a cruel dismemberment and a disaster, for life in the physical world is a curse. Dionysus could stand only to lose by abandoning his true nature, and this is true also of the fallen soul of man:

> Flying from an indivisible and Dionysiacal life, and energising according to a Titannic and revolting energy, the soul becomes bound in body as in a prison.[39]

Minerva, however, rescues and preserves the God's heart, this being a symbol of his eventual liberation and resurrection into the spiritual world:

> The heart of Dionysus, too, is with the greatest propriety said to be preserved by Minerva, for this goddess is the guardian of life, of which the heart is a symbol.[40]

The ceremony of cutting out the heart as a symbol of eventual resurrection, Taylor might have added, dates back to Egyptian funeral rites.[41] When Jupiter takes the body of the slain god from the Titans and commits it into Apollo's keeping, the myth represents the rescue of the spirit of man from a merely material existence and its conversion to a life of reason and harmony, for Apollo is connected with these qualities. The worshippers are being advised to live purposively and purely, to cultivate what Platonism calls the intellectual life, for by this process they experience a spiritual regeneration while still living, and after death arrive at union with the divine mind:

> The soul . . . being purified from Titannic defilements, and collected into one, becomes a Bacchus; that is, she passes into the proper integrity of her nature according to the Dionysus that is on high. . . . Intellect remains entire during its participations in matter, and the participations themselves are continually converted to their source, with which they become finally united.[42]

Therefore, Taylor concludes: 'the design of the mysteries is to lead us back to the perfection from which, as a principle, we first made our descent'.[43] Dionysus, who points the way to salvation, is a type of the victim-god.

There is clearly a considerable gulf between Taylor's scholarly interpretation and the orgiastic practices with which the god was vulgarly associated. Before being converted into a saviour god, Dionysus had been the centre of a fertility cult, and some elements of the earlier cult, such as ritual prostitution, continued to attach to the god in the popular mind. Yeats was well aware of this fact. In the narrative of *The Resurrection*, he describes a popular ceremony in full detail,[44] drawing perhaps upon Flaubert's *Temptation of St. Anthony*; but in the songs in the same play, the legend is put before us in its essential dignity:

> I saw a staring virgin stand
> Where holy Dionysus died,
> And tear the heart out of his side,
> And lay the heart upon her hand
> And bear that beating heart away;
> And then did all the Muses sing
> Of Magnus Annus at the spring,
> As though God's death were but a play.[45]

There is the same dignity in his allusion to the myth in 'Parnell's Funeral', where he is interpreting the scene pictured on a Sicilian coin:

> Rich foliage that the starlight glittered through,
> A frenzied crowd, and where the branches sprang
> A beautiful seated boy; a sacred bow;
> A woman, and an arrow on a string;
> A pierced boy, image of a star laid low.
> That woman, the Great Mother imaging,
> Cut out his heart.[46]

Here there are two protagonists; a woman, equated with Minerva, and a seated, wounded boy, equated with Dionysus as being the 'image of a star laid low'; for in Yeats's symbolism of the Incarnation, we read elsewhere, 'a star fell, and a star was born'.[47] A fallen star, a fallen angel; one imagines he made the connection. The reference in 'Parnell's Funeral' is particularly interesting, for the poem was published together with *A Full Moon In March*, and this confirms Yeats's interest in the Dionysus myth at the time he wrote his play.

IV

In *A Vision* and his dance-play *The Resurrection* Yeats frequently alludes to the Dionysus legend. He sees it as connected with his theory of personality: his distinction, that is, between the subjective (ecstatic) and objective (Christian-depressive) types of mind. The texts in question are notoriously difficult, but I propose now to consider them: they show, beyond doubt, the meaning he gives the myth.

At the centre of Yeats's arguments in *The Resurrection* is his cyclic theory of history, which has often been compared to Vico's. His preface sets out his point of view. The pattern of history is meaningful, and the time needed for the complete evolution of the pattern can be considered under the symbol of the Great Year of the Ancients. Great Years follow one another, each representing one complete statement of the historical pattern in all its detail; their length can be variously computed, but they can be subdivided into shorter, alternating cycles. The earliest philosophers had understood this:

> Whatever its [the Great Year's] length, it divided, and so did every unit whose multiple it was, into waxing and waning, day and night, or summer and winter. There was everywhere a conflict like that of my play between two principles, or elemental forms of the mind, each 'dying the other's life, living the other's death'.[48]

These two principles are Yeats's own 'objectivity' and 'subjectivity', and their symbols, in his poetry, are sun and moon. In each cycle of a Great Year, he explains, one or the other predominates, and there is no such thing as progress, for the cycles alternate endlessly, and the two principles are mutually exclusive; there is merely conflict. This conflict, the preface concludes, he has made the subject of his play.

In *The Resurrection*,[49] the Greek civilisation is presented as a subjective manifestation, and the Christian, Hebraic culture which follows is seen as an objective phase. The Greek in Yeats's play personifies the subjective point of view, with its insistence on the 'radical innocence' of the Self:

> —all hatred driven hence
> The soul recovers radical innocence
> And learns at last that it is self-delighting,
> Self-appeasing, self-affrighting,
> And that its own sweet will is Heaven's will.[50]

As Yeats himself does in these lines from 'A Prayer for My Daughter',
the Greek maintains that the personality is essentially pure. He has no
sense of shame either in himself or in his race, and the classical culture
is for him a source of pride:

The Syrian: What is human knowledge?
The Greek : The knowledge that keeps the road from here to Persia
free from robbers. . . that has made the modern world,
that stands between us and the barbarian.

He stands as Yeats did, for an essentially non-Christian order, whose
keynote is man's sense of his own nobility and self-sufficiency. The
Greek thinks of the Gods as entirely self-contained, and of man as
equally independent, for in a pagan, subjective cycle the Self seems to
be divine:

The Greek : What seems their [the Gods'] indifference is but their
eternal possession of themselves. Man too remains
separate. He does not surrender his soul. He keeps his
privacy.

An objective cycle on the other hand is characterised by man's sense of
his 'weakness and dependence', and of his essential impurity. 'The
divine suffering' has to descend 'into one's mind and soul and make
them pure'. To follow Christ, the Hebrew says:

One had to give up all worldly knowledge, all ambition, do nothing
of one's own will. Only the divine could have any reality. God had
to take complete possession.

In an objective cycle men tend towards annihilation of the Self, and
reliance on an external Saviour-God.

In this play Yeats uses the Dionysus legend as a subjective equivalent
for the Christian story of the Incarnation. It is not a pure equivalent,
for purely subjective man has no sense of his own inadequacy, and
consequently knows no need for salvation. Thus the Greek can see no
meaning in the myth of divine victimage:

We Greeks understand these things. No God has ever been buried;
no God has ever suffered.

The element of self-abandonment in Dionysiac ecstasy would be repugnant to the subjective mind:

> I cannot think that all that self-surrender and self-abasement is Greek, despite the Greek name of its God. When the Goddess came to Achilles in the battle she did not interfere with his soul, she took him by his yellow hair.

The cult, then, is Greek and not Greek, and Yeats stresses the racial impurity of the worshippers:

> the most ignorant and excitable class of Asiatic Greeks, the dregs of the population.

The atonement-myth in itself, I think he means, is characteristically primary or Christian; in so far as the popular mind distorted it into a ritual in praise of life, it is antithetical or subjective; but when they carried their ecstasy to excess, overstepping the golden mean of classical tradition, this was again a primary trait. No pure subjective could subscribe to an ecstasy that robbed the individual of his self-respect. But as the wheel of history began to turn towards objectivity, and as the first inklings of objective feeling began to permeate men's minds, these half-Asiatic rituals were taken over by pagan worshippers to express their spiritual apprehension of the coming world-order. The real Christ was something very different; he stood for spirituality and renunciation and not at all for the delight in the manifested world with which Pound★ and Nietzsche had taught Yeats to connect the Dionysiac rituals; but this was the nearest pagan man could get to him. Dionysus is thus a figure of mixed significance; the representation of an objective divinity seen through subjective eyes. But he is analogous to the Christ figure, and the songs which begin and end the play assert the essential identity of the two myths.

In the revised version of *A Vision*, Yeats elaborates his theory. The cycles of the Great Year begin at the vernal equinox; Christ's resurrection was celebrated at this period, as also was that of Dionysus and for that matter that of Attis, whom Yeats now equates with Dionysus.[51]

★'Christ follows Dionysos/Phallic and ambrosial/Make way for macerations/Caliban casts out Ariel'
　　　　—E.P. *Ode pour l'election de son sepulchre.*

Nietzsche teaches also that the Bacchic worshipper found joy in the manifested world, but that he did so by escaping from his sense of his personal isolation—that is, from the Self, which he feared and hated—into a state of 'oneness with nature'.

Yeats imagines that there was a received tradition that the objective victim-god would be manifested at this time, and that the pagan cults availed themselves of it. He carries his argument to great lengths. As Henn has noted,[52] he even relates to it the apotheosis of Julius Caesar, though he does so in a passage so confused by argument as to calendars and dates that it is not easy to quote from it. His intention is to suggest that the fact of Caesar's death at the Ides of March, and of his subsequent apotheosis, led a large part of the Roman empire to regard him as the Messiah prophesied in the Sibylline books. For, he says, the Roman empire had not yet lost the conviction that the expected saviour would rise from the dead at a full moon in March:

> Did the Julian house inherit from that apotheosis and those prayers the Cumaean song? Caesar was killed on the fifteenth day of March, the month of victims and saviours. Two years before he had instituted our solar Julian calendar, and in a few years the discovery of the body of Attis among the reeds would be commemorated on that day.[53]

March is 'the month of victims and saviours'; Attis has now been found a place in Yeats's gallery of godhead. The symbolism of *A Full Moon In March* has to be related to the general theory set out in passages such as this.

Yeats's symbolic system proliferated rapidly, and in the same context we find a further, even more significant, identification taking place. St. John the Baptist, begotten 'when the grape was ripe', is being compared to Dionysus:

> Coventry Patmore claimed the Church's authority for calling Christ supernatural love and St. John natural love, and took pleasure in noticing that Leonardo painted a Dionysus like a St. John, a St. John like a Dionysus.[54]

This difficult passage refers to an essay by Patmore called 'The Precursor',[55] which Yeats no doubt read in the 'nineties; the prose style of Patmore seems to me to come close to Yeats's own, and I imagine there was an influence. In his essay, quoting in support St. Augustine and St. Bernard of Clairvaux, Patmore argues that it is impossible to consider the legend of St. John on a literal level; he was a precursor of Christ, which is something much more than a mere prophet; the story, he suggests, must be treated as symbolism. Here he enters upon his theory of 'natural love' as at once a symbol of the divine love and a necessary preliminary to it. By natural love Patmore often means pure love between the sexes, and his theory would have attracted Yeats. St. John, Patmore suggests, symbolises natural love; he is 'the Precursor of Christ, as natural love is the precursor of the Divine':

> His baptism was necessary even to Christ as the representative of Christianity, for none can receive effectually Christ's baptism of fire and the holy spirit without the previous baptism of the purifying water of natural love—water itself always signifying, in the parabolic vocabulary of all primitive religions, the life of the external senses, or of nature.[56]

Patmore goes on to claim precedent in traditional symbolism for the interpretation of the honey on which St. John fed as 'natural good', and reads a parallel meaning into his clothing of camel's hair and leather girdle, 'skin and hair being those things which are most natural'. St. John's death, 'sacrificed to Herod's passion', completes the symbolism, for it represents

> the usual fate of pure natural love when brought into conflict with the sensuality that apes and profanes it.[57]

Yeats clearly accepted Patmore's interpretation, and brought in Renaissance painting to bear him out. He had seen Leonardo's 'St. John The Baptist' and a Dionysus of the same school in proximity at the Louvre. Leonardo so thoroughly rejected the concept of St. John as a penitential figure, and so thoroughly converted him into a representation of natural love, that in the eighteenth century his picture was taken to be a Bacchus.[58]

The scheme of symbolic reference has now become so complex that I think I should recapitulate. Yeats saw Dionysus worship as something very different from Christianity; the subjective popular mind connected the God with generative powers and love of the natural world, making him stand for everything that Christian asceticism renounced. But Christ and Dionysus are to be associated in that they stand for two opposite types of saviour, Dionysus the victim-god mankind can imagine in a subjective, pagan period, and Christ the redeemer in an objective, self-obliterating cycle. On the other hand, Yeats saw St. John as the precursor and necessary antithesis of Christ, natural love

where Christ was supernatural, 'a midsummer child' where Christ was
'a midwinter', as he himself puts it; and in so far as he was Christ's
antithesis, the legend of St. John could be thought of as a parallel or
late variant to the Dionysus myth. It is by this rather devious chain of
associations that Yeats comes to relate the St. John and Dionysus legends
in his two plays. When the Queen dances with the Stroller's head, we
are moving among memories of Wilde's *Salome*, but when Yeats's
hero rises from the dead, and at a full moon in March, we are in the
presence of Dionysus.

There is, however, still a further connection between the two legends,
which may help to bridge the gap between them. Dionysus is associated
almost as closely as St. John with the dance with the severed head. As
we have seen, there is no such association in the story of the god himself, but in Euripides' *Bacchae*, which Yeats can hardly not have read,
Agâvê kills Pentheus while possessed by the god, and, at the climax of
the play, appears in Dionysiac frenzy with his severed head.[59] There is
also a connection in religious myth. Orpheus is dismembered by Thra-
cian women in a Bacchic frenzy, after which his severed head floats
down to Lesbos singing, and is possessed of prophetic powers.[60] Pentheus and Orpheus, or so Yeats was taught by Taylor,[61] were thought
of as ritual victims, whose deaths symbolised on the human plane the
death of the God himself; they are lay figures in the likeness of Dionysus. All this no doubt confirmed Yeats in the parallelism he saw between
the Bacchus and St. John the Baptist myths, and strengthened their
association in his mind.

V

There is still a further text to be considered before the preparatory
data on Yeats's plays can be complete, and this is the most essential of
all, for from it will follow their meaning. I have shown that Yeats
considered the myths of Dionysus and of Attis to be synonymous, and
it remains to be shown why he did so, and why the legend of Attis
was in his mind at the time he began to prepare for *The King Of The
Great Clock Tower*:

> And he that Attis' image hangs between
> That staring fury and the blind lush leaf
> May not know what he knows, but knows not grief.[62]

I think there can be no doubt that Yeats was at this time reading the
works of the Emperor Julian, which were found in his library when he

died. Julian may not seem to us a considerable Platonic philosopher, but we must remember that he was preoccupied with the interpretation of religious legend. What Yeats enjoyed most in Platonism was perhaps the element of myth it contained.

Julian in his 'Hymn to the Mother of God',[63] which is in fact a prose dissertation, discusses at length the legend of Attis:

> Attis or Gallus is a God of generative powers. Of him the myth relates, that, after being exposed at birth near the eddying stream of the river Gallus, he grew up like a flower, and when he had grown to be fair and tall, he was beloved by the Mother of the Gods. And she entrusted all things to him, and moreover set upon his head the starry cap. But if our visible sky covers the crown of Attis, must one not interpret the river of Gallus as the Milky Way? For it is there, they say, that the substance that is subject to change mingles with the passionless revolving sphere of the fifth substance. Only as far as this, did the Mother of the Gods permit the fair intellectual God Attis, who resembles the sun's rays, to leap and dance. But when he passed below this limit and came even to the lowest region, the myth said he had descended into the cave and had wedded the nymph. And the nymph is to be interpreted as the dampness of matter. . . .[64]

In this difficult passage, we must first understand that the Mother of the Gods (Cybele) symbolises intellective deity, that part of the divine mind that does not participate in union with matter, just as Attis symbolises 'generative powers', divinity that does descend. The words Julian uses to make this point are important to an understanding of *The King Of The Great Clock Tower*:

> Who then is the Mother of the Gods? She is the source of the intellectual and creative gods, who in their turn guide the visible gods. She is both the mother and spouse of mighty Zeus; she came into being next to and together with the great creator; she is in control of every form of life.[65]

In Julian's interpretation, the Mother of the Gods forbids Attis to descend below the Milky Way; that is, since the Milky Way is the conventional Platonic symbol for the point of juncture of the spiritual and material worlds, she is unwilling to countenance the descent of spirit into matter. But Attis disobeys her (here we have the theme of the rebellion of the angels) and descends into the cave of the nymph, which Julian very properly reads as symbolic of the union of spirit with matter. The nymph is the conventional Platonic symbol for the material world, as Yeats well knew.* Julian continues:

> The Mother of the Gods exhorted Attis not to leave her or to love another. But he went further and descended even to the lowest limits of matter.[66]

Then 'since it was necessary that his limitless course should halt at last' the goddess brought about his castration. By this is symbolised the curtailment of the generative powers of the spirit in matter; and the god's death follows, representing the withdrawal of spirit from the natural world:

> After that [i.e. the castration], the Hilaria must by all means follow. For what could be more blessed, what more joyful, than a soul which has escaped from limitlessness and generation and inward storm, and has been translated up to the very Gods?[67]

At this point Julian pauses to explain the identity of this myth and that of Dionysus:

> Does it not still remain for me to celebrate the Goddess in her union with Minerva and Dionysus? ... I recognise the kinship of Minerva and the Mother of the Gods... and I discern also the divided creative function of Dionysus which great Dionysus received from the single and abiding principle of life that is in mighty Zeus. For from Zeus he proceeded, and he bestows that life on all things visible, controlling and governing the creation of the whole divisible world.[68]

I quote merely to show that Julian concedes the identity of Minerva and Cybele, and of Dionysus and Attis as two representations of spirit proceeding into matter; I do not think I need go into the argument from mythology by which he justifies his contention.

In the perfectly archetypal situation on which Yeats based *The King Of The Great Clock Tower*, King, Queen, and Stroller stand in exact symbolic relation to Zeus, Cybele, and Attis-Dionysus. The Stroller symbolises spirit in its fallen condition, after the descent into matter,

*My sixth chapter will demonstrate how Yeats used both nymph and Milky Way symbolism in his poetry.

but spirit which is nevertheless in love with and beloved by the Mother of the Gods (Yeats's Queen). That is to say, on the human or microcosmic level, the Stroller symbolises man in the physical world, who is nevertheless in love with the idea of Heaven. In Julian, Attis has to suffer symbolic mutilation and death at the hands of Cybele before he can return to the heavenly world. So also in Yeats, the Stroller must die a ritual death, and the Queen tacitly acquiesce in it, before they can consummate their love. As for the hints Yeats gives in his notes, which might seem to lead away from this interpretation, they in fact go to confirm it. Julian's editor, in the translation Yeats used, points out the connection with the ritual myth of the year:

> Originally the myth of Cybele symbolised the succession of the seasons; the disappearance of Attis, the sun-god, is the coming of winter. His mutilation is the barrenness of nature when the sun has departed; his resurrection the renewal of Spring.[69]

Yeats clearly read and remembered this, and it was as much of the explanation of his plays' purpose as he cared to give.

Julian is also the clue to a number of minor points connected with poems I have mentioned above, and I will corroborate my argument by noticing some of them here. In 'Parnell's Funeral', it cannot have been immediately apparent why Yeats called Minerva 'the Great Mother':

> That woman, the Great Mother imaging.

Minerva had been a 'staring virgin' in his previous poem on the theme. It is now clear that he gave her this title in deference to the association Julian makes with Cybele. Again, 'Vacillation' is full of memories of Julian. When Yeats advises us to turn from the world with middle age—

> No longer in Lethean foliage caught
> Begin the preparation for your death[70]

—he is echoing his author. In Julian's phrase, philosophy is 'a preparation for death'.[71] We find in Julian, furthermore, an elaborate description of the tree consecrated to Attis, and an explanation of its symbolism:

> the tree grows from the earth, but it strives upwards as though to reach the upper air, and it is fair to behold and gives us shade in the

heat, and casts before us and bestows on us its fruits as a boon. Such
is its superabundance of generative life. Accordingly, the ritual en-
joins on us, who by nature belong to the heavens but have fallen to
earth, to reap the harvest of our constitution here on earth,—and
then strive upwards to the goddess of our forefathers, to her who is
the principle of all life.[72]

Yeats takes over this tree, with its two symbolic functions, 'superabundance of generative life' and spiritual striving, and represents it in
'Vacillation' by the burning tree of the *Mabinogion*,* half leafage, half
flame. Flame is his common symbol for spirituality: 'Look on that fire,
salvation walks within'. The verse ends with a symbol for the reconciliation of these two activities:

> And he that Attis' image hangs between
> That staring fury and the blind lush leaf
> May know not what he knows, but knows not grief.[73]

Attis, as we have seen, is an antithetical Christ, and the fixing of his
image on the tree is an antithetical symbol for the crucifixion. He is in
his mutilation, like Jesus in his martyrdom, the rose on the cross, the
reconciler of opposites; and the worshipper in Yeats's moving lines, as
Ellmann rightly points out, 'experiences the ecstasy of seeing beyond
the cross or gyres into the rose or sphere of things'.[74]

VI

We have in *The King Of The Great Clock Tower* a reconstruction of
the Platonic myth of the relation between spirit and matter, but in
saying this I still have to indicate why Yeats makes his hero a strolling
minstrel. This suggests Orpheus rather than Dionysus, but it is equally
a concession to the Celtic element in the play. Yeats had originally
planned to give his fable an Irish setting. He himself refers us to the
legend of Dectira and Aodh, which can be found in one of his own
stories in *The Secret Rose*.[75] To look at that story now will bring us
a stage closer to the heart of his symbolism.

Aodh is a strolling minstrel who comes to the court of Queen Dectira and falls in love with her while watching her bind up her hair.

*It has often been pointed out that Yeats's symbol here derives from the *Mabinogion*
(Lady Charlotte Guest's translation, 1902 edition, p. 275). The tree is in fact Peredur's
tree. Peredur's tree, Julian's tree, the tree of life in the Kabbala, all seemed to Yeats variant
forms of the one archetype.

He kneels down before her and is about to sing her his love when he is prevented by a disturbance in the hall: the Queen's territories have been invaded by her enemies:

> But the Queen sat there straight and still; and Aodh half-knelt before her, with bowed head, and slowly touched the five-stringed cruit as though he were half sunk into a Druid sleep.[76]

As in *The King Of The Great Clock Tower* she is an immobile figure, and Aodh's voluntary abasement before her is almost masochistic. I personally feel that even in this early story something of the atmosphere of the plays is already in the prose.

Aodh promises to sing his song before morning whatever the result of the battle which has interrupted him; but he is killed in the battle, and Queen Dectira goes out at dawn to search for him. She finds 'a head hanging from a bush by its dark hair, and the head was singing'. The head sings one of the most famous of Yeats's early lyrics:

> Fasten your hair with a golden pin,
> And bind up every wandering tress . . .[77]

The story ends with Dectira in rapture before the head, though there is as yet no suggestion that she has connived at her lover's death.

In the song on this subject which Yeats incorporated into *The King Of The Great Clock Tower* and subsequently into *A Full Moon In March*, he is at pains to twist the legend to suit his Platonic theme. Dectira sings:

> He had famished in a wilderness,
> Braved lions for my sake,
> And all men lie that say that I
> Bade that swordsman take
> His head from off his body
> And set it on a stake.
>
> He swore to sing my beauty
> Though death itself forbade.
> They lie that say, in mockery
> Of all that lovers said,
> Or in mere woman's cruelty,
> I bade them fetch his head.

The first two lines relate Aodh to John the Baptist; and in those that follow Yeats has to connect him also with the Attis-Dionysus myth. If the parallel was to be exact, Aodh must seem to die at the Queen's own hand, as Attis was mutilated through the agency of Cybele. Yeats intimates this indirectly. He will not falsify legend and have Dectira kill Aodh, so he foists on her an imaginary accusation and has her answer it with extreme evasiveness. For she goes on to say:

> O what innkeeper's daughter
> Shared the Byzantine crown?
> Girls that have governed cities,
> Or burned great cities down,
> Have bedded with their fancy-man
> Whether a king or clown;
>
> Gave their bodies, emptied purses
> For praise of clown or king,
> Gave all the love that women know!
> O they had their fling,
> But never stood before a stake
> And heard the dead lips sing.

Theodora and Helen knew ecstasy, but not ecstasy to compare with hers after her lover's mutilation and death. As with several of the women in Yeats's gallery, ecstasy and cruelty are associated in Dectira's mind:

> The joy of woman is the death even of her most beloved
> Who dies for love of her
> In torments of fierce jealousy and pangs of adoration.[78]

Yeats's preoccupation with 'beauty's cruelty' has roots in literature, as well as in his unhappy love. I quote these lines from *The Four Zoas* to suggest a source in Blake, who is full of the idea. 'The Mental Traveller' comes to mind at once, and since Blake composed this poem round the Dionysus myth,* it must have been much in Yeats's thoughts when he wrote his plays.

In his last plays, as we shall see in these essays, Yeats frequently alludes to his early stories, his early poems such as 'The Wanderings Of Oisin', and even to his anthology, *A Book Of Irish Verse*. He felt a strong impulse to take up the thread of his immature work:

*I am drawing here on an unpublished essay by Kathleen Raine.

What can I but enumerate old themes?[79]

The representation of the Attis-Dionysus figure as a strolling minstrel is a first example of this; Yeats is remembering Aodh. He continues the Irish reference in *The King Of The Great Clock Tower* by using Tir-nan-Oge as his symbol for heaven, by including a song to describe a hosting of the Sidhe, and by allusions to Oisin and his early story 'The Wisdom Of The King'.* But the legend of Dectira and Aodh is the central Irish reference, and I imagine that Yeats saw in it a Celtic variant on the Orphic myth.

VII

In *The King Of The Great Clock Tower*, a hero in the Attis-Dionysus mould comes to the court of a Queen to woo her, and succeeds in alienating her affections from her husband the King. This King and this Queen represent Zeus and Cybele, or the masculine and feminine principles in deity. For Yeats, as an occultist and a Kabbalist, saw deity as both male and female:

> . . . Man, woman, child (a daughter or a son),
> That's how all natural or supernatural stories run.[80]

Quite early in his life, following Blake and Boehme, he had postu-lated:

> besides the trinity, a fourth principle, a universal matrix. . . . To this emanation is applied constantly by Boehmen [*sic*] the word looking-glass . . . God looking into this mirror ceases to be mere will, beholds himself as the Son . . . and enters on that eternal meditation about himself which is called the Holy Spirit.[81]

It is by this process that, as we are told in 'Supernatural Songs', 'God-head begets Godhead',[82] or in the language of *The Herne's Egg*, divinity mates with the feminine principle to beget 'his image in the mirror of my spirit'.[83] The belief is a convention in what Yeats called heterodox mysticism, and it is hardly surprising that he should have adopted it.

Beyond this, and emerging from it, we should not forget another significance of Yeats's King and Queen. In his system, history divides into alternating cycles, subjective and objective, pagan and Christian, lunar and solar, and each cycle is dominated by an appropriate mani-

---

* 'The king who had feathers instead of hair,' mentioned in the poem, is in fact the hero of that story.

festation of Godhead; that is, it sees God in a certain light. God's symbol, for Yeats, is alternately King and Queen, 'wisdom and beauty':

> There is that continual oscillation which I have symbolised elsewhere as a King and Queen, who are Sun and Moon also, and whirl round and round as they mount up through a round tower.[84]

These are the 'golden king and silver lady' of Billy Byrne's vision,[85] and the symbolism of *The King Of The Great Clock Tower* obviously has to be related to the earlier poem. Behind Yeats's imagery is a distinction between the Platonic conception of divinity as absolute beauty, and the Hebraic idea of God as a patriarchal, omniscient Lord of Hosts. It is thus most apposite that the Saviour mankind can imagine in a lunar, subjective era should have eyes only for the Queen (intellectual beauty): one takes it that the Victim-God in an objective cycle would love only the patriarchal King. Yeats's King and Queen are of course no less Zeus and Cybele in that they have secondary symbolic functions also; and my argument is profitable and necessary in that it clarifies a further, difficult symbol. The Clock Tower the King and Queen govern represents Time.

The Minstrel in Yeats's play loves the Queen though he has never seen her. If we interpret the archetypal symbolism, this means that the fallen God loves the principle from which he emanated, but from which he has been divorced since his incarnation. We must also interpret on the human, or microcosmic, level, since Yeats's symbolism throughout the play is clearly operative on two planes: at this level, we are being told that humanity is in love with pure spirituality, though it has no real cognisance of what pure spirituality may be, since it has been separated from that state from the time of its descent or fall into the world. The Queen is also in love with the Minstrel, and for his sake she has turned away her face from her husband the King:

> The King: Why sit you there
> Dumb as an image made of wood or metal,
> A screen between the living and the dead?

By this lovely and moving symbol Yeats means much more than that divinity loves the Victim-Saviour it has sent into the world. At the human level, he indicates that heaven has as much need of the fallen spirit of man as man has of heaven. 'Eternity is in love with the productions of time.'

The Minstrel behaves with the coarseness which we are to expect from spirit sunk in the material world:

> He seems a most audacious, brazen man,
> Not caring what he speaks of, nor to whom,
> Nor where he stands.

He is as little able to conduct his love affair as we should expect from spirit in its divorce from its heavenly origin; he cannot even appreciate the heavenly beauty when he sees it:

> Neither so red, nor white, nor full in the breast
> As I had thought. What matter for all that
> So long as I proclaim her everywhere
> Most beautiful?

Yet he remains convinced, having been told so by divine revelation, that he is 'a sacred man'. The King has him executed for his insolence, with the Queen's tacit acquiescence: this is the Attis-motif, symbolising the bodily death both Godhead and man must undergo in their separation from the physical world. But the Minstrel first prophesies his own resurrection:

> On stroke of midnight when the old year dies.

Midnight is Yeats's common symbol for the moment of death or of entry upon the mystery of heaven:

> At stroke of midnight God shall win . . .[86]

> At stroke of midnight soul cannot endure
> A bodily or mental furniture . . .[87]

In the play, the 'Alternative Song' reinforces the symbol by reminding us that the Sidhe ride at midnight, the hour consecrated by folklore to the spirit world.

When the clock strikes, the Minstrel's resurrection takes place; the Queen dances with the singing severed head, and the drama ends with their symbolic kiss. This symbolises, of course, on the macrocosmic plane the final liberation of the Victim-God, at the beginning of a new cycle of the Great Year. Yeats reminds us of Virgil's fourth eclogue, to establish this meaning:

Sacred Virgil never sang
All the marvel there begun.

On the microcosmic plane, the symbolism is of the liberation of each
individual spirit after death, when man enters upon the joys of heaven.
This microcosmic meaning is brought to the surface in the lovely song
for the severed head:

Clip and lip and long for more,
Mortal men our abstracts are;
What of the hands on the great clock face?
All those living wretches crave
Prerogatives of the dead that have
Sprung heroic from the grave.
A moment more and it tolls midnight.

Crossed fingers there in pleasure can
Exceed the nuptial bed of man;
What of the hands on the great clock face?
A nuptial bed exceed all that
Boys at puberty have thought,
Or sibyls in a frenzy sought.
A moment more and it tolls midnight.

The Queen and the Stroller are the macrocosmic realities whose patterns all human life must follow, and, like them, all living beings crave
for death. For humanity longs for love, and only after death is real love
possible. Yeats is remembering Swedenborg's description of the intercourse of angels as 'a conflagration of the whole being', which he had
already used in that unforgettable poem, 'Ribh at the Tomb of Baile
and Aillinn'.[88] In heaven, a nuptial bed is more passionate than a young
boy's desire at puberty, when as we know from 'Long-Legged Fly'[89]
he constructs a mental image of the first Eve; it is more passionate than
the desire of a Sibyl for possession by the God. Here I think Yeats
has in mind the Sibyl in *Othello*, whose 'prophetic fury'[90] as the God
descends to her is vividly described.

To so passionate a nuptial bed the liberated spirit proceeds. The
meaning is in one sense symbolic of the union of spirit with the principle from which it emanates, but it is also literal. For Yeats really
believed in 'the intercourse of angels'.

The dead, as the passionate necessity wears out, come into a measure of freedom . . . they are moved by emotions, sweet for no imagined good but in themselves, like those of children dancing in a ring, and I do not doubt that they make love in that union which Swedenborg has said is of the whole body and seems from far off an incandescence.[91]

The song for the severed head is concerned with realities, and it is not mere metaphor.

From these heights of emotion the final song subtly leads us down. It presents us with a situation as archetypal as the main body of the play, though this may not at once be obvious:

> O but I saw a solemn sight;
> *Said the rambling, shambling, travelling-man;*
> Castle Dargan's ruin all lit,
> Lovely ladies dancing in it.
>
> What though they danced? Those days are gone,
> *Said the wicked, crooked, hawthorn-tree;*
> Lovely lady or gallant man
> Are blown cold dust or a bit of bone.
>
> O, what is life but a mouthful of air?
> *Said the rambling, shambling, travelling-man;*
> Yet all the lovely things that were
> Live, for I saw them dancing there.
>
> Nobody knows what may befall
> *Said the wicked, crooked, hawthorn-tree.*
> I have stood so long by a gap in the wall
> Maybe I shall not die at all.

Yeats's image of the lit house has a complex origin, being compounded of memories of the burning house he saw as a child,[92] and the vision of a miraculously lit ruin which an old Irish peasant woman described for him, and which he records at the end of the preface to *The Words Upon The Windowpane*.[93] To this he could add visions that came sometimes in his own dreams. In *Per Amica Silentia Lunae* he tells of

those elaborate, brightly lighted buildings and sceneries appearing in a moment, as I lie between sleeping and waking.[94]

Like many of the symbols in the last plays, this depends for proper elucidation upon our knowledge of its past uses; for at this stage in his work Yeats quite rightly expects from the reader an acquaintance with his past verse. The lit house is a symbol of the mansions of heaven, where 'all lives that has lived': it was used in this sense in 'All Souls' Night', where we hear of the 'immense miraculous house the Bible promised us' being 'lit up' for a moment by love.[95] It is also a symbol of permanence in 'Crazy Jane On God':

> Before their eyes a house
> That from childhood stood
> Uninhabited, ruinous,
> Suddenly lit up
> From door to top.
> *All things remain in God.*[96]

The old beggar is Yeats's Platonic symbol for humanity, in the rags of mortality, here sustained by the vision of its future beatitude. Nothing is ever lost.

> All the lovely things that were
> Live, for I saw them dancing there.

Yeats makes his poem a conversation between the beggar and the thorn tree under which he is standing, and this is a very Irish detail. We remember, perhaps, the legend of the beggar-poet Raftery:

> He was the greatest poet in Ireland, and he'd make a song about that bush if he chanced to stand under it. There was a bush he stood under from the rain and he made verses praising it, and then when the water came through he made verses dispraising it.[97]

The tree by the gap in the wall, however, is an extremely complex image. Where the lit house is a Biblical and the beggar a Platonic symbol, we shall probably be right to connect it with Attis's tree, in its function as the symbol of the 'antithetical crucifixion', and with the 'dry tree' of medieval symbolism and the 'barren' tree of the Kabbala[98]: all of them symbols of human suffering. The beggar converses with the embittered *alter ego* of his own disillusion:

> What though they danced? Those days are gone,
> Said the wicked, crooked, hawthorn-tree.

The tree then cynically voices the clinging belief of humanity in its own immunity to change. Yeats is a hard poet, and a poet of integrity. If he has voiced, through his beggar, the universal desire of man for his transfiguration and future beatitude, integrity leads him to balance it against man's obdurate belief in his material indestructibility, and his unwillingness to face the fact of death. The play thus closes on a mocking note, and with a brilliantly dramatic twist.

VIII

I have left until now the Musicians' opening song, because I think it discloses its meaning more readily when we have the whole play with which to balance it, and also because it was probably written later than the main text. It is not in fact very well integrated with the narrative that follows. Yeats's aim is to give us an introductory picture of heaven, and in the song he originally wrote, it is the Platonic heaven he describes. There, the lovers 'touch nerve to nerve throughout the sacred grove'; and this is the heaven described in 'The Delphic Oracle Upon Plotinus'; the Greek paradise, the Isles of the Blessed:

> Scattered on the level grass
> Or winding through the grove
> Plato there and Minos pass,
> There stately Pythagoras
> And all the choir of love.[99]

But in the song that he finally printed he defers to the Irish element in the play and gives us an alternative form of the same archetype: Tir-nan-Oge, the paradise of Irish superstition:

> 2nd. Attendant: They dance all day that dance in Tir-nan-Oge.
> 1st. Attendant: There every lover is a happy rogue;
> And should he speak, it is the speech of birds.
> No thought has he, and therefore has no words.
> No thought because no clock, no clock because,
> If I consider deeply, lad and lass,
> Nerve touching nerve upon that happy ground,
> Are bobbins where all time is bound and wound.

Tir-nan-Oge is a timeless country, like Byzantium. In Byzantium, the poet stands outside time and is able to sing at will 'of what is past, or passing, or to come'; and here the lovers are subject to no change, for their bodies are spools on which all time, like a thread, is wound. The image comes from Yeats's memories of the 'pern-mill' at Sligo,[100] but it derives equally from the Greek mystery religions and from Plato's myth of Er, where the three fates weave the destinies of men on 'the spindle of necessity':[101]

> Who talks of Plato's spindle;
> What set it whirling round?
> Eternity may dwindle,
> Time is unwound,
> Dan and Jerry Lout
> Change their loves about.[102]

Here we have the symbol of the unwinding spool, and in the present poem the symbol is reversed. Yeats's central meaning is, I think, that every individual soul in heaven is a part of the divine will and yet at the same time the whole of it, so that each individual soul is, in a sense, the spindle upon which all creation turns. As he was fond of quoting at this time:

> The bright eternal self that is in thunder, the bright eternal self that lives in the voice, are one and the same.[103]

That is to say, the pure self at the centre of each individual personality is identical with God (thunder). Another possible reading of the lines is that the whole universe is motivated by love.

In heaven, the happiness of the soul in its liberation from time is such that it knows only 'the speech of birds', the pure language of joy. The bird is the traditional symbol for the purified soul, as I have used my preface to demonstrate, and Yeats employs it consistently in this sense. One thinks of his manuscript reference to the 'birds that I shall be like when I get out of the body',[104] or of several other uses, for this was his first dramatic symbol, as it was one of his last. In *Time and the Witch Vivien*, Vivien hears a 'bird walk on the doorstep', and this is a symbol of the nearness of her death.[105] In *The Death Of Cuchulain*, the hero sees in a vision

> The shape that I shall take when I am dead,
> My soul's first shape, a soft feathery shape.[106]

'Sailing to Byzantium' gives us the symbol in its most developed form.

In the second verse of this lyric Yeats is remembering his early poem 'The Wanderings Of Oisin':

2nd. Attendant: O never may that dismal thread run loose.
1st. Attendant: For there the hound that Oisin saw pursues
               The hornless deer that runs in such a fright,
               And there the woman clasps an apple tight
               For all the clamour of a famished man.
               They run in foam, and there in foam they ran,
               Nor can they stop to take a breath that still
               Hear in the foam the beating of a bell.

'The Wanderings Of Oisin' was much in Yeats's mind in the 'thirties, and he discusses its meaning at length in *Wheels and Butterflies*. When he wrote it, he says, he tried to keep symbolism out of the text, but it was not easy to deny hound and prey, man and running woman, their full meaning:

[Oisin] rides across the sea with a spirit, he passes phantoms, a boy following a girl, a hound chasing a hare, emblematical of eternal pursuit,* he comes to an island of choral dancing, leaves that after many years, passes the phantoms once again, comes to an island of endless battle for an object never achieved, leaves that after many years, passes the phantoms once again, comes to an island of sleep, leaves that and comes to Ireland, to S. Patrick and old age. I did not pick these images because of any theory but because I found them impressive, yet all the while abstractions haunted me. . . . How hard it was to refrain from pointing out that Oisin after old age, its illumination half accepted, half rejected, would pass in death over another sea to another island.[107]

In this passage Yeats clearly refers to the Platonic symbol for the prenatal state, or heaven, the Isles of the Blessed. He knew this symbol from several sources, one of which was no doubt Taylor's *Dissertation*:

the fortunate islands are said to be raised above the sea; and hence a condition of Being transcending this corporeal life and generation, is denominated the islands of the blessed; but these are the same with the Elysian fields.[108]

*There are of course traditional symbols: the woman with the apple a variant form of the Atalanta-image; and the hound and deer (or hare) alchemical emblems for the two sexes.

They also correspond, in traditional symbolism and in Yeats's mind, with the islands of the dead in Irish mythology and with Avilion and Hy-Brasail:

> Renowned Hy Brazel, where he who touches shall find no more labour or care, nor cynic laughter, but shall go walking about under shadiest boscage, and enjoy the conversation of Cuchulain and the heroes.[109]

As for the images of man and running woman, they are patently as Yeats explains them in an early note, symbols of 'the immortal desire of Immortals', and so of that love which is unending in the heaven Yeats inherited from Swedenborg and the classical tradition.[110] Hound and deer are identical, in the words of the note 'plain images of the desire of the man that is for woman and the desire of the woman which is for the desire of the man'.[111] It remains to add that this heavenly desire is not carnal. In Yeats's heaven, the lovers desire that absolute beauty which each sees reflected in the other's whole being.

The second verse begins with a prayer that the souls who have entered into paradise may never suffer rebirth into the world of time:

> O never may that dismal thread run loose.

In Yeats's source in Plato and the Greek mystery religions, the thread run off by the spindle and sorted by the fates represents the destiny of the reincarnated soul.[112] The First Musician then resumes the description of heaven, Oisin's island (identified now with the Islands of the Blessed), where desire is everlasting, and lovers do not tire. They are continually resuscitated by the sound of a perpetually beating bell ('still' here means 'always'), and this takes us back to Tir-nan-Oge, of which Yeats had written:

> many have seen it in many places; some in the depths of lakes, and heard rising therefrom a vague sound of bells.[113]

The sound of bells, then, is characteristic of the Irish paradise, and I think Yeats means us to connect his image also with the bell which rings midnight in the Great Clock Tower. In heaven, time stands still and it is perpetual midnight; lovers never tire, for they remain always in the first joy of their resurrection into the spiritual world.

The beginning of the play thus prepares us for the symbolism in which the action culminates, and introduces us to the heaven to which we are later to be returned. It does not, however, prepare us fully, for it fails to make explicit the point that love in time is an unreal shadow, an argument Yeats was presently to stress:

> All those living wretches crave
> Prerogatives of the dead that have
> Sprung heroic from the grave.

I think the omission unfortunate, particularly since the discarded version of the song[114] did make this preparation, and in powerful verse. It begins with a direct reference to the Great Clock Tower, for it is much more closely integrated with what follows than the version Yeats kept:

First Musician: I wait until the tower gives forth the chime
And dream of ghosts that have the speech of birds;
Because they have no thoughts they have no words;
No thought because no past or future; Time
Comes from the torture of our flesh, and these,
Cast out by death and tethered there by love,
Touch nerve to nerve throughout the sacred grove
And seem a single creature when they please.

What one is sorry to lose here is the direct statement that 'time comes from the torture of our flesh'. The second verse runs:

Second Musician: I call to mind the iron of the bell
And get from that my harsher imagery,
All love is shackled to mortality,
Love's image is a man at arms in steel;
Love's image is a woman made of stone;
It dreams of the unborn; all else is nought;
Tomorrow and tomorrow fills its thought;
All tenderness reserves for that alone.

The physical body is a mere shell, insensitive as armour or as stone. The lover 'shackled to mortality' thinks always of the far side of death, for love cannot be fully realised in the flesh. Here again we remember 'Ribh at the Tomb of Baile and Aillinn', where Yeats tells us that in heavenly love:

There is no touching here, nor touching there,
Nor straining joy, but whole is joined to whole.[115]

I find the early version of the Musicians' song impressive, though the
last line suggests that it was not brought up to a final polish before
being discarded. But it is clear that, whichever version Yeats might
have adopted, he could not have prepared us fully for what was to
come. The theme was so complex as to demand a longer introduction
than he had space for. Neither of his drafts seems to me to be fully
adequate, and this I feel to be a weakness in the play.

IX

When he wrote *A Full Moon In March*, Yeats had so pared down his
theme that he hardly needed an introduction at all:

First Attendant: What do we sing?
Second Attendant: 'Sing anything, sing any old thing,' said he.
First Attendant: Come then and sing about the dung of swine.

In this play, Yeats abandons the technique of identifying man's fate and
that of Dionysus, and there is no attempt to bring home the kind of
'microcosmic meaning' enforced in *The King Of The Great Clock
Tower*. We are presented with a simple account of the Saviour-God
myth, and it is left to our discretion whether to read the story as a
history of the individual soul also. Since the poetry of *The King Of The
Great Clock Tower* had been at its most powerful at what I will call the
human level, this was a considerable sacrifice; but there seems little
doubt that Yeats's decision strengthened the dramatic structure of his
play, and made it more immediately intelligible. The change is also
significant in a more radical sense: this I shall take up later.

Instead of Tir-nan-Oge we now begin with Pythagoras, and this is
at least not out of place in a play centring upon the Platonic theology.
Pythagoras began the process of translating the Greek mystery religions
into philosophy, and the Platonists followed his example. He is presented as the type of wisdom; but the real function of the lyric is to
define the nature of love:

Every loutish lad in love
Thinks his wisdom great enough,
What cares love for this and that?

> To make all his parish stare
> As though Pythagoras wandered there.
> *Crown of gold or dung of swine.*
>
> Should old Pythagoras fall in love
> Little may he boast thereof.
> *What cares love for this and that?*
>
> Days go by in foolishness.
> O how great their sweetness is.
> *Crown of gold or dung of swine.*

Love is an absolute, whether we think of it as absolute spirituality, 'crown of gold', or absolute grossness, 'dung of swine'; it has nothing in common with the intermediates between the two extremes. The crown of gold we may connect with the crown of melodious diamonds which served Yeats's early prose as a very orthodox symbol for the object of the mystic vision,[116] but it is also to be associated with his Queen, and so underlines her significance as the type of pure spirituality. In the same way, 'dung of swine', a symbol probably derived from Blake,[117] represents carnal love; but it is also the emblem of the hero, now a swineherd, and so suggests his function as representing spirit on the lowest, material plane. Yeats also stresses that love converts all human life into its opposite; it 'can make the loutish wise', as the song goes on to tell us, or it can make a scholar[118] write in praise of folly, and a Pythagoras pass his days in 'foolishness' and find that foolishness 'sweet'. This was a common thesis with Yeats, who had made the point in a note on *Fighting The Waves*:

> Young, we discover an opposite through our love; old, we discover our love through some opposite neither hate nor despair can destroy, because it is another self, a self we have fled in vain.[119]

Love teaches the young to seek the negation of all that they are, and the old can love only an opposite to themselves, which reminds them of some facet of the self they have left undeveloped. This theory of opposites is an argument to which the play returns.

In the action which follows, the cast has been reduced to Queen and suitor, and the hero has become a Swineherd. This is in deference to the almost universal legend where a Queen offers her throne to the man who can woo her best, and is won by a countryman of humble origin. There is also, I think, an allusion to the parable of the prodigal

son, and even perhaps to the story of Odysseus and Eumaeus.* The
reason for the change is clear: Yeats clearly felt that the hero in *The
King Of The Great Clock Tower* had been too romantic a figure for his
purpose, and the change in his status helps to make the drama more
forceful. The Swineherd 'wears a half-savage mask', and Yeats indicates the fallen condition of spirit in the material world in vigorous and
bitter verse, sometimes almost Rabelaisian in its strength:[120]

> Queen, look at me, look long at these foul rags,
> At hair more foul and ragged than my rags;
> Look on my scratched foul flesh. Have I not come
> Through dust and mire? There in the dust and mire
> Beasts scratched my flesh; my memory too is gone,
> Because great solitudes have driven me mad.
> But when I look into a stream, the face
> That trembles upon the surface makes me think
> My origin more foul than rag or flesh.

Here we have the symbolism of 'dust and mire' which I have noted as
a Platonic symbol of the material world; and there may also be some
allusion to the origin in Europe of the cult of Dionysus, which first
entered the Western World through the forests of Northern Greece.
The Swineherd has lost his memory; that is, in Platonic terms, he has
lost the pre-natal memory, as spirit must do on entering the material
universe. He remembers nothing of his existence in the intellectual
world before his incarnation; Yeats ironically has him think his origin
'more foul than rag or flesh'. The rags he is dressed in symbolise the
garment of mortality. There is also some hint of the legend of St. John
the Baptist, as there had to be if Yeats was to universalise his myth.

The Queen warns him of her cruelty in verse equally ferocious:

> Remember through what perils you have come;
> That I am crueller than solitude,
> Forest or beast. Some I have killed or maimed
> Because their singing put me in a rage,
> And some because they came at all. Men hold
> That woman's beauty is a kindly thing,

---

*In the Platonic interpretation of the *Odyssey* (which I shall reconstruct in all detail
in my sixth chapter) Odysseus in the swineherd's hut symbolises man at the very outset
of his search for the spiritual life, and the palace of Ithaca the goal of spirituality to which
he must attain. This symbolism is central to Neoplatonism, and Yeats—who uses 'dung
of swine' and palace in a precisely similar sense—can hardly not have had it in mind.

But they that call me cruel speak the truth,
Cruel as the winter of virginity.
But for a reason that I cannot guess
I would not harm you. Go before I change.

Here the central purpose is clearly to prepare us for the ritual death of the God that is to follow, and to provide us with one of those shreds of characterisation Yeats found necessary in his dance-plays; but there is more in the lines than this. When Yeats turned back from his study of the absolute, as I have shown him doing, to the celebration of 'the whole man', he did so partly because he found the life of sanctity hard and unsympathetic, 'external' as he called it. In his symbolic system he placed the saint next to the hunchback at the dark of the moon.[121] A quotation from Von Hügel will make clear what he found to dislike. This quotation comes at the heart of Von Hügel's study of St. Catherine of Genoa, and St. Catherine is used by Yeats as his symbol for primary sanctity in *A Vision*,[122] so that we know the text was significant to him:

Not only is there no trace about her, at any time, of moral vulgarity of any kind, or of any tendency to it; and this is, of course, a grand strength; but she seems at all times to have been greatly lacking in that quite innocent and normal sensuousness, which appears to form a necessary element of the complete human personality.[123]

Only on rare occasions, Von Hügel continues, was St. Catherine able to become fully human, or in his own memorable phrase to show

the beautiful tenderness and daring of a great positive purity, the purity of flame and not of snow.[124]

It was on the strength of such passages as this that Yeats spoke of 'the sincere and noble Von Hügel'. In his own play, the Queen is the principle of pure spirit and thus at once the type and goal of all sanctity, and she has for Yeats the purity of snow rather than that of fire. His sympathies are with the Swineherd. One remembers a magnificent prose passage in his essay on Balzac, written at about this time:

I have lived from boyhood in the shadow, as it were, of that enumeration of famous women in 'La Recherche de l'absolu' ending with the sentence 'Blessed are the imperfect for theirs is the kingdom of love'. Dante might have made it or some great mediaeval monk.[125]

There is no doubt that Yeats took his stand with imperfection, here and throughout his last verse.

As in the previous play, the Swineherd conducts his love-affair with the crude insolence we may expect from spirit in its fallen condition. ' What do I know of beauty?' he asks the Queen contemptuously, when asked to sing his love for her, and he has nothing more to offer her than

> . . a song—the night of love,
> An ignorant forest and the dung of swine.

This means that he is aware of his own grossness, for the forest, as Taylor points out,[126] is a common Platonic symbol for the fallen world. The Queen has him beheaded, and the severed head sings as before, but in this play the resurrection is at the vernal equinox. The curiously haunting song Yeats gives to the head uses the personae of Jack and Jill to avoid particularisation as far as possible, for Yeats is bringing together many myths; but it leaves us in no doubt that we are present at the ascent of the God:

> I sing a song of Jack and Jill.
> Jill had murdered Jack;
>> *The moon shone brightly.*
> Ran up the hill, and round the hill,
> Round the hill and back.
>> *A full moon in March.*
>
> Jack had a hollow heart, for Jill
> Had hung his heart on high;
>> *The moon shone brightly.*
> Had hung his heart beyond the hill,
> A-twinkle in the sky.
>> *A full moon in March.*

The reference here is patently to Minerva and Dionysus, and to the excision of the god's heart as a symbol of his eventual resurrection. One should not read too much into so simple a lyric, but I imagine the 'hill' stands both for Calvary and the Mount Abiegnos of the mystics, the penitential mountain.

The play ends with the Musicians' song for the closing of the stage curtains, and this song is remarkable for its formal, stately beauty, which contrasts strongly with the dynamic thrust of the remainder of the play. It is perhaps the nearest Yeats ever came in a dance-play to the realisation of the formal ideal he took over from the Japanese. The Queen and the Swineherd appear carrying 'pitchers', and this we are told will symbolise 'to understanding eyes' that they are now outside time, having conquered it:

Tight
Therein all Time's completed treasure is.

The use of this symbol is a glance back to the story of Jack and Jill, the water-carriers, and it is also an allusion to the wineskins of Dionysus. Carrying her pitcher, the Queen is led down by her lover to their marriage bed, Yeats's 'symbol for the solved antinomies':

2nd. Attendant: Why must those holy, haughty feet descend
                 From emblematic niches, and what hand
                 Ran that delicate raddle through their white?
                 My heart is broken, yet must understand.
                 What do they seek for? Why must they descend?
1st. Attendant: For desecration and the lover's night.
2nd. Attendant: I cannot face that emblem of the moon
                 Nor eyelids that the unmixed heavens dart,
                 Nor stand upon my feet, so great a fright
                 Descends upon my savage, sunlit heart.
                 What can she lack whose emblem is the moon?
1st. Attendant: Her desecration and the lover's night.

These verses do indeed 'delight my heart with sound', but it is their symbolic meaning that makes them so impressive, and provides as completely satisfying a conclusion as the trick ending had been in Yeats's previous play. For to our surprise we see that in this resurrection it is the Queen who descends. Yeats's aim is to stress that 'eternity is in love with the productions of time'. We are returned to the argument I have quoted from the Yeats-Ellis *Blake*:

that the mobility of heaven is distinguished from its eternity, that this mobility is Christ, that it fell, or went out into the void which thus became nature, and that on returning it formed the joys of heaven with what it took from the energy or 'eternal hell' outside.

The Queen represents perfect beauty, symbolised by the moon, 'unmixed' spirituality as distinct from that energy whose symbol in Yeats

is the sun.[127] But she in her cold impassivity had been as imperfect as
the Swineherd in his brutal oblivion of his divine nature; heaven is no
heaven until it has been fertilised by its opposite, the energy which is
the property of time. For as Yeats had said in *A Vision*, to 'separate the
Eternal Ideas from Nature and show them self-sustained' is 'a form of
death'.[128] We remember what the Queen had sung to the severed head:

> Child and darling, hear my song.
> Never cry I did you wrong;
> Cry my wrong came not from me
> But my virgin cruelty.

This coldness, this monumental cruelty which the Queen could not
restrain, is the mark that Godhead itself is imperfect when divorced
from the spirit which has gone out into matter: heaven is incomplete
in its separation from man, the timeless in its separation from the
world of time.

X

That this is the radical meaning of *A Full Moon In March* there can
be no doubt: Yeats enforces it by the title and by systematic allusion
to the Attis-Dionysus myth in the lyrics. There are, at the same time,
subsidiary connotations to the symbolism. Yeats does not insist upon
them, and there is no compulsion on the audience to read them into
the play; but they are there beneath the surface, and the critic cannot
afford to ignore them.

By eliminating the King from his cast, Yeats does much more than
simplify the structure of his dance-play. The change affects the whole
balance of his argument. For as long as the Queen had been a mere
puppet, powerless to act in her own right, she could not play a very
prominent part in the symbolism; in the reorganisation of the story,
however, she is promoted to the forefront of the action. We are now
clearly able to see her for what she really is, the type of the 'eternal
feminine', while the Swineherd represents equally the masculine principle in nature, brutal, violent and disruptive. One function of *A Full
Moon In March* is to strip bare the relations between the sexes. All
women, Yeats tells us, inherit from the Great Mother; all men resemble
Dionysus in his essential savagery, through the primitive nature of the
male sexual urge. The love of man and woman follows the pattern of
that of their great archetypes: man is the suitor, dying a spiritual death

from 'beauty's cruelty'; though on the far side of this death woman will admit him to her love.

This theme, suggested rather than stated, is the undercurrent to Yeats's symbolism, and to it is sacrificed the 'microcosmic argument' of *The King Of The Great Clock Tower*. In that play, Yeats's intentions were too complex for him to realise the symbolism on the sexual plane: he was preoccupied with showing that his male protagonist represented the individual soul. Thus we are told that the stroller has, and has left for the Queen's sake, 'a wife fat, slow, thick o' the limbs' —a detail by which Yeats symbolises the attractions of matter, from which the individual soul has to break away; while the Queen, so far from representing woman, is called 'a screen between the living and the dead', a religious image which connects her with the Virgin Mary. All such details could only confuse the new, sexual argument, and so they are eliminated from *A Full Moon In March*; instead, we have a few vivid strokes in which the subsidiary function of Yeats's symbolism is indicated. The Queen is allowed one speech, her speech of warning to her suitor, to establish herself as the great principle of all femininity:

> Men hold
> That woman's beauty is a kindly thing,
> But they that call me cruel speak the truth,
> Cruel as the winter of virginity.

Similarly, there is one place where the Swineherd is presented as the masculine archetype: when he first looks upon his lover's face.

> What do those features matter? when I set out
> I picked a number on the roulette wheel.
> I trust the wheel, as every lover must.

The economy of means here is remarkable: a single suggestive phrase serves to convey to the audience that the Swineherd is the type of 'every lover'; but it is, I think, enough.

The two strata of Yeats's theme are integrated in the final tableau. Here, more than anywhere else, we are simultaneously aware of the sexual and theological elements in the argument: they are, in fact, presented as parallel examples of the working of a single spiritual law. The Queen descends to her inescapable violation, and the chorus provides us with their commentary on what is taking place:

2nd. Attendant: What can she lack, whose emblem is the moon?
1st. Attendant: Her desecration and the lover's night.

Here, on the sexual plane, there is a connection with 'Crazy Jane And
The Bishop':

> A woman can be proud and stiff
> When on love intent;
> But love has pitched his mansion in
> The place of excrement;
> For nothing can be sole or whole
> That has not been rent.

As the poem does, the play also broadens out at its conclusion into a
general statement of the Platonic theory of opposites. Every quality
cries out to be combined with that which is most alien to it, and without such fusion cannot be called complete: 'without contraries is no
progression'. The consummation of virginity lies in its 'desecration',
just as the consummation of the divine order lies in its reconciliation
with the fallen world.

CHAPTER THREE

THE HERNE'S EGG

I

*T*he *Herne's Egg*[1] was written in a period of considerable excitement, after Yeats's Steinach operation, and when he had just completed the study of contemporary poetry he made for *The Oxford Book of Modern Verse*. This was also the time of his friendship with Dorothy Wellesley, and a letter to her compares the projected play and *A Full Moon In March*:

> I have asked Macmillan to send you my new book [*A Full Moon In March*]. I don't like it—it is a fragment of the past I had to get rid of. The swift rhythm of 'Fire', and the study of rhythm my work for the anthology entailed, have opened my door.[2]

The rhythms of Yeats's last period do not really derive from Dorothy Wellesley's poem 'Fire', or from any other modern poet he had been reading, but his discovery of contemporary poetry did have an important effect on his new play, for it encouraged him to break free from the blank verse convention. The letter goes on to make this point:

> I have a three-act tragi-comedy in my head to write in Majorca, not in blank verse, but in short lines like 'Fire', but a larger number of four-stress lines—as wild a play as Player Queen, . . but with more philosophic depth.[3]

I think we can say that the general incentive to write a philosophical play, and to do so in fast-moving rhythms and colloquial language, all probably came to Yeats from Dorothy Wellesley, for these were all qualities he associated with her verse;[4] but the philosophical argument of *The Herne's Egg* owes very little to her. A letter written a little later brings us closer to Yeats's source:

> Shri Purohit Swami is with me, and the play is his philosophy in a fable, or mine confirmed by him.[5]

When Yeats wrote *The Herne's Egg*, the Indian holy man Purohit
Swami was a guest in his house, and they were working together on
a translation of the Upanishads.[6] Yeats had been interested in Indian
thought from adolescence, when he came into contact with Mohini
Chatterjee and with Madame Blavatsky, and he returned to it in what
is for me his most exciting play.

Yeats saw in Platonic and Vedic philosophy the complete antithesis
to Christianity, and he came to prefer the Indian to the Greek. As I
have said, he related all human thought to his cyclic theory of history:

> I . . . saw in the changes of the moon all the cycles; the soul realising
> its separate being in the full moon, then as the moon comes to
> approach the sun and dwindle away, all but realising its absorption
> in God.[7]

Here, Yeats implies that man's mind changes as mechanically as the
moon does, the full moon, as always in his system, symbolising a subjective era and the dark of the moon an objective phase: the distinction
he makes is between the Christian absorption in an external Saviour-
God and the non-Christian tendency to see deity in the Self. Yeats
himself, it is important to realise, had not given his allegiance to the
subjective principle without a knowledge of both forms of visionary
experience. As a young man, he had known the sense of Christian
dependence:

> Close to Inchy Wood . . . I felt an emotion which I said to myself
> was the root of Christian mysticism. There had swept over me a
> sense of weakness, of dependence upon a great personal Being some-
> where near at hand.[8]

This was the objective vision, the sense of the limitation of the Self
and of its reliance upon an external power; but in maturity Yeats could
balance it against a sense of the strength of the personality, whose 'own
sweet will' is 'Heaven's will', and which is dependent upon no external
reality at all:

> I am always, in all that I do, driven to a moment which is the reali-
> sation of myself as unique and free, or to a moment which is the
> surrender to God of all that I am. I think that there are historical
> cycles when one or the other predominates.[9]

The sense of the Self as 'unique and free', as in fact divine, Yeats felt to be the distinguishing feature of Indian philosophy.

Though he had written two plays out of the Platonic theology, Yeats was not altogether a convinced Platonist, and it would be wrong to think that he subscribed even to Plotinus without reservation. At the time of Plato and Aristotle, the pendulum of history was already beginning to swing away from the Self towards the idea of an objective God:

> To Aristotle and to Christian orthodoxy only God has value in himself, even Spirit is contingent. At the fall of Hellenism and its exaltation of personality, instinct demanded an extreme objectivity. Man had to annihilate himself.[10]

The development of Greek philosophy coincided with 'the fall of Hellenism', and thus even Plato to some extent repelled Yeats because of the element of objectivity in his thought:

> Even the truth into which Plato dies is a form of death; for when he separates the eternal Ideas from Nature and shows them self-sustained, he prepares the Christian desert and the Stoic suicide.[11]

But Indian philosophy, and particularly the thought of the Upanishads, knew nothing of this strange dualism; it was purely subjective:

> In the Brihadaranyaka-Upanishad there is a certain Yadnyawalkya into whose mouth are put profound thoughts, litanies, variations upon a theme: 'Thunder is the honey of all beings; all beings are the honey of thunder. The bright eternal self that is in thunder, the bright eternal self that lives in the voice, are one and the same: that is immortality, that is spirit, that is all' . . . He had substituted the eternal Self for all the Gods.[12]

In words which Spengler might have written, Yeats compares Yadnyawalkya to Pythagoras, the earliest and most subjective of his Greek authorities; Pythagoras' teaching derived from the mystery religions as Yadnyawalkya's did from Vedic religious legend. He then compares Socrates to Buddha, for in their thought objective reasoning had begun to set in. Buddha thought life essentially evil, Socrates that reality was something outside life and time:

Like Pythagoras, who occupied the same place in Greek civilisation, Yadnyawalkya substituted philosophic reason for custom and mythology, put an end to the Golden Age and began that of the Sophists, an intellectual anarchy that found its Socrates in Buddha.[13]

Between the composition of *A Full Moon In March* and *The Herne's Egg*, Yeats turned away from Platonism to Pythagoras and the Upanishads, from the abstract to the concrete. Indian philosophy is remembered in this play and in the prose, Pythagoras in the poem 'The Statues',[14] which makes him the fountainhead of all that is best in European thought.

I have suggested what, centrally, Yeats learned from Indian religion: it taught him that the pure Self is identical with God. The hermit 'upon Mount Meru or Everest', Yeats tells us, knows this well:

If to Brahma's question—'Who are you?' he can answer 'Yourself' [he can] pass out of the three penitential circles . . . and find some cavern upon Meru, and so pass out of all life.[15]

The ascetic, knowing the truth, can enter upon that solitary meditation where mundane realities disappear. In his own poem 'He and She', Yeats goes further than this; the soul substitutes for the answer 'I am Yourself' the proud 'I am I'. By this it realises its own divinity and so attains to the object of all human existence:

All creation shivers
At that sweet cry.[16]

But to arrive at such an identification some discipline was necessary, and we find Yeats preoccupied with the meditation used in the system of Yoga, as a means by which complete self-realisation can be brought about:

Through states analogous to self-induced hypnotic sleep the devotee attains a final state of complete wakefulness called, now conscious Samadhi, now Tureeya, where the soul, purified of all that is not itself, enters upon its own timelessness.[17]

Having accepted this discipline, Yeats ranges through history to find parallels to it in heterodox mysticism. Christianity, he thought, had lost the habit, but it was rediscovered:

In the seventeenth century conscious samadhi reappeared in the 'waking trance' of Boehme, when truth fell upon him 'like a bursting shower', and in the eighteenth, much contaminated by belief in the literal inspiration of scripture, in the visions of Swedenborg . . . we may, I think, concede to Swedenborg an impure samadhi.[18]

By this means Yeats associates Boehme and Swedenborg with the disciplines of Indian mysticism, and it is worth pointing this out. In *The Herne's Egg*, they are as much in his mind as the Upanishads.

It may be objected that *The Herne's Egg* does not appear to be about Boehme and Swedenborg, or Indian philosophy, at all; the setting, characterisation and plot are distinctively Irish. It is the strength of the play that Yeats clothed what might have been an exotic fable in a Celtic dress, but it is not hard to show that he did so. The process began with 'Supernatural Songs', where Ribh is an Irish hermit, but is afforded a distinctively Indian philosophy, as the notes Yeats wrote for the Cuala Press edition make clear.[19] For Yeats had come to see primitive Ireland and India as complementary:

It pleases me to fancy that when we turn towards the East, in or out of Church, we are turning not less to the ancient west or north; the one fragment of pagan Irish philosophy come down, 'The Song of Amergin', seems Asiatic.[20]

The comparison Yeats is making here is continued in one of the most beautiful passages of his late prose, where he is contrasting subjective and objective morality. In it the 'Russian mystic' serves as the type of objective thought, and Yeats stresses that subjective vision persisted into the first four centuries of the Christian era, after which it died out in Europe:

The Russian, like most European mystics, distrusts visions though he admits their reality, seems indifferent to Nature, may perhaps dread it like St. Bernard who passed the Italian lakes with averted eyes. The Indian, on the other hand, . . . speaks continually of the beauty and terror of the great mountains, interrupts his prayer to listen to the song of birds, remembers with delight the nightingale that disturbed his meditations by alighting upon his head and singing there, recalls after many years the whiteness of a sheet, the softness of a pillow, the gold embroidery upon a shoe. These things are indeed part of the 'splendour of that Being'. The first four Christian centuries shared his thought, Byzantine theologians that named their great church 'The Holy Wisdom' sang it; so too did those Irish monks who made innumerable poems about bird and beast, and spread the doctrine that Christ was the most beautiful of men. Some Irish saint, whose name I have forgotten, sang 'There is one among the beasts that is perfect, one among the fish, one perfect among men.'[21]

The Self, which is both Godhead and the core of each individual personality, is diffused into every particle of life; 'everything that lives is holy', as Blake had said. India and ancient Ireland shared the perception of this fact.

At the time he was planning *The Herne's Egg*, Yeats was casting about for some other European writer who could support him in the attitude to experience he had come to adopt. He thought much of Balzac at this period, and wrote the moving essay on him called 'Louis Lambert'.[22] Like him, Balzac had renounced the cold, Christian view of sanctity; had he not written 'Blessed are the imperfect, for theirs is the Kingdom of love'? Yeats came even to think that the example of Balzac's novels, read when he was a young man, had rescued him from a sterile Platonism:

> Me at any rate he saved from the pursuit of a beauty that seeming at once absolute and external requires, to strike a balance, hatred as absolute.[23]

Like him, again, Balzac had turned to esoteric mysticism and the study of the occult in his search for an imaginatively consistent basis for his art; he had read Grosseteste and Bonaventura, and had written a whole novel, *Seraphita*, based on the teaching of Swedenborg. Like him, Yeats felt that Balzac accepted the visionary world:

> When Balzac speaks through Seraphita, or describes the Duchesse de Longuet playing upon the organ, he thinks of the Choir of Heaven.[24]

But, as Yeats was now doing, this man 'whose rhythm seems to combine the bull and the nightingale'[25] had turned back from the cold climate of Seraphita's ecstasy: he had preferred life, and had seen something approaching sanctity in everything that lived:

Balzac leaves us when the book is closed amid the crowd that fills the boxes and the galleries of grand opera; even after leaving Seraphita amid her snows we return to that crowd which is always right because there is so much history in its veins, to those kings, generals, diplomats, beautiful ladies, to that young Bianchon, to that young Desplein, to all those shabby students of the arts sitting in the galleries. Tolstoi, Dostoieffsky, Flaubert, draw to their support scholars and sectaries, their readers stand above the theme or beside it, they judge and they reject; but there in the crowded theatre are Balzac's readers and his theme; seen through his eyes they have become philosophy without ceasing to be history.[26]

It was because Balzac's art accepted, in this way, the whole of life, that Yeats found room to write an essay on him among his Indian studies and the preparations for his new play. The essay is magnificent, and it is profoundly moving; and where Yeats is profoundly moved by a writer, that writer is commonly remembered in his own subsequent work.

II

The Herne's Egg is a difficult play for at least three reasons. Like much of Yeats's mature work, it does not yield its full meaning to the reader who goes to it without a knowledge of philosophy, for it is nothing if not a philosophical play. It is also quite unapproachable without a knowledge of the whole body of Yeats's symbolism, for in it he takes up, without explaining them, a number of wholly or partly traditional symbols which he has used in the past; the Herne himself and the symbol of the fool are two of the more obvious. But it is also difficult in a way in which not many of Yeats's works are, in that it contains several oblique literary allusions. I think it is definitely part of Yeats's design that we shall make the connections he hints at, and it will be best to begin by seeing what works he has in mind.

The most obvious set of allusions is to Shakespeare's *Julius Caesar*. Congal is to some extent the Brutus to Aedh's Caesar; he and his men surprise Aedh and kill him in a comic brawl, and there is talk of treachery:

> Congal: Tara knew that he was overmatched;
> Knew from the start he had no chance;
> Died of a broken head; died drunk;
> Accused me with his dying breath

> Of secretly practising with a table-leg,
> Practising at midnight until I
> Became a perfect master with the weapon.
> But that is all lies.

In fact, Aedh says that his death is 'a murderous drunken plot'. After it, Congal's man Pat plays the Antony over his body:

> . . . Let all men know
> He was a noble character
> And I must weep at his funeral.

Congal himself falls into the Shakespearean idiom:

> I would not have had him die that way,
> Or die at all, he should have been immortal.

Like Brutus, again, Congal is persecuted by misfortune after the murder, which at first seemed to promise him nothing but advancement, and he kills himself in a manner obviously suggestive of Brutus's suicide. The Fool assists him much as Strato did Brutus:

> Congal: Give me that spit.
> I put it in the crevice of the rock,
> That I may fall upon its point.
> These stones will keep it sticking straight.

I have little doubt that this parallelism is intentional, that Yeats wishes the reader to be aware of it, and that it is not mere burlesque, but is meant to assist us in coming to an understanding of the play. Even so, it is not at first easy to see its significance.

An allusion which is less obvious, and which, in fact, has not been noticed before, is to the little-known Irish legend of the battle of Magh Rath, and to Samuel Ferguson's now forgotten poem *Congal* which is based upon it.[27] Yeats knew the myth itself in English translation,[28] and he knew and to some extent admired Ferguson's rather unwieldy epic:

Ferguson is frequently dull, for he often lacked the 'minutely appropriate' words necessary to embody those fine changes of feeling which enthral the attention, but his sense of weight and size, of action and tumult, has set him apart and solitary, an epic figure in a lyric age.[29]

One cannot say that the Irish myth provides Yeats with a complete source for his narrative, but at least it gives him justification for choosing an Irish setting for his play.

In the original legend,[30] Congal and Domhnall (not Aedh) are two rival Irish rulers. Congal is invited to a banquet by the high King Domhnall, and they decide upon 'goose eggs' as a delicacy for the feast. Domhnall (not, as in Yeats, Congal) sends out 'purveyors'; they come to a 'hermitage', and steal eggs from a woman who is the housekeeper to a Christian saint. The saint curses them, with the result that, at the banquet, Congal is accidentally given a hen's egg, 'though a goose egg, in a silver dish, stood before every king in the house'. Congal uses this trivial incident as a pretext to rebel against the high king, but, after a series of adventures, none of which finds its way into Yeats's text, he is killed in battle. This story gives Yeats a precedent for his episode of the banquet, though in his own version it is of course Aedh who meets his death there.

Ferguson's romantic epic adds a good deal of embroidery to the essential myth, and two of the additions he permits himself are remembered in Yeats's text. One of these is the incident of Congal's death 'at the hands of a fool'. Greatly expanding a detail in the original, Ferguson has Congal slain 'by an idiot youth, whom he passed by in the battle, on account of his imbecility'.[31] The boy, in his poem, is named Cuanna, and after Congal has refused his challenge to single combat, Cuanna gives him 'a mortal blow with a billhook'.[32] Though we still have to decide precisely *why* Yeats chose to adopt this detail, it is clearly at the root of his own narrative of Tom Fool.

Another incident which Yeats converts to his own ends is Ferguson's story of Lafinda. She, in the rather sentimental poem, is the betrothed of Congal, and after his rebellion against the high king enters a Christian nunnery. At the climax of the battle, when Congal lies dying upon the ground, she comes from her cell to tend his wounds, though she rejects his love:

'Bride now of Christ,' she answered low, 'I know thee but as one
For whom my heavenly spouse has died.'[33]

Lafinda is not in any way to be associated with the 'housekeeper of the saint'—an old woman who, in Ferguson's poem as in the Gaelic, is a very minor character and speaks only a few words—but Yeats clearly combines both these personages in the figure of his Attracta. Just as the housekeeper serves the saint, so Attracta is the keeper of the Herne's eggs, and, like Lafinda, she succours Congal at the moment of death.

So much can be done to provide Yeats's play with a Gaelic source, though the source, when it is found, leaves out of account the Herne himself, the Herne's egg, Aedh, the stylised battle at the beginning, Congal's six accomplices, almost all the action after the banquet itself and—if we consider it as a full-length portrait—the character of Attracta. Ferguson's Lafinda does not resemble Attracta in point of detail, but fills a conventional and hardly very important role.[34] All we can say, then, is that Yeats took over three incidents from the Irish— the banquet, the wounding of Congal by a fool, and his death in the presence of a woman figure—with full determination to add to them whatever he pleased; and he chose such a framework, I think, for two reasons. He probably hoped, in the first place, that a Dublin audience would recognise the mythological basis of his narrative, and that the non-initiates among them would be content to take his play at the level of Irish heroic legend. With this, I think he saw symbolic potentialities in the three incidents he retained: they were not, as they stood, archetypally communicative, but they could by very skilful handling be made so. Yeats therefore adds to them a great deal of extraneous matter, building, as Melchiori notes,[35] round the symbol of the egg. As I shall later demonstrate, this added material is usually Indian in origin. *The Herne's Egg* reflects nothing so much as Yeats's studies with Purohit Swami, and the strain of Irish allusion it contains will not bring us to the heart of his play.

III

Whatever *The Herne's Egg* owes to Irish, or even to Indian, sources, a principal borrowing is certainly from Balzac's novel *Seraphita*.[36] Attracta, as Yeats characterises her, *is* in fact Seraphita, and in everything she says and does he is building upon Balzac's heroine.

In Balzac, Seraphita is an imaginary daughter of Swedenborg who is endowed from her birth with the utmost purity and beauty, and the course of the novel leads through her triumph over temptation to her final mystic union with God, after which she ascends into heaven.

The being we call Seraphita is one of those rare and awe-inspiring spirits to whom it is given to constrain man, to coerce nature, and to share the occult powers of God.[37]

'In the same way, Yeats's Attracta is the dedicated priestess and the beloved of the Great Herne, whom I shall presently demonstrate to represent pagan, subjective Godhead, and the play leads up to their mystic union, when the God begets, as Attracta says, 'his image in the mirror of my spirit', an illusion to Boehme's mirror I have already clarified.[38]

In describing this mystic marriage, the correspondences are so close as to be verbal. Seraphita says, in the translation Yeats read:

My marriage was decided upon at my birth; I am betrothed.[39]

Attracta, using the same archaism, speaks of herself as:

Being betrothed to the Great Herne.

A character in Balzac's novel describes Seraphita, shortly before her transfiguration:

To me she is a sorceress who bears in her right hand an invisible instrument to stir the world with, and in her left the thunderbolt that dissolves everything at her command.[40]

Yeats preserves the exact image:

Nor shall it end until
She lies there full of his might,
His thunderbolts in her hand.

Seraphita is permeated by the symbolism of midwinter, for snow and ice are the images of Seraphita's virginity, and her marriage is the 'first springtime of the new century', when at last they are dissolved:

'I promise, if my father will grant it, to invite you to that mysterious wedding.'
'Is it to be soon?'
'I am waiting.'
A long silence ensued.

'The spring is come,' said Seraphita. 'The noise of waters and of breaking ice has begun; will you not come to hail the first spring-time of the new century?'[41]

Similarly in Yeats's play 'snow' lies among the 'wintry rocks', and this is symbolic of Attracta's virginity:

> Women thrown into despair
> By the winter of their virginity
> Take its abominable snow,
> As boys do common snow, and make
> An image of god or bird or beast
> To feed their sensuality.

Congal says that 'seven men/ Are needed to melt down that snow', and when he and his followers finally rape Attracta and fulfil the prophecy, they are possessed by the God, who consummates through their agency his mystic marriage with his priestess. The imagery of snow in the play has perhaps a compound origin, for we should not forget the symbolism in Von Hügel which I have quoted, but I think it derives principally from Balzac. In the same way, the marriage in *The King Of The Great Clock Tower*, taking place at midnight on the last day of the old year, is probably a reminiscence of Balzac's sym-bolism of the century's end.

Seraphita, though she has no concern on earth but the purification of her soul which will make her mystic marriage possible, still finds time for the trivial affairs of her village, and helps to bring about the marriage of Wilfred and Minna, two young countryfolk.[42] Yeats no doubt realised the dramatic possibilities inherent in this, and exactly parallels it in a moving scene. Attracta finds time to give advice to three young country girls, just before going into the trance that leads her to her bridebed:

> Attracta: Sit round upon these stones.
> Children, why do you fear
> A woman but little older,
> A child yesterday?
> All, when I am married,
> Shall have good husbands. Kate
> Shall marry a black-headed lad.

Agnes: She swore but yesterday
        That she would marry black.
Attracta: But Agnes there shall marry
        A honey-coloured lad.
Agnes: O!
Attracta: Mary shall be married
        When I myself am married
        To the lad that is in her mind.

Again—and this is perhaps the most important reminiscence of all—
Seraphita, like Attracta, is tempted by 'seven devils' to prove her
worthiness of her marriage. In Balzac, these represent the forces of
desire; Seraphita overcomes them by meditation; for she 'remains
praying':

Spirits marvelled at her constancy; they stood there in a motionless
chorus, weeping and saying 'Courage'. At last she had triumphed
over desire, unchained to rend her in every shape and species.[43]

In Yeats, the seven tempters are of course Congal and his six followers,
and in tempting Attracta they test her absolute purity of intention.
But her meditation remains unbroken, and when her constancy has in
this way been proved, the God descends into them, and uses their
bodies to consummate his love. The analogy here is crucial, for we
must, I think, use Balzac to ascertain the precise significance of the
symbolism of the 'seven men' in Yeats.

Attracta's marriage takes place when she is in deep trance—a condition no doubt analogous to the mystical state of *samadhi* I have referred to—and, after her union with the God, she advises us obliquely
that her whole personality has been changed:

When beak and claw their work began
What horror stirred in the roots of my hair?
    Said the bride of the Herne and the Great Hearne's bride.
But who lay there in the cold dawn
When all that terror had come and gone?
Was I the woman lying there?

Balzac also advises us obliquely that Seraphita will change her whole
nature after her marriage.

According to Swedenborg God did not create angels independently; there are but those who have been human beings on earth. The angels are not angels by original nature; they are transformed into angels, by an intimate union with God.[44]

When, after her marriage, Attracta goes out to tend Congal on the mountainside, she is not—as Ferguson's Lafinda is—a 'sister of mercy' merely: she has been 'transformed' into an angelic spirit, and in this condition tries to save Congal from the punishment of metempsychosis decreed for him upon his death. This detail of her transfiguration Yeats clearly derives from Balzac, and through him from the teaching of Swedenborg on the function of angels, who 'are kept to loving and valuing' the souls still in the world.[45] The teaching of Swedenborg here corresponds with Indian tradition, for as Yeats himself wrote in his translation of the Brihadaranyaka-Upanishad, 'when all desires of the heart are gone, mortal becomes immortal, man becomes spirit, even in this life'.[46]

IV

The analogy between Attracta and Seraphita cannot be dismissed as in any sense casual. Yeats does not merely take some of his incident from Balzac; he takes over an entire relationship. If we are to discover the precise significance of the love-affair between Attracta and the Great Herne, we must do so by understanding Seraphita's love-affair with God, and the meaning here is complex.

Previous Yeats criticism has already made the salient point. Carl Benson, in his essay on 'Yeats and Balzac's "Louis Lambert" ' has explained the argument that underlies Seraphita as it does that book:

One of Lambert's key notions is a Swedenborgian one, that all men have a dual nature. The angelic side is emphasised if the inner man conquers the external. If, on the other hand, man allows simple physical action to dominate, 'the angel slowly perishes through the materialisation of both natures.'[47]

This definition is hardly comprehensive, and I will implement it from Swedenborg himself. At the centre of Swedenborg's argument is the idea that the Self is essentially impure:

Every individual in the heavens is aware and believes, aye, perceives, that he wishes and does nought of what is good, of himself; and thinks and believes nought of what is true, of himself, but of the Divinity, thus, of the Lord; and that the good and the true which are from himself, are not good and true, because there is not life from the divinity in them.[48]

Faith in the Self is in fact the passport to eternal damnation:

Spirits, who, while they lived in the world, fixed themselves in the belief, that the good which they do and the truth which they believe, are from themselves . . . are not received into heaven; the angels shun them; they look on them as dolts and thieves; as dolts, because they are continually looking to themselves and not to the Divinity; as thieves, because they take away from the Lord what is his.[49]

Man's separation from God has taken place for this very reason:

because man has broken his connection with heaven, by having turned away his inner parts from heaven, and turned them round to the world and to Self, through the love of Self and of the world, and has thus withdrawn himself, so as to serve for a basis and foundation to heaven no longer.[50]

Balzac's mystical novels reproduce this argument, and Seraphita's virtues are Swedenborgian, objective, and as negative as those of Lafinda—a fact which may explain why Yeats associated the two figures. Here is Seraphita's own definition of her religion:

I have conquered the flesh by abstinence; I have vanquished false speech by silence; I have vanquished false knowledge by humility; I have vanquished pride by charity; I have vanquished the earth by love; I have paid my tribute of suffering; I am purified by burning for the truth; I have striven for life by prayer; I wait adoring, and I wait resigned.[51]

Attracta lives by the same principles:

> Attracta: Being betrothed to the Great Herne
> I know what may be known; I burn
> Not in the flesh but in the mind;
> Chosen out of all my kind

> That I may lie in a blazing bed
> And a bird take my maidenhead.
> To the unbegotten I return,
> All a womb and a funeral urn.

Attracta has no desires but the intellectual desire for union with God; her bridebed is pure spirituality, fire being Yeats's symbol for the spiritual life, as I have shown. The 'blazing bed' gives us also a connection with the phoenix, a traditional alchemical symbol for rebirth into the heavenly world. She wishes to escape from the wheel of birth and death, and knows—as Yeats will have learned from the Buddhist *Sutras*—that there is no escape save by union with the divine principle:

> There is, disciples, an Unbecome, Unborn, Unmade, Unformed; if there were not this Unbecome, Unborn, Unmade, Unformed, there would be no way out for that which is become, born, made and formed.[52]

But she effects her escape by making herself 'all a womb and a funeral urn', that is, a compound of the death-wish and the desire for her mystic marriage. She has made herself this, and nothing more. In so doing she has renounced the whole of life and with it the Self, in so far as the Self is manifested in everything that lives. Congal, in a magnificent passage, rebukes her for this:

> It may be that life is suffering
> But youth that has not yet known pleasure
> Has not the right to say so: pick,
> Or be picked by seven men,
> And we shall talk it out again.

If we remember how much Yeats's sympathies were with the Self when he wrote *The Herne's Egg*, we shall see that Congal's stricture here is also his own.

Yeats faithfully reproduces Balzac's Swedenborgian arguments in describing Attracta's relationship with God, and his integrity in doing justice to these arguments, with which he was not altogether in sympathy, is a mark of his stature as an artist. What could be more passionate than the speech of Attracta I have just quoted, or more human and moving than her conversation with Kate, Mary, and Agnes, before she goes, in *samadhi*, to her wedding; how could this side of Yeats's theme be given more complete expression than in the lines which then follow:

> Mary: And must he be all feathers?
> Agnes: Have a terrible beak?
> Kate: Great terrible claws?
> Attracta: Whatever shape he choose,
> Though that be terrible,
> Will best express his love.
> Agnes: When he comes—will he?——
> Attracta: Child, ask what you please.
> Agnes: Do all that a man does?
> Attracta: Strong sinew and soft flesh
> Are foliage round the shaft
> Before the arrowsmith
> Has stripped it; and I pray
> That I, all foliage gone,
> May shoot into my joy.*

The path of renunciation, where the Tree of Life is stripped bare of all 'superabundance' of sensual foliage, could not be more vividly symbolised; and we do not question that we have witnessed the consummation of a life of extreme purity when Attracta is raped and the God possesses her:

> The Herne is my husband.
> I lay beside him, his pure bride.

But Attracta's is a negative and not a positive purity, to use Von Hügel's phrase. In an early essay Yeats tells us that Blake prayed to be delivered from 'the spectral and formal intellect of Swedenborg',[53] and in *A Vision* he dismisses Swedenborg with extreme contempt:

> a mind incredibly dry and arid, hard, tangible, and cold, like the minerals he assayed for the Swedish government.[54]

The rest of *The Herne's Egg* is an argument to offset the Swedenborgian teaching.

The first stages of the reaction can be seen in the symbol employed

---

*This passage in fact derives directly from Indian traditional symbolism. Compare Yeats's translation of part of the Katha-Upanishad (*The Ten Principal Upanishads*, p. 38): 'Man should strip him of the body [i.e. renounce the sensual life] as the arrow-maker strips the reed, that he may know God as perpetual and pure.'

for the God himself. Yeats could not be satisfied with the objective deity of Swedenborg. The image of the bird as God is specifically Indian in its origin, for as Purohit Swami says 'by analogy we endow God with a name and a form to meditate on him';[55] but Yeats did not need Purohit Swami to introduce him to this symbol, for he had learned it from Madame Blavatsky and Mohini Chatterjee in the 'eighties. The swan, Madame Blavatsky says, is the traditional Hindu symbol for divinity, 'representing, for instance, Divine Wisdom, Wisdom in darkness beyond the reach of man'.[56] In primitive legend, therefore:

> Bramah became the Swan of Eternity, who lays at the beginning of each Mahâmanvantara a Golden Egg.[57]

'The egg or the circle', she explains, archetypally represents the quintessence of the manifested world, for

> in Occultism, the primordial form of everything manifested, from atom to globe, from man to angel, is spheroidal, the sphere having been with all nations the emblem of eternity and infinity.'[58]

The myth, she goes on, was widely disseminated, and she compares 'the egg of the Universe in which Ra gestates'[59] and the Orphic egg of the Greek mystery religions. In another context she postulates that 'Pythagoras brought Bramah's doctrines from the eastern sanctuaries' and that they were then translated into the Orphic hymns.[60] Her theory here Yeats cannot have accepted, for he knew that Pythagoras learnt from the mystery religions and did not inaugurate them, but her symbolism of bird, egg and sphere he took over in his verse.

In Yeats's system, every cycle of the Great Year begins from the manifestation of Godhead under the symbol of the bird:

> I imagine the annunciation that founded Greece as being made to Leda, remembering that they showed in a Spartan temple, strung up to the roof as a holy relic, an unhatched egg of hers . . . and when in my ignorance I try to imagine what older civilisation that annunciation rejected, I can but see bird and woman blotting out some corner of the Babylonian mathematical starlight.[61]

His poem 'The Mother Of God'[62] suggests that he saw the Christian dispensation in a similar light; the dove is the Christian symbol for the

Holy Spirit, and at the annunciation to Mary, she is aware of 'wings beating about the room'. In *The Herne's Egg* he recalls the myth of Leda, which he clearly regarded as the European version of the swan archetype:

> Women thrown into despair
> By the winter of their virginity
> Take its abominable snow,
> As birds take common snow, and make
> An image of God or bird or beast
> To feed their sensuality:
> Ovid had a literal mind,
> And though he sang it neither knew
> What lonely lust dragged down the gold
> That crept on Danae's lap, nor knew
> What rose against the moony* feathers
> When Leda lay upon the grass.

Here, Congal is mocking Attracta, and suggests that the Godhead she loves is a mere fabrication of her morbid imagination, but we are of course not expected to believe him. As Attracta says in reply:

> There is no reality but the Great Herne.

For, as Yeats and Purohit Swami wrote in their translation of the Upanishads:

> Invisible, he sees; inaudible, he hears; unthinkable, he thinks; unknowable, he knows. None other can see, hear, think, know. He is your own Self, the immortal; the controller; nothing else matters.[63]

The Herne is divine Selfhood ('thunder is the honey of all beings'), of which each individual Self constitutes a part.

Yeats translates the 'swan of Bramah' into an Irish heron in deference to the guiding principle of his play; the exotic has to be subordinated to the Celtic. The heron was an excellent choice, for several reasons. As I have said, Yeats could not accept Swedenborg's objective deity; he wanted a deity in which it would be possible for the 'whole man' to believe, and he wanted, therefore, a subjective symbol. Further, since

---

*'Moony' because this incident will have taken place at a full moon in March.

the setting of the play is clearly in primitive, non-Christian Ireland, the
Ireland whose philosophy he had equated with the Indian, he wanted
a pagan symbol. The heron had for him strong pagan associations. In
the Irish myth, the pagan men of learning at the court of King Leag-
haire are turned into herons by St. Patrick, and he himself tells this
story in *The Secret Rose*.[64] Again, in his play *Calvary*, he had used the
heron as a symbol for 'subjective life';[65] for that part of the soul of man
quite unaffected by the Christian revelation, and for which the death
of Jesus had no meaning:

> Motionless under the moon-beam,
> Up to his feathers in the stream;
> Although fish leap, the white heron
> Shivers in a dumbfounded dream.
> God has not died for the white heron.[66]

The heron here is preoccupied with the Self, and this went to enhance
its suitability. Yeats therefore took it over into *The Herne's Egg* and
did all he could to give immediate impact to his symbolism by the
stage direction at the beginning of the play:

> Men and rocks; high up on backcloth a rock, its base hidden in mist;
> on this rock stands a great Herne.

The image is of a *great* Herne, and the high rock on which it stands no
doubt has affinities with the mountain symbol in Hindu tradition, with
its three penitential rings, representing stages of the meditative life; the
mountaintop is sacred to God.[67] The mountain-side is littered with
herne's eggs, and here, though the precise meaning is best left until
later, we must clearly understand a connection with the archetypal egg
of Brahma. Yeats shows his awareness of this symbolism in an early
note on Blake:

> The egg of Los, sometimes called the mundane egg ... is the micro-
> cosmic aspect of that 'circle pass not' so much talked of in theoso-
> phical mysticism, and is identical with the egg of Bramah.[68]

Here Yeats makes an association with forbidden things, with the know-
ledge-barrier beyond which the adept in theosophy was not permitted
to pass, and this point will later be returned to. For the present, it is
enough to show that he knew the symbolism. What he understood so

well as the editor of Blake, we cannot suppose him to have forgotten as the author of *The Herne's Egg*.

The Herne, then, was suitable to Yeats's purpose because it was a traditional Celtic symbol, and he was also, no doubt, attracted to it because it was a grotesque symbol. *The Herne's Egg* is a strange and an extremely uninhibited play; it hides a profoundly serious intention behind a mask of flamboyant levity. This tragicomic levity is not unique in our drama (a near parallel, perhaps, is provided by long stretches of *Hamlet*) and, though Yeats's practice has been condemned by most of his critics, it seems to me to be creative and fully justified.* At all events, Yeats needed a tragicomic God—an image as irreverent as Blake's Nobodaddy—to balance his tragicomic hero Congal, and 'the old, old herne who had but one leg' provided him with the grotesque figure he required.

I still have to show why the Great Herne does not make love to Attracta in his own person, why he chooses instead a substitute-relation, through the bodies of Congal and his men. This incident, of course, is mere metaphor,** but Yeats was a traditionalist in all things, and this case he had an authority he had been drawing upon for years. His authority was Plutarch, though Plutarch himself states that he is merely summarising the teachings of Egyptian theurgy on the subject.

Yeats refers us to Plutarch's views on divine cohabitation in *Visions and Beliefs in The West of Ireland*, where he also tells the traditional legend of Cuchulain and Fand.[69] The reference is to the *Morals*, and Plutarch's real point is to make a distinction between the ethereal and corporeal bodies, properties in which Yeats of course believed. By the ethereal body, Yeats explains in *A Vision*,[70] is meant in occultism the pure embodiment of the soul after death. Plutarch points out that it is impossible for a soul in this pure state to have physical contact with a living being, and that it is therefore improper to represent goddesses as having contact with men:

*I should like to suggest, as a comparison for Yeats's poetry in this vein, the archetypal paintings produced by Picasso in the nineteen-thirties. Beside *The Herne's Egg* I would set, say, 'Minotaur Carrying a Dying Horse', and beside 'News for the Delphic Oracle' perhaps 'Ulysses and the Sirens'. These paintings of Picasso are full of comic invention, but their comedy is a very subtle thing: it flows up, together with a profound archetypal symbolism, from the depths of the subconscious mind.

**I imagine it is no more than a reconstruction, in concrete terms, of Seraphita's— transcendental—mystic marriage. But there is a difficult passage in *A Vision*, in which I think Yeats has the Mandukya-Upanishad in mind, where he says that humanity is so fallen from the spiritual world that God may first have to make his presence felt to the worshipper on the sexual plane; by a transfiguration of 'natural craving'. 'Such experience is said, however, to wear itself out swiftly, giving place to the supernatural union.'

The Egyptians . . . think that no mortal can beget anything on a goddess, because they believe the goddesses are made of thin air, and subtle heat and moisture.[71]

Yeats remembered Plutarch when he soon afterwards made the ingenious reconstruction of myth that is *The Only Jealousy Of Emer*, a play in which he completely recasts the traditional legend as he himself had already set it out. Fand loves Cuchulain, but being unable to make love to his corporeal body, she 'gives him the touch', or spirits away his soul, putting an alien soul in its place.[72] Another reference to the intractability of the ethereal body to mortal touch occurs in *The Death of Cuchulain*. The harlot cannot make love with the Sidhe:

> I adore those clever eyes,
> Those muscular bodies, but can get
> No grip upon their thighs.[73]

In the passage I have mentioned, Plutarch next considers whether Gods can have physical contact with women:

> For my part, I am afraid to beget, as well as to be begotten, is repugnant to the incorruptibility of the deity. For that implies a change and passion, as Alexander implied when he said that he knew himself to be mortal as often as he lay with a woman or slept. For sleep is a relaxation of the body, occasioned by the weakness of our nature; and all generation is a corruptive parting with our own substance.[74]

Plutarch concedes that it might be possible for a God to beget on a woman, but he would first have to assume some form less alien than his own:

> It seems no incredible thing that the deity, though not after the fashion of a man but by some other certain communication, fills a mortal creature with some divine conception.[75]

In another passage of the *Morals*[76] he gives an example of this 'other certain communication', which suggests a substitute-relation like that of Yeats's play. Hercules plays dice with a gambler with a beautiful courtesan as stake. He wins the throw but, since it is repugnant to him to consummate a relationship with her in his own person, he has her go out in the street and cohabit with the first man she meets; the

suggestion clearly is that this man will be possessed by the God. I do
not know whether Yeats remembered this particular story in *The
Herne's Egg*, but Indian religious legend certainly bears it out. As Yeats
records in *A Vision*, the God might sometimes descend to a supplicant
by possessing the body of a 'wandering priestess', a 'living symbol of
himself':

> In the most ascetic schools of India, the novice tortured by his
> passion will pray to the God to come to him as a woman and have
> with him sexual intercourse.[77]

All these precedents in tradition Yeats had before him, and he could
not have failed to note than he could employ them to great dramatic
effect in his play.

So much for the Attracta group of symbols in *The Herne's Egg*.
Yeats reconstructed Balzac's heroine with the utmost fidelity, though
he substituted for Balzac's God a deity in which he himself could wish
to believe. His feeling was, I think, that while Seraphita's way was one
path to the divine union—for he did not discredit objective mysticism
—it was not the most natural path, nor indeed the most rewarding. It
did not even satisfy Balzac himself for long:

> Even after leaving Seraphita amid her snows, we return to that crowd
> which is always right because there is so much history in its veins.

Balzac turned back from the contemplation of divinity to the celebration of life, and Yeats in *The Herne's Egg* follows his example.

V

Congal is the antithesis of Attracta. He represents pride in the Self,
or if we prefer it that 'energy' which in Blake's phrase is 'eternal delight'. We see his absolute self-reliance most clearly at the climax of
the play, when he decides to kill himself to frustrate the Herne's prophecy that he must die 'at the hands of a fool'. After a moment's
natural hesitation, he has no doubt of his place in the scheme of things,
or of his ability to overcome the curse:

> Congal: Fool! Am I myself a Fool?
>   For if I am a Fool, he wins the bout.
> Fool: You are King of Connacht. If you were a Fool
>   They would have chased you with their dogs.

> Congal: I am King Congal of Connacht and of Tara,
> That wise, victorious, voluble, unlucky,
> Blasphemous, famous, infamous man.
> Fool, take this spit when red with blood,
> Show it to the people and get all the pennies;
> What does it matter what they think?
> The Great Herne knows that I have won.

The scene shows us the full powers of the Self, even if it sets itself up in opposition to Godhead instead of identifying itself with it. It can effect anything; it can defeat a God; there is no obstacle to its will that it cannot overcome. In life it has a kind of absolute freedom, but its autonomy ends with death, and it is powerless when out of the body. This Yeats drives home in the scene in question by a brilliant juxtaposition. Attracta, now Congal's guardian angel, comes in while he is dying:

> Congal: Attracta!
> Attracta: I called you to this place,
> You came, and now the story is finished.
> Congal: You have great powers, even the thunder
> Does what you bid it do.
> Protect me, I have won my bout,
> But I am afraid of what the Herne
> May do with me when I am dead.
> I am afraid that he may put me
> Into the shape of a brute beast.
> Attracta: I will protect you, if, as I think,
> Your shape is not yet fixed upon.

Attracta intercedes for Congal much as a Homeric goddess may intercede for a hero, and we remember that in Yeats's 'hero's crescent' 'Athene takes Achilles by the hair';[78] but it is Congal's tragedy that he should need her protection. He is alternately strong and weak, self-sufficient and abjectly dependent, for power is 'a property of the living'[79] and the 'mere shade' 'transparent like the wind' has no strength of its own.[80] After death he is at the Herne's mercy. This is the fate of the Self, if it sets up its part of divinity against the whole, for a part cannot conquer the whole, though it may hold its own in life.

Congal is the type of the hero, though Yeats is careful not to romanticise:

> I am an old campaigner,
> Robber of sheepfolds and of cattle-trucks,
> So cursed from morning until midnight
> That there is not a quarter of an inch
> To plaster a new curse upon.

Because of his stubborn self-reliance, we are meant to sympathise with him, and he wins our sympathy because he accepts the whole of life. The destiny of humanity, he says, is to live, and not to contemplate the mystical escape:

> It may be that life is suffering,
> But youth that has not yet known pleasure
> Has not the right to say so: pick
> Or be picked . . .

When Congal tries to dissuade Attracta from her mystic marriage, he may be terribly mistaken, but his arguments are intended to tell upon us. They are the arguments of experience against ignorance, of energy against spirituality, of life against the absolute:

> Seven men packed into a day—
> Or dawdled out through seven years—
> Are needed to melt down the snow
> That's fallen among these wintry rocks.

Congal's splendid speech in passing judgment upon Attracta makes this point in the most passionate poetry: it is the verdict of 'the galleries at the opera' upon the externality of objective mysticism, rejecting it for its coldness and its impervious, unnatural chastity. Yeats makes very clear that the choice lies between the affirmation of the ego and its rejection. 'I am the Court', Congal says; for how is he to judge, save from the divinity that is in the Self?

> This man who struck these seven blows
> Means that we seven in the name of the law
> Must handle, penetrate, and possess her,
> And do her a great good by that action,
> Melting out the virgin snow,
> And that snow image, the Great Herne.

> For nothing less than seven men
> Can melt that snow, but when it melts
> She may, being free from all obsession,
> Live as every woman should.
> I am the Court; judgment has been given.

This speech has obvious designs on our emotions; we are of course
expected to endorse that arrogant 'live as every woman should'. Congal wishes Attracta to accept life, and to accept her station in life; to
become, as he later supposes she has become:

> A sensible woman; you gather up what's left
> Your thoughts upon the cupboard and the larder.

He is hard, and Yeats admired hardness, but his conduct after the rape
is not unnaturally cruel:

> The seven that held you in their arms last night
> Wish you good luck.

The romantic phrase 'held you in their arms' emphasises the generosity
in Congal's nature. Sexual violence and tenderness were not divorced
in Yeats's mind.

The hero, for Yeats, is the type of pure subjectivity, or 'self-exaggera-
tion', as he calls it in *A Vision*;[81] his crescent is the twelfth of the phases
of the moon, shortly before the full. He is characterised by 'the greatest
belief in all values created by personality', and his study should be
'subjective philosophy', but he is 'fragmentary and violent'.[82] He is also
associated with folly and with impassioned opposition; Nietzsche is
given as the example of this type, and Yeats's definition of the hero's
function suggests nothing so much as romantic rebellion:

> [He] is pursued by a series of accidents, which . . . drive him into all
> sorts of temporary ambitions opposed to his nature, unite him per-
> haps to some small protesting sect; and these ambitions he defends
> by some kind of superficial intellectual action, the pamphlet, the
> violent speech, the sword of the swashbuckler.[83]

Congal is as unwise and as much a subjective rebel as Cuchulain, for
they are two of a kind. His rebellion, the crime on which the tragedy
turns, is the theft of the Herne's egg:

> Only the women of these rocks,
> Betrothed or married to the Herne,
> The God or ancestor of Hernes,
> Can eat, handle or look upon those eggs.

The Herne's egg represents the egg of Brahma, 'boundless infinity', and it is also in a sense forbidden fruit, since Yeats has connected it with the 'circle pass not' of theosophy. Infinity is the province of the mystic, Attracta and her kind, and Congal's crime is that he tries to arrogate the egg to himself; that he claims for himself what is God's, and what man can only come to share through the meditative life.

Yeats's use of this symbolism—which was already latent in his Gaelic original—is the clearest confirmation of Congal's function in the play: Congal substitutes the part for the whole, and recognising his own Self as divine will subscribe to no other divinity. In stealing the egg for himself he equates himself with Godhead in a sense that is clearly *hubris*. We can compare his act, if we choose, with the theft of the forbidden fruit from Eden, for as in that myth, the act is followed by his fall, and makes him subject to the Herne's curse:

> He that a Herne's egg dare steal
> Shall be changed into a fool
>
> And to end his fool breath
> At a fool's hand meet his death.

Congal's crime, like Adam's, is that he trespasses on the divine prerogative, and recognises no law but his own. It is clear that his proper course would have been that of Yeats's Indian mystics: not to deny his own divinity but to recognise it as a fraction of a great whole, and to spend his life on contemplation of that whole, from which it would follow that the egg of divine wisdom would become his by right. Instead of this, he throws stones at the Herne, and ravishes his bride.

But Yeats's sympathies remain with him. The meaning is clear: energy, proceeding from the Self, is always beautiful, and misdirected energy is not less beautiful in that it is also tragic. 'Everything that lives is holy.' This is made plain in the scene after Attracta's rape. When they see that the God means vengeance, all Congal's men try to deny that they took part in the act:

Thunder. All prostrate themselves except Attracta and Congal. Congal had half knelt, but he has stood up again.

He is too proud to deny what he has done, and too self-reliant, even now, to believe fully either in the God or in the reality of Attracta's mystic marriage. She then pronounces their punishment:

Attracta: He will come when you are dead,
        Push you down a step or two
        Into cat or rat or bat,
        Into dog or wolf or goose.
        Everybody in his new shape I can see,
        But Congal there stands in a cloud
        Because his fate is not yet settled.
        Speak out, Great Herne, and make it known
        That everything I have said is true.
        (*Thunder. All now, except Attracta, have prostrated
        themselves.*)
Attracta: What has made you kneel?
Congal: This man
        That's prostrate at my side would say,
        Could he say anything at all,
        That I am terrified by thunder.
Attracta: Why did you stand up so long?
Congal: I held you in my arms last night,
        We seven held you in our arms.

In this way, even at the moment when he is forced at last to acknowledge the Herne's supremacy, Congal keeps his tragicomic dignity. Even in the half-farcical atmosphere with which Yeats surrounds him, his actions have a stubborn beauty. A more purely tragic moment comes when the Herne summons him to his death on the mountainside:

Congal: I know the place and I will come,
        Although it be my death, I will come.
        Because I am terrified, I will come.

In these fine lines, all the stress falls on the last 'because'. By this simple device Yeats puts before us the crux of Congal's personality. The terrible exerts this attraction only upon the hero.

The final scene between Congal and Tom, the fool who has been
sent to kill him on the mountainside, is for me the most moving in all
Yeats's dramatic work:

> Congal: Here, take a drink and have no fear.
> All's plain at last; though I shall die
> I shall not die at a Fool's hand.
> I have thought out a better plan.
> I and the Herne have had three bouts,
> He won the first, I won the second.
> Six men and I possessed his wife.
>
> Fool: I ran after a woman once.
> I had seen two donkeys in a field.
>
> Congal: And did you get her, did you get her, Fool?
>
> Fool: I almost had my hand upon her,
> She screamed and somebody came and beat me.
> Were you beaten?
>
> Congal: No, no, Fool.
> But she said that nobody had touched her,
> And after that the thunder said the same,
> Yet I had won that bout, and now,
> I know that I shall win the third.

Congal has learned by now an odd humility, and in this beautifully
modulated dialogue we feel that he accepts the fool on terms of complete equality; but he has not lost his personal pride. He still retains the
passionate conviction that he is not inferior to the Herne, that he has
beaten him in the past, and will beat him again. Then the fool wounds
him, and confirms him in his growing realisation that he has nothing
to live for:

> Congal: The Herne has got the first blow in;
> A scratch, a scratch, a mere nothing.
> But had it been a little deeper and higher
> It would have gone through the heart, and maybe
> That would have left me better off,
> For the Great Herne may beat me in the end.
> Here I must sit through the full moon
> And he will send up Fools against me,
> Meandering, roaring, yelling,
> Whispering Fools, then chattering Fools,

> And after that, morose, melancholy,
> Sluggish, fat, silent Fools.
> And I, moon-crazed, moon-blind,
> Fighting and wounded, wounded and fighting.
> I never thought of such an end.
> Never be a soldier, Tom;
> Though it begins well, is this a life?
> If this is a man's life, is there any life
> But a dog's life?

Yeats has taken pains not to romanticise this 'robber of cattle-trucks'; he is hard, arrogant, violent, coarse-mouthed, if humanised by a robust wit and a certain tenderness. His life has been a process of stubborn opposition to the source of all good, an opposition he will not even now relinquish. But at this moment we have, I think, to judge for ourselves whether there is not something noble in his obstinate self-reliance, something even divine. Yeats himself judges him in what Attracta says of him: 'one man will I have among the Gods'.

VI

We are now able to go through the play scene by scene, clarifying the minor difficulties which remain. The opening stage direction presents an immediate problem, for the action begins from a stylised battle:

> Many men fighting with swords and shields, but sword and sword, shield and sword, never meet. The men move rhythmically as if in a dance.

Congal and Aedh finally stop fighting and begin to talk:

> Congal: Where is the wound this time?
> Aedh: Here, left shoulder-blade.
> Congal: Here, right shoulder-blade.
> Aedh: Yet we have fought all day.
> Congal: This is our fiftieth battle.
> Aedh: And all were perfect battles.

Their losses are equal; they always have been and will be; this is a formal, endless battle, and it is a very puzzling one. A clue to this symbolism is given later, when, after his theft of the Herne's eggs and subsequent fall, Congal kills Aedh. Previously, he says, they had

> . . . fought like gentlemen, but now
> Knowing the truth must fight like the beasts.

The stylised battle, then, is converted by Congal's fall into a savage brawl.

Yeats took over this symbol from Blake; the contrast, I think, is basically between the 'mental' and 'corporeal' war in the preface to Blake's *Milton*. The distinction there is between heaven and the material world, for Blake speaks of

> the Gods of the Kingdoms of the Earth: in contrarious
> And cruel opposition: Element against Element, opposed in War
> Not Mental, as the Wars of Eternity, but a Corporeal Strife.[84]

When man enters Blake's heaven, he does not enter into a merely passive state, but an essentially active condition where the whole personality may recreate itself in 'mental' combat. Thus *The Four Zoas* ends:

> Urthona rises from the ruinous walls
> In all his ancient strength to form the golden armour of Science
> For Intellectual War. The War of swords departed now,
> The dark religions are departed and sweet Science reigns.[85]

Behind this symbolism lies Blake's conviction that war is not essentially evil, but could be a pure activity if its sole purpose were joy: but in the physical world:

> War and Hunting, the two Fountains of the River of Life,
> Are become Fountains of bitter Death and of corroding Hell.[86]

Yeats elaborated this symbolism in his early, romantic verse and prose, where it is very prominent. In heaven, he tells us in 'The Happy Townland':

> When their hearts are so high
> That they would come to blows,
> They unhook their heavy swords
> From golden and silver boughs;
> But all that are killed in battle
> Awaken to life again.[87]

This activity, if we read the poem in its proper prose context, is contrasted with 'the warring and the perishing . . . the wars and bitterness' that illicit love brings into the material world.[88] In the same book Hanrahan, dying, hears 'the continual clashing of swords':

> 'I am after my death,' he said, 'and in the very heart of the music of heaven.'[89]

The 'continual clashing of swords' symbolises 'paradise' as late as *Where There Is Nothing*.[90] *The Secret Rose* associates this symbol also with the Sidhe, as in the description of Hanrahan's meeting with Dermot and Dervorgilla which 'The Happy Townland' is used to introduce.[91] We remember that the Sidhe fight endless, joyous battles among themselves:

> The countryman has need of but Swedenborg's keen ears and eagle sight to hear the noise of swords in the empty valley.[92]

Valhalla, of course, is our central archetypal parallel to the stylised battle image, but I imagine that the warfare of the Sidhe is also relevant.*

This gives us an Irish connection for the beginning of Yeats's play and it also gives its essential meaning. Yeats reverts to a favourite early symbol for heaven because he wishes to show that the play begins from spiritual equilibrium, or if we will, from Eden. Congal's theft of the herne's eggs is analogous to Adam's theft of the apple; it is on one plane a subjective version of the fall, or separation of man from God. But it has not yet taken place, nor has Congal even been tempted to steal the egg; the action begins from harmony. After the fall, Yeats manipulates his symbolism savagely to emphasise the distinction between 'mental' and 'corporeal' war. Congal and Aedh no longer use sword and shield:

> To arms, to arms—but if you have not got any
> Take a table-leg or a candlestick,
> A boot or a stool or any old thing.

For the men 'drop their swords and shields into a basket' before going

---

*In reverting, in the present context, to the use of his stylised battle symbolism, after an interval of some years, it may be that Yeats was influenced by his reading of the Bhagavad-Gita. The Gita certainly influenced the symbolism of a poem I shall discuss later: 'What Was Lost'.

in to eat the forbidden eggs, and this I think is symbolic. Now, too, the fighting is no longer stylised but Congal murders Aedh, and the action continues by using the most commonplace and tawdry objects to bear out the symbolism, by which I think Yeats is stressing the coarseness of the fallen, material world. Congal and his men throw caps at a mark to decide who shall first ravish Attracta, and Tom Fool fights Congal with a cauldron lid for a shield, a cooking pot for helmet, and a kitchen spit for sword. By the grotesque humour of this symbolism, Yeats brings home to us what Congal has lost by his temptation and fall.

If the symbolism of *The Herne's Egg* is as complex as I have tried to demonstrate, it is possible that Aedh himself has specific symbolic significance. This is the kind of point which can, I think, be pressed too closely, for it can lead us into that abstraction which Yeats so much hated, but a simple distinction between the two kings is not hard to make. Aedh plays the Caesar to Congal's Brutus; he is not tempted and Congal is tempted; the first consequence of Congal's fall is his murder. Now in Swedenborg, on whom Yeats is so largely drawing, the first consequence of man's fall is the murder of his higher nature by the 'proprium' or 'black knot of the ego'.[93] As I have quoted to show, man's separation from God comes about:

because man has broken [the] connection with heaven, by having turned away his inner parts from heaven, and turned them round to the world and to Self.[94]

'Aedh', furthermore, is the Irish word for fire, Yeats's symbol for spirituality, and—since the name is not in his Gaelic original—he cannot have used it here without reason. In the only other place where he adopts it, in poems like 'Aedh wishes for the Cloths of Heaven', he is at pains to tell us by a note that Aedh symbolises 'fire burning by itself' and is thus the type of the spiritual lover.[95] I think a similar reading permissible in *The Herne's Egg*, and that Aedh represents Congal's own 'higher nature', the selfless or objective part of his personality, since in Swedenborg's system the objective is the pure. Or we may say that Aedh represents the *satwa* of the Upanishads and Congal the *rajas*. These qualities represent the purity which is removed from action and the impulse to passionate action respectively.[96]

It is possible that Yeats implies this in the symbol of the dog, which it is so hard to account for. I have already quoted to show him using this homely image to represent the life of man.

> If this is a man's life, is there any life
> But a dog's life?

At the beginning of the play there is also talk of a dog, in lines I do not suppose Yeats included without an ulterior purpose:[97]

> Aedh: A story is moving round
>   Concerning two rich fleas.
> Congal: We hop like fleas, but war
>   Has taken all our riches.
> Aedh: Rich, and rich, so rich that they
>   Retired and bought a dog.
> Congal: Finish the tale and say
>   What kind of dog they bought . . .
> Aedh: A fat, square, lazy dog,
>   No sort of scratching dog.

One would not suggest symbolism here in any play but *The Herne's Egg*; but where cauldron and kitchen spit are symbolic properties, I do not see why this should not be. Are not Congal and Aedh, man's higher and lower natures, two fleas on one dog; if man's life is a dog's life, is not the dog the type of fallen humanity, tormented by the itch for purity and the itch for action? I do not stress this point: the Brutus-Caesar analogy provides an equally good road to the same conclusion. One remembers Aedh's funeral oration:

> He was a noble character
> And I must weep at his funeral.

There may be logic beneath the irony of this twice-repeated epitaph.

The Herne's Egg begins from Eden, where man's lower and higher natures are in perfect harmony. Heaven, as Yeats had written, is the reconciliation of the subjective and objective elements in man's mind:

> Could these two impulses . . . be reconciled . . . all life would cease.[98]

Nothing of Yeats's symbolism was present in his Gaelic source, and this is why he had to reorganise the myth so completely. Only the central episode, the theft of the sacred eggs, was to the purpose, and all the detail of the play's beginning—Aedh, the Great Herne himself, the stylised battle—had to be invented. By doing so, Yeats converted a naturalistic legend into an archetypal play.

VII

The next few scenes present little difficulty. In Scene Two, Congal
sets out to steal the Herne's eggs from Attracta, and it is made clear that
his motive, like Eve's, is merely frivolous:

> Congal: We have set our minds upon
>   A certain novelty or relish.
> Mike: Herne's eggs.

Aedh has nothing to do with the theft, though he may have tacitly
acquiesced in it; this could mean that the whole personality is to some
extent involved in the fall, but the matter is designedly left vague, and
there seems no point in pursuing it. Congal summons Attracta, and we
are told that this can only be done in one way:

> Corney: A flute lies there upon the rock
>   Carved out of a herne's thigh.
>   Go pick it up and play the tune
>   My mother calls 'The Great Herne's Feather'.
>   If she has a mind to come, she will come.[99]

The flute is simply another device to indicate Attracta's position in the
play: she has ears for nothing but the god. It is later played by the god
himself when she is summoned to her marriage, and its music sends her
into a trance much as the fairy music does in so many Irish tales.[100]
Yeats puts his music to excellent dramatic effect, for the tune haunts
Congal throughout the play. Whenever he hears it, we know the god
is near.

Attracta refuses to sanction Congal's theft, and the argument that
follows is used to underline his and her function in the play. He finally
takes the eggs by main force, and Attracta pronounces the curse. Then
he sets out for Tara, pursued by the God, whom he and his men
unsuccessfully try to stone and beat down. The God is inviolable as
he is also ubiquitous. Yeats's symbolism here is eclectic and traditional,
for he is remembering the Meena-Upanishad:

Everything owes life and movement to Spirit—Spirit strikes terror,
hangs like a thunderbolt overhead. Find it, find immortality.[101]

The scene where the herne flies menacingly above Congal's head is thus one of the most interesting pieces of symbolism in the play.

Congal has with him six men, and their significance may now be discussed. If we take Congal to symbolise *rajas*, or passion, his six men will represent the 'six enemies' which in Indian tradition wait upon passion: vanity, jealousy, sloth, anger, greed, and lust.[102] If we prefer to think of Congal as pride, his followers will make up the number of the seven deadly sins. That they have to be taken in this way is best seen from the rape of Attracta, where, as in Balzac, she is possessed by 'seven devils'. This scene is clearly her temptation by the seven deadly sins. It is possible to differentiate some of Congal's men by means of the rape scene. Mathias—'I first'—may represent lechery, and Pat gluttony:

> Here is my bottle,
> Pass it along, a long, long, pull;
> Although it's round like a woman carrying,
> No unmannerly, disloyal, bottle,
> An affable, most loyal bottle.

Congal's lieutenant Mike, who speaks always in monosyllables, may symbolise sloth, though I doubt whether Yeats intended this; Mike is far too hard and virile to represent sloth, even if he is laconic. By and large, Yeats is content with the merest suggestion of particularisation. He had a strong dislike of allegory.

Attracta is put into *samadhi* by the Great Herne, who has her substitute a hen's egg for the herne's egg Congal is about to eat, though all Congal's men get herne's eggs. The hen's egg is traditionally the symbol of folly or of grossness:[103]

> Herne's egg, hen's egg, great difference.
> There's insult in that difference.

We must remember that Congal, in the first place, probably stands for *rajas*, rather than any specific sin. His crime is *hubris*, in that he steals the egg and so arrogates himself above God. He gets no real benefit from his action, nothing in fact but a hen's egg, the mark and seal of his folly. The fact that his men do get Herne's eggs is probably mere dramatic necessity, though one could justify it by saying that the benefit of man's *hubris* goes merely to the dark powers who tempt him to it; they are the 'six enemies', and Congal acts always upon their advice, as it is given him in the promptings of his lieutenant Mike.

Attracta's *samadhi* leads her to her rape and mystic marriage; she is raped as punishment for substituting the hen's egg. In making the discipline lead up to union with the Self, Yeats was merely giving it the powers it claimed. Attracta's transfiguration is of course synchronous with her rape, and this detail probably interested Yeats on several levels. I have referred to his sources in *Seraphita* and Plutarch, but there is also a literal sense in which the symbolism holds good. In *The Aphorisms of Patanjali* Yeats tells the story of a monk in *samadhi* whose escape from the world of becoming is brought about when his Abbot cuts off his finger. Under *samadhi*, he explains, 'escape is precipitated by shock'.[104]

Nothing in *The Herne's Egg* is more vivid from the theatrical point of view than Attracta's trial:

Congal: Here where I put down my hand
         I will put a mark, then all must stand
         Over there in a level row.
         And all take off their caps and throw.
         The nearest cap shall take her first,
         The next shall take her next, so on
         Till all is in good order done.
         I need a mark, and so must take
         The Herne's egg, and let her wake.

This symbolism is self-explanatory. In coveting Attracta, Congal and his men set their caps at what is God's. Yeats is here giving us advance notice that further retribution must follow.

Here and throughout these scenes Yeats is of course making a new departure in method. He had never before used undistinguished objects, caps, stones, a table leg, a snowman, in such thick symbolic clusters, or with such gusto. These are symbols of the fallen world, and the technique they inaugurate continues into *Last Poems*. Stilts, a rag-and-bone seller, a coathanger, a jack-knife, even urine, are all brought into the verse, and, as here, the contrast is with heaven, Oisin's islands, Eden's 'garden', 'grass-green Avalon'.[105] But the focal point is always the squalor of the material world; even if Eden is described, it is seen in distortion through the eyes of an old lecher;[106] if Yeats himself has a vision of the spirit world, of 'the begotten or unbegotten Perning in a band', he at once turns away:

I bend my body to the spade
Or grope with a dirty hand.[107]

This technique, and this bitter contrast between the two planes of being, originates from *The Herne's Egg*, which is thus almost more important in its influence than in itself; and it originates largely from the middle scenes. The final scene, though the symbolism persists, discards harshness for tragedy.

VIII

The last scene takes place on 'the mountain top', and since this is traditionally where 'the gods move in adoration', the suggestion is that Congal is now face to face with the God. Attracta has called him here; he has not so much passed through as bypassed the three penitential circles, and is now, whatever his faults, almost divine. The full moon, symbol of death and resurrection, is in the sky, though Yeats preserves the tragicomic atmosphere; it is 'the moon of comic tradition, a round, smiling face'. This is the symbol that death is near to Congal, and of his eventual resurrection.

Congal fights with Tom Fool, and even if he defeats him he knows the Herne will send up other fools against him:

> Whispering Fools, then chattering Fools,
> And after that, morose, melancholy,
> Sluggish, fat, silent Fools.

The meaning of this beautiful and pregnant episode has been much confused by an error in past Yeats criticism, which has tried to derive Yeats's theory of the fool from the Elizabethan. No doubt Yeats takes into account Shakespeare's fools, but his practice is essentially Irish, and originates from folk tradition. The fool in Yeats's poetry is intimately associated with 'the fool of faery, wide and wild as the hill'; that is, as he explains in *The Celtic Twilight,* the Amadan:

> The boy . . . saw the Amadan coming at him. He had a big vessel in his arms and it was shining, so that the boy could see nothing else; but he put it behind his back then and came running, and the boy said he looked wild and wide, like the side of the hill.[108]

The Amadan is divine, and Yeats connected him with the messenger of Aengus, god of love, a man in cap and bells who is remembered in the early poem of that name.[109] All mortal fools were like him, and like him held the secret of wisdom; for this was the meaning of his cup:

I cannot think it wonderful that men should see a fool with a shining vessel of some enchantment or wisdom or dream too powerful for mortal brains. . . . The self, which is the foundation of our knowledge, is broken in pieces by foolishness, and is forgotten in the sudden emotions of women, and therefore fools may get, and women do get of a certainty, glimpses of much that sanctity finds at the end of its painful journey.[110]

This is why the fool comes next to the saint at the dark of the moon in Yeats's system, where he is called 'the child of God';[111] why Teigue, in *The Hourglass*, knows heaven so intimately:

when it is summer with us the snow is falling there, and have I myself not heard the lambs that are there all bleating on a cold December day?[112]

This is why a fool is made to speak that exquisite early poem 'Running to Paradise'.[113] And this is also why Yeats adapts Ferguson to his own ends and has the Herne send fools against Congal: the saint and the fool are the Herne's messengers, in contact with the divine will. The God acts through his own: Attracta is used to recover the stolen egg and the Fool to kill Congal and complete the curse.

Together with this, the Fool is used to humiliate Congal, and to bring home to us the squalor of human life. Congal is not to be permitted a hero's end, but must die on a kitchen spit, at the hands of a halfwit wearing a cooking pot for a helmet. All life in the material world is sordid, and death is the most sordid event of all; grotesque and farcical, a bad joke. But Congal transcends his humiliation by receiving the fool on terms of complete equality, equality in suffering:

> Never be a soldier, Tom.
> Though it begins well, is this a life?
> If this is a man's life, is there any life
> But a dog's life?

He defeats the Herne even in death by impaling himself on the spit, and dying with real, if tragicomic dignity. Such is the power of the Self.

After his death, Attracta, now an angel, tries to save his soul. Corney comes in with his donkey:

> Attracta: Come lie with me upon the ground,
>   Come quickly into my arms, come quickly, come
>   Before his body has had time to cool.

She wishes to have him reincarnated into human shape, for his soul will pass into whatever body is first conceived after his death. But they are too late; Corney's donkey breaks loose and couples with another donkey in the field below:

> King Congal must be born a donkey.

This story Yeats certainly took over from Indian folk-tradition. Perhaps Purohit Swami told it him, or perhaps he read it in Alexandra David-Neel's *With Mystics and Magicians in Tibet*. In her version, a young girl is accosted by a holy man, who attempts to violate her. She runs away, but her mother sends her back, telling her the man is holy and she must submit to his will. But the saint explains that it is now too late:

> 'My child,' he said, 'women awake no desire in me. However, the Grand Lama of the neighbouring monastery has died in ignorance, having neglected all occasions of instruction. I saw his spirit wandering in the Bardo, drawn towards a bad rebirth, and, out of compassion, I wished to procure him a human body. But the power of his human deeds has not permitted this. You escaped, and while you were at the village, two asses in that field nearby coupled. The Grand Lama will soon be reborn as a donkey.'[114]

Corney's function in the play is merely to make this scene possible. He represents '*l'homme moyen sensuel*', though his villager's natural piety is shocked by Congal's acts. When he and Attracta fail in their plan, Congal's defeat is at last established and the play ends.

In making Congal end in final defeat Yeats was following Vedic philosophy. Only the ascetic can escape the wheel of rebirth; and of those who do not choose this path, only the pure in heart can escape punishment after death. I will substantiate this by giving one of the most striking passages from Yeats's little-known translation of the Upanishads. The prose is designedly unEuropean, and it is mystifying, but it is very beautiful:

> Householders who know and worship sacrificial fire, ascetics who know it in solitude, and worship it as faith and truth; pass after death

into light, from light to day, from day into the moon's brightening
fortnight, from the moon's brightening fortnight into the six months
when the sun moves northward, from these months into the territory
of the Gods, from the territory of the Gods into the sun, from the
sun into lightning. The self-born Spirit finds them there, and leads
them to heaven. In that kingdom of heaven they live, never returning
to earth.

But they who conquer the lesser worlds by sacrifice, austerity,
almsgiving, pass into smoke, from smoke into night, from night into
the six months when the sun travels southwards, from these months
into the world of fathers, from the world of fathers into the moon,
where they become food. As priests feed on the moon, so Gods feed
on them. When their Karma is exhausted, they return to air, from
air to wind, from wind to rain, from rain into the earth, where they
become food, where they are offered as sacrifice to the fire in man,
offered as sacrifice to the fire in woman; there they are born again.
Once more they rise, once more they circle round.

Those who do not know any of these roads are born as poisonous
worms and insects.[115]

This is 'the soul's journey, how it is whirled about' which Yeats first
mentions in 'All Souls' Night'.[116] The 'householder' and 'ascetic' represent two stages on the path of holiness, and only those of their kind
who worship the fire of the Self in absolute purity can reach heaven.
The rest are allotted to favourable or unfavourable rebirths according
to their acts.[117]

It is hardly necessary to explain that we are not to understand literally the 'poisonous worms and insects' above, or the statement that
Congal will be reborn as a donkey. Yeats did not believe in metempsychosis. The preface to *The Tibetan Book of The Dead*★ explains the
difference between the 'exoteric' and 'esoteric' interpretations of traditional Indian rebirth symbolism. Country folk take the symbols
literally, but ascetics understand that all that is implied is unprofitable
rebirth; rebirth into an inferior position in the scale of human life.[118]

Congal's punishment is reincarnation into a subservient position. The
justice in this is apparent, but we remember him as a hero:

> moon-crazed, moon-blind,
> Fighting and wounded, wounded and fighting.

★This book was in Yeats's library.

Yeats even suggests in these lines that Congal is not to be blamed for his own failings; he is at the mercy of his phase, among the 'phases of the moon', and his whole life is governed by a force beyond his control, by the workings of Yeats's own determinist system. For our acts are predestined: 'we all complete a task or circle' as Congal himself fatalistically says. Even so, perhaps the dominant note in his character is joy, joy in heroic achievement. We are meant to feel for him much as we do for the hero in 'The Wild Old Wicked Man'. Like him, the old man knows that life is terrible, and like him he knows the necessity of choice between sanctity and man's lower nature:

> All men live in suffering,
> I know as few can know;
> Whether they choose the upper road
> Or stay content on the low.[119]

Like Congal, the old man chooses 'the low', and how passionately Yeats extols the decision:

> That some stream of lightning
> From the old man in the skies
> Can burn out that suffering
> No right-taught man denies.
> But a coarse old man am I
> I choose the second best.
> I forget it all awhile
> Upon a woman's breast.[120]

To reject the divine illumination and prefer life is the hero's path; but Congal's road is even more heroic than the old man's. He needs no 'woman's breast' to console him; he is absolutely self-sufficient.

CHAPTER FOUR

PURGATORY

I

YEATS WROTE *Purgatory*[1] rapidly and quietly; he did not send bulletins of progress to his friends, as he did when composing *The Herne's Egg*. We have only one published reference to the projected work, in a letter to Edith Shackleton Heald:

I have a one-act play in my head, a scene of tragic intensity.[2]

With this Yeats sat down to the text, which he quickly completed. The play, written early in 1938, was given in Dublin in September, and its performance excited a minor 'religious controversy'.[3] Yeats made a speech in his own defence, in which he stressed that the philosophy on which it depended seemed to him literally true, and was in fact an integral part of his own system of life and death:

I have put nothing into the play because it seemed picturesque; I have put there my own conviction about this world and the next.[4]

After the production of *Purgatory*, Yeats wrote little about it, and when he did so, it is important to note, it was primarily in connection with its theology. He clearly thought of it above all else as a ghost play, if with political and social involvements; and in approaching it from the point of view of its theology, I imagine I am documenting it as he would have wished.

Purgatory is for me, in the first place, an essay in the 'psychology of the supernatural'; but it can also be read against *A Vision* in several other respects. The play is remarkably concise: within the limits of a single scene, Yeats combines a treatise on the Platonic theory of 'the body of air' with a bitter commentary on the collapse of the aristocratic Ireland he loved; and behind all this we are conscious of the workings of his determinist gyres and of history moving inexorably towards the final cataclysm, humanity falling a prey to that 'natural declension of the soul'[5] which Yeats detected not only in Ireland but throughout the world. To fuse all these elements into a coherent whole, a construction very different from that of *The Herne's Egg* was necessary; and the two plays could not be more unlike. The free verse of *Purgatory* is disciplined and severe: there is nothing of the exuberance of the earlier experiment, and one misses at once the ferocious levity of the previous play's humour, and the sheer extravagance of its symbolism and plot. On the other hand, *Purgatory* is a stark and even a terrible play, and it has its own austere beauty. It has, too, an immediacy of impact and a dramatic intensity beside which *The Herne's Egg* seems sprawling and diffuse.

Perhaps the most striking change lies in the new note of harshness that has come into the verse; an element of exhilaration has gone out of it. With this we must couple Yeats's determination to write on a small scale. *The Herne's Egg* had been a full-length stage play, cosmic in scope and at once tragic and gay in intention, as Yeats thought all great art should be. With *Purgatory* he limits himself to a single scene, restricts the scope of his action to the history of a single family, and tells his story simply and directly, in a spare and bitter verse. It is easy to explain this shift in technique in terms of the growing disillusion of Yeats's last years, and *Purgatory* certainly reflects his hatred of the new Ireland and his increasing despair before the human situation generally; but I do not think this explanation is enough. Yeats's growing disillusion did not inhibit the lyric poetry he was writing at this time, curb the exuberance of 'News For The Delphic Oracle' or restrict the vast historical panorama of 'The Statues', and since these are characteristic works of his last period, the concision of *Purgatory* makes it to some extent unique. It is not as if Yeats's verse generally was moving towards a classical clarity and economy; we are left to suppose that his dramatic work was subject to pressures from which his lyric poetry was exempt.

I think Yeats was led to shape *Purgatory* as he did by the resurgence of an old ambition. For years he had been writing on the model of the Japanese Noh plays, and it is clear that what attracted him most was the Noh of ghosts. He knew and followed the rigid rules Japanese tradition had laid down for plays of this kind:

The hero or heroine, or the secondary character, sets out upon a journey, generally in search of some person or to fulfil some duty or religious object, and on this journey passes some famous spot. In the course of long and generally wearying wanderings, a recital of which gives an opportunity for the description of natural beauties,

this living person meets some god, or the ghost or reincarnated
spirit of some person of note, or perhaps the altered and melancholy
wreck of some person of former grand estate. . . . Often a priest
forms one of the characters, then the ghost may be soothed by his
prayers and exhortations.[6]

Thus in *Nishikigi*,[7] perhaps Yeats's favourite Noh play, the prayers of a
wandering priest rescue the souls of two lovers from purgatory; and
in *Motomezuka*,[8] the play to which he next most frequently refers, the
whole action is concerned with a girl's sufferings in the several circles
of the Buddhist hell, from which in this case no prayer can set her free.
In *Purgatory*, a wandering beggar comes to the ruin of a once famous
house, formerly his own home, and meets there the ghost of his own
mother, whose fall from 'grand estate' came about with her marriage
to a drunken groom. The finest speech in the play is the incidental
description of the vanished beauty of the house, and the plot centres
about his attempt to liberate the ghost from its purgatorial torment
both by action and, when that fails, by prayer. The analogy with the
Noh technique is closer than in any play since *The Dreaming Of The
Bones*; and I imagine that in returning to his Japanese models Yeats was
trying both to write a better ghost play than he had yet done, and to
insure his new drama against failure on the stage. He knew from experience that plays on the Noh pattern could be successful on the stage,
whereas *The Herne's Egg*, a new departure, could not even be performed.

One result of the Japanese correctness of *Purgatory* is that the play is
perfectly clear. The superficial meaning can be taken from a first reading, and, if we are content with what Yeats allows to come to the
surface of his verse, we shall have no need for a commentary at all. The
present essay is written in the belief that we should not be satisfied so
easily. Yeats presents his philosophy with tragic conviction, and it is
easy to suspend disbelief in it while the play is being performed, which
is enough for its justification as theatre; but where the thought is
apparently so eccentric, and is in fact so purely traditional, a scholarship which avoids the issue of the full meaning has not, perhaps, done
enough. In his own criticism, Yeats always insisted on full understanding of his author's thought, because he thought that great art had a
profound moral purpose, and whether we accept his general critical
attitude or no, it seems necessary as well as just that he should at some
time be approached as he approached other poets. The purpose of this
essay is to consider Yeats's philosophy as Yeats did Blake's in the

Quaritch edition and Shelley's in his two splendid essays,[9] and to do justice to his thought.

II

If the tragic catastrophe of *Purgatory* presents no difficulties, this is because Yeats has prepared for them in advance. At the beginning of the play, the Old Man explains how 'souls in Purgatory' revisit 'familiar spots' on earth, where they expiate their past lives:

> Relive
> Their transgressions, and that not once
> But many times; they know at last
> The consequence of those transgressions
> Whether upon others or upon themselves;
> Upon others, others may bring help,
> For when the consequence is at an end
> The dream must end; if upon themselves,
> There is no help but in themselves
> And in the mercy of God.

This speech sounds logical enough on the stage, though it is an over-simplification and does not perhaps fully explain the tragedy of what follows. To understand this clearly, we need to know something of the theory that underlies it.

It is easy to elaborate Yeats's argument from *A Vision*. There, he divides the soul's life after death into two main phases: the expiatory phase, represented by the *Dreaming Back*, *Shiftings* and the *Return*, and the purified condition, called the *Marriage*.[10] In the Dreaming Back, souls 'examine their past'; they relive each event of their past lives, exploring both its consequences and its causes, until they have 'turned it into knowledge', and are incapable of being moved by it either to pleasure or pain:

> Every event so dreamed is the expression of some knot, some con-centration of feeling . . . and the dream is as it were a smoothing out or an unwinding. Yet it is said that if [the ghost, while alive] had great intensity and the consequences of the event affected multitudes, he may dream with slowly lessening pain and joy for centuries.[11]

After releasing itself from the bondage of an event by means of the Dreaming Back, the soul relives the event in the Return, a state in which it passes through all the circumstances of its past life in reverse order, working from death to birth; and when this has been accomplished it is subjected to the Shiftings, where it experiences a fantasy life precisely the opposite to that it has in fact enjoyed:

if the surroundings of a past life were good, they are now evil, and if evil good, and if a man has had good motives they are now evil, and if evil good.[12]

After this the soul is free to proceed to its beatitude, a temporary 'marriage' or union with God which (unless it has earned liberation from the cycle of material existence) is quickly followed by its reincarnation into the world. But not all souls are capable of the Marriage:

If a spirit cannot escape from its Dreaming Back to complete its expiation, a new life may come soon and be, as it were, a part of its Dreaming Back and so repeat the incidents of its past life.[13]

It is thus essential for the soul to complete the Dreaming Back, both so as to be able to proceed to the Marriage, and so as to be properly reborn and to progress through its predestined cycle of incarnations in the material world.

It is perhaps easier to understand why Yeats found these states of the soul necessary than why he gave them the names and characteristics he did. Yeats did not believe in absolute evil,[14] but he did believe that the soul of man, in time, is necessarily imperfect; and the purpose of the successive expiatory states is to enable it to shake off its imperfections. The Self at the centre of each individual personality was for him 'pure intelligence', but this 'spiritual intellect' is contaminated by emotion and sensation. Physical sensation evaporates with the physical body, but the purpose of the Dreaming Back is the conquest of emotion, which for Yeats continues to affect the shade. In the Return and Shiftings, the shade's purpose is to acquire knowledge, for it must learn to see things as they really are; and reality, for Yeats, involved the acceptance of a higher morality, beyond good and evil, as he himself puts it.[15] This belief Yeats shared with Blake (whose Lilly is the symbol of the higher synthesis),[16] with the commentators on the Kabbala and with most of the other authorities on whom he relied, the Japanese dramatists he was imitating, for instance, for it is a characteristic of Zen Buddhism:

absolute purity is absolute affirmation, as it is above purity and non-purity and at the same time unifies them in a higher synthesis.[17]

When the soul has overcome pleasure and pain, and all the evil consequences following from reliance upon 'a common wrong and right', it attains to what Plotinus, one of Yeats's sources, called 'the impassivity of the unembodied',[18] and needs only to be 'purified of complexity' to be perfected, and to be able to enter upon the beatitude of union with God.

For Yeats, as for Blake, all religions were essentially one, and he found support for the general outlines of his system in most of the received beliefs of the world. Yeats could not bring himself to believe in the possibility of eternal damnation, but his prose explicitly relates the Christian purgatory and heaven with the expiatory and purified phases his philosophy sets out.[19] Damnation, for Yeats, was the inability to escape from the Dreaming Back. He also relates the Buddhist hell and heaven, for hell, to the Buddhist, is an illusion created by the unpurified imagination of the sufferer; if Unai, the heroine of the Noh play *Motomezuka*, 'can but cease to believe in her punishments', and will divest herself of all emotion and passion, 'they will cease to exist'.[20] In the same way, *A Vision* makes an association with Indian philosophy:

> Certain Upanishads describe three states of the soul, that of waking, that of dreaming, that of dreamless sleep, and say that man passes from waking through dreaming to dreamless sleep every night and when he dies.[21]

In this passage Yeats equates 'dreaming' with the fantasy life of his purgatory, and 'dreamless sleep' with his own heaven, where the soul surrenders its individuality to God; Indian philosophy, he says, had always equated dreaming with the impure dead:

> The Indian ascetic passing into his deathlike trance knows that if his mind is not pure, if there is anything there but the symbol of his God, some passion, ambition, desire or phantasy will confer upon him its shape or purpose, for he is entering upon a state where thought and existence are the same . . . The ascetic would say, did we question him, that the unpurified dead are subject to transformations that would be similar.[22]

In reading passages of this kind, which compare heaven to a sleep without dreams, we should always remember that Yeats envisaged also 'a fourth state' spent 'not in dreamless sleep, but in contemplation and wakefulness', and justified himself from the Mandukya Upanishad. This was the condition of those souls who had earned final liberation from the wheel of incarnation, and were united in heaven 'to the blessed dead'.[23]

These are interesting associations, but it would be as wrong to suppose that they are central to Yeats's system as it would to think of his philosophy as personal occult knowledge imparted by his ghostly instructors. While oriental philosophy may have confirmed Yeats in his beliefs, and his wife's automatic writing have helped him to fill in gaps of detail in his system, these things cannot possibly be at the root of his theory of life and death, for the simple reason that he had evolved that theory, in all but its minutiae, before he began to take them into account.* Platonism is beyond doubt Yeats's primary source; his Return can be traced to a text in Plato and to the Orphic mysteries, and the ethical theory behind his Shiftings he himself refers to Plotinus; [24] the successive steps to the Marriage compare closely with the stages of the intellectual life as Diotima sets them out in the *Symposium*.[25] As for the Dreaming Back, he had met with the theory in adolescence, in Madame Blavatsky's interpretation of Proclus:

'After death,' says Proclus, 'the soul continues to linger in the aerial body till it is entirely purified from all angry and voluptuous passions ... then doth it put off by a second dying the aerial body as it did the earthly one. Whereupon, the ancients say, there is a celestial body always joined with the soul, which is immortal, luminous and star-like.'[26]

Here Madame Blavatsky introduces us to the Platonic theory of the three 'vehicles' of the soul: the material body, which the soul wears during life, the aerial body, the less gross but still impure substance which is its purgatorial dress, and the celestial body, the absolute purity in which it is clothed in heaven. When Yeats read More's essay on *The Immortality of the Soul*, which he did in the winter of 1914–15, he was returned to these ideas, and his theory began to shape itself in his mind.

*The first statement we have of Yeats's theory, the very detailed essays he contributed to *Visions And Beliefs of the West of Ireland*, was in existence some years before his wife's automatic writing began.

Yeats's philosophy of the soul thus has basically the same sources as
the theosophical doctrine of the aerial and ethereal planes, but while
theosophy is a vulgarisation of the Platonic teachings,[27] *A Vision* preserves them in a relatively pure form. In an essay he wrote for one of
Lady Gregory's collections of occult folklore, Yeats numbers his
authorities, and introduces us to a tradition that went back to Egyptian
theurgy and persisted through Greece and Alexandria, Avicenna, Paracelsus and Agrippa, into comparatively modern times:

> Much that Lady Gregory has gathered seems but the broken bread
> of old philosophers, or else of the one sort with the dough they made
> into their loaves. Were I not ignorant, my Greek gone and my
> meagre Latin all but gone, I do not doubt that I could find much
> to the point in Greek, perhaps in old writers on medicine, much in
> Renaissance or Medieval Latin. As it is, I must be content with what
> has been translated or with the seventeenth-century Platonists. . . .
> These writers quote much from Plotinus and Porphyry and Plato
> and from later writers, especially from Synesius and John Philo-
> ponus in whom the school of Plato came to an end in the seventh
> century.[28]

From the Cambridge Platonists Yeats learned primarily the doctrine,
central to his system, that the soul has two 'vehicles' after death, the
unpurified and the purified, and lives through corresponding states;
and he quotes More when he writes that, after the soul has entered
purgatory:

> there is another birth or death, when we pass from the airy to the
> shining or ethereal body and 'in the airy the soul may inhabit for
> many ages and in the ethereal for ever'.[29]

His classical authorities confirmed all this and taught him also that the
purgatorial condition is that of his own dreaming back, for, to use his
own words:

> Synesius, who lived at the end of the fourth century, and had
> Hypatia among his friends . . . describes the spirit body as capable
> of taking any form and so enabling us to work out our purgation;
> and says that for this reason the oracles have likened the state after
> death to the images of a dream.[30]

Synesius does indeed treat of 'the similarity of the soul's way of life in another world to the imaginings of the dream condition';[31] and Porphyry explains that it is because of the soul's 'enduring affection to the body' that 'the form of the phantasy is impressed on the spirit'.[32] Proclus and Yeats's other authorities bear this out; perhaps the most quotable is Hermes Trismegistus. After death, he says, 'the vehicle of passion and desire' which is the aerial body must be combatted, and 'the soul or reason gradually separated from it; or rather, its true nature [will show] forth in the man as he gradually strips off the irrational tendencies of the energies'.[33] Together with all this we must consider the beautiful words of Plotinus which describe the necessity of stripping the soul of good and evil, pleasure and pain:

> The purification of the soul is simply to allow it to be alone; it is pure when it keeps no company; when it looks to nothing without itself.[34]

From such authorities as these Yeats's own theory took shape.

In the winter of 1914–15, while reading the authorities from whom I have been quoting, Yeats was also occupied on a reconsideration of Swedenborg, and in comparing the beliefs of folklore with the superstitions of spiritualism, 'amused to make Holloway interpret Aran', as he himself puts it. All these sources of information seemed to corroborate his own developing philosophy,[35] as did also the detail of the Japanese Noh plays which he was then first reading: as the authorities accumulated, it is interesting to note, his findings won the grudging assent of Ezra Pound.[36] The value of Swedenborg's teachings was much offset, for Yeats, by his 'abstraction, his dryness, his habit of seeing but one element in every thing',[37] and he could not see, as Blake did, that the dead reached heaven by their own exertions, but he could be allowed a real if contaminated insight into the nature of the spiritual world. In a famous passage, Swedenborg had remarked that 'the whole life of everyone is laid open after death, even to the most minute particulars';[38] he had maintained that 'impure spirits' are occupied with 'phantasies';[39] and he had in fact, as Yeats read him, a clear knowledge of the nature of the Dreaming Back. After death, according to Yeats's paraphrase of the *Arcana Coelestia*:

> 'the most minute particulars which enter the memory remain there and are never obliterated' [making] us live again all our transgressions and see our victims 'as if they were present, together with the

place, words and motives', and that suddenly, 'as when a scene bursts upon the sight' and yet continues 'for hours together'. And like the transgressions, all the pleasure and pain of sensible life awaken again and again, all our passionate events rush up about us, and not as seeming imagination, for imagination is now the world.[40]

All this, of course, sorted very well with the Platonic theory, while as for the apparitions of folklore, Yeats had precedent for believing that they were quite real. Philoponus had investigated this problem in the seventh century:

> What account can be given of those spectres and phantoms which appear shadow-like about graves or sepulchres, since the soul itself is neither of any figure, nor yet at all visible. . . . Impure souls, after their departure out of this body, wander here, up and down, for a certain space, in their spirituous, vaporous, and airy body.[41]

Philoponus thought that the soul, in its airy body, exercised 'plastic life' and was able to materialise and change its shape at will, a theory which Yeats felt was rediscovered in the twentieth-century psychical researches of d'Orchorowicz and Myers.[42] Yeats adopted it (with variations I need not mention here) to explain the manifestations at those seances he did not discredit.

It will now be clear that Yeats's theory of the life after death was rooted in tradition; and the symbolism he uses for purgatory is always equally traditional. His most commonly employed imagery is Homeric, for he had Platonic authority for reading the Book of the Dead in the *Odyssey* as an illustration of his theory. Yeats quotes Porphyry and Philoponus, and he might have given Plutarch and Henry More also, as authorities for supposing that Hades is a symbol of life in the aerial body, 'that Invisible region of the dead' into which the impure soul must pass with death.[43] Following these authorities, we find Yeats using the Book of the Dead in many passages of his mature prose, where my card-index shows it to be the most persistent of all his symbols after Ahasuerus: his ghostly instructors are 'voices that speak as to Odysseus but as the bats'; Achilles in Hades, describing his past life to Odysseus, is given as an example of a shade imprisoned in the Dreaming Back; the blood-pool from which Homer's shades had to drink before they could communicate with the living is called 'an ancient substitute for the medium'.[44] There are also verse allusions, in the minor poem 'Let cubes of basalt',[45] and even, I think, in 'Byzantium':

> A mouth that has no moisture and no breath
> Breathless mouths may summon.[46]

Particularly since the word 'Hades' has just gone before, I think we must take this as an indirect reference to Tiresias, Homer's Summoner of the shades. When Yeats did not use Homeric symbolism for the life after death, he sometimes turned to Dante:* 'News For The Delphic Oracle' consigns the Platonists, after death, to Dante's limbo, and 'Cuchulain Comforted' places the ghost of Cuchulain himself in the Valley of the Rulers, a feature of the 'Purgatorio'.[47] Alternatively, Yeats might use the imagery of folklore: he had, as I have said, Platonic authority for treating it seriously, and he and Lady Gregory had done too much research among the Irish peasantry to incline them to disbelieve. The miraculously lit ruin that the old peasant woman saw was real enough for them.

In *Purgatory*, which is the account of a vision seen by a wandering beggar and his son, Yeats naturally uses the symbolism of folklore: the lit house and the popular, almost tangible ghost. The ghost (a woman) is imprisoned in the Dreaming Back, and the Old Man, whose mother she is, kills his own son in order to cut short her dream: she is meditating on the consequences of her marriage, and he supposes that by ending a family line which has brought her nothing but shame he will be able to release her from her meditation. But he is mistaken: he can rescue her from her horror at what might otherwise be an endless chain of circumstances following from the single tragic event of her marriage; but he cannot rescue her from her personal emotion, the mingled 'pleasure and remorse' that she feels as she relives the 'sexual act' from which he was conceived. Not until she has purified her own memory of all emotion can she 'unloose the knot'; the dreamer must find a footing in a world beyond pleasure and pain.

III

Behind the theology of *Purgatory* we are allowed to glimpse Yeats's philosophy of history, and his conviction that the present, objective cycle of civilisation was nearing an end. It is impossible to come at the full meaning of the play without some idea as to what Yeats's attitude to history was, and since past criticism has hardly done justice to the subject, it will be useful to take it up here.

*No doubt because Dante's philosophy of the ghost came very close to his own—*vide* Purgatorio XXV.

Yeats's philosophy of history was certainly not personal and arbitrary, as has commonly been supposed: nor was it 'revealed' to him by his instructors. As with so much of his thought, his acquaintance with the tradition on which it depends can be traced back to Madame Blavatsky, whose writings are full of the gyres. Classical philosophy, she tells us:

> divided the interminable periods of human existence on this planet into cycles, during each of which mankind gradually reached the culminating point of highest civilisation and gradually relapsed into abject barbarism.[48]

Here already are the salient features of Yeats's own system: the progress towards unity of culture, arrived at towards the middle of a cycle, and after this the slow degeneration into 'abstraction' and, finally, violence. Yeats himself thought that this essentially Platonic theory of degeneration and renewal was the central premise of his early verse and prose, though work like *The Adoration Of The Magi* and *The Secret Rose* has a bias towards the mystical and apocalyptic and could not be called in any sense Platonic in tone:[49] this is because Yeats took up the tradition at the point where it merged into heterodox medieval thought and did not, at first, trace it to its source. In his early period he was preoccupied with the teachings of the eleventh-century monk Joachim de Flora, and was content with merely visionary authority for supposing 'that our civilisation was about to reverse itself, and receive from Joachim de Flora's holy spirit a multitudinous influx'.[50] It was not until middle life that he went back to the 'Great Year of the Ancients' and arranged his authorities 'in one clear view', an orderly sequence embracing Empedocles, whose theory of life as a cyclic alternation between 'concord' and 'strife' is much discussed in *A Vision*;[51] Plato, whose alternating gyres are met with in the *Statesman*;[52] Joachim himself, who arrived at a similar cyclic theory in the early middle ages and founded an influential sect which had the painter Hieronymus Bosch as a member, and influenced Paracelsus and Agrippa;[53] Swedenborg, who knew Joachim's teachings well and took him as one of his authorities;[54] through Swedenborg, Blake, and, through the Platonic tradition, Shelley:

> The world's great age begins anew;
> The golden years return.[55]

At the time Yeats made this review of the authorities, it much excited him to find their general theory being rediscovered, as he believed, in modern thought. Just as he had been impressed by the parallelism between Philoponus' theory of the plastic powers of the aerial body and the researches of d'Orchorowicz and Myers, so in this field also he was impressed to find Empedocles and Agrippa being borne out by Vico and Spengler.

Purgatory is particularly concerned with the condition of humanity at a reversal of the gyres, and Yeats's conclusion is that as a cycle nears its end, brutality, violence and 'terror' are to be expected. It is interesting to see what traditional authority he had for this view. In the system of Empedocles, every cycle ends in 'strife',[56] and Yeats refers to this in his poem 'The Gyres':[57] the line 'Empedocles has thrown all things about' is, I think, a succinct and epigrammatic way of saying that Empedocles' theory can be seen working itself out in the gradual disintegration of modern life and thought. Plato also has a terrible passage describing the end of a cycle when, 'deprived of the care of God who had possessed and tended them', men are left 'helpless and defenceless', 'without skill or resource', to die of famine or be 'torn in pieces by the beasts'.[58] But Yeats's central source is here what he calls the Stoic tradition,* especially as he knew it in a famous text in Hermes Trismegistus. This passage, a favourite text of theosophy, and which Yeats knew in Taylor's and in Mead's translations,[59] has even in the English versions a grim and terrible beauty. At the end of a cycle:

No-one shall look up to heaven. The religious man shall be accounted insane, the irreligious shall be thought wise, the furious brave, and the worst of men shall be considered a good man. For the soul and all things about it, by which it is either naturally immortal, or conceives that it shall attain to immortality, conformably to what I have explained to you, shall not only be the subject of laughter, but shall be considered as vanity. Believe me likewise, that a capital punishment shall be appointed for him who applies himself to the religion of intellect. New statutes and new laws shall be established, and nothing religious or which is worthy of heaven, or celestial concerns, shall be heard, or believed by the mind. There shall be a lamentable departure of the Gods from men, evil daemons will alone

---

*One might add, however, that a Jungian psychologist, Joseph Campbell, has written a whole book on the persistent tendency of the human psyche to evolve, in all periods, cyclic theories of history, and gives parallels to the 'Stoic tradition' from Hindu and Jainist myth, and even from St. Matthew.—*vide The Hero With a Thousand Faces.* pp. 255–378.

remain, who being mingled with human nature will violently impel the miserable men of that time to war, to rapine, to fraud, and to every thing contrary to the nature of the soul. Every divine voice shall be dumb by a necessary silence.[60]

When this happens, God:

washing away all malignity by a deluge, or consuming it by fire, or bringing it to an end by disease and pestilence dispersed in different planes, will restore the world to its ancient form.[61]

This seems to me to be beyond doubt a main source of Yeats's poem 'The Second Coming',[62] and it is an attitude to history he believed had been rediscovered by Vico. As Yeats interprets him, Vico believed that civilisation at length 'grew malicious and treacherous, fell into "the barbarism of reflection" and after that into an honest plain barbarism accepted with relief by all and started on its round again.'[63] It is easy to see what Yeats found to support Vico in his theory.

Purgatory was printed together with *On the Boiler*, and *On the Boiler* contains a direct allusion to 'the old Stoic prophecy of earthquake fire and flood at the end of an age',[64] so that I am sure Yeats wrote his play with the text in Hermes Trismegistus in mind. It is just possible that it contains a half-conscious reminiscence of the words 'a capital punishment shall be appointed for him who applies himself to the religion of intellect'; they are terrible enough to remain in memory, and *Purgatory* provides a verbal parallel:

> ... to kill a house
> Where great men grew up, married, died,
> I here declare a capital offence.

At any rate, we need have no doubt what lies behind the 'studied violence' of *On the Boiler*, where Yeats denounces modern civilisation:

Unless there is a change in the public mind, every rank above the lowest must degenerate, and as inferior men push up into its gaps, degenerate more and more quickly. The results are already visible in the degeneration of literature, newspapers, amusements, and, I am convinced, in benefactions like those of Lord Nuffield, a self-made man, which must gradually substitute applied science for ancient wisdom.[65]

Yeats thought that these changes and 'the growing frenzy' of public
life were all products of the 'violence' at a reversal of the gyres, which
was responsible for creating 'the hell we live in', and though he com-
plained to Dorothy Wellesley elsewhere that he could see 'no solution',
and that the process could not be finally halted,[66] *On the Boiler* does at
least contain suggested measures to stave off final disaster. Yeats proposes a return to 'the religion of intellect', to the subjective philosophy
of Plato and of Berkeley:

> No educated man today accepts the objective matter and space of
> popular science, and yet deductions made by those who believed in
> both dominate the world, make possible the stimulation and con-
> donation of revolutionary massacre and the multiplication of mur-
> derous weapons by substituting for the old humanity [of the middle
> ages] with its unique irreplaceable individuals something that can be
> chopped and measured like a piece of cheese; compel denial of the
> immortality of the soul by hiding from the mass of the people that
> the gravediggers have no place to bury us but in the human mind.[67]

Since Ireland seemed to him close enough to ancient habits of thought
and feeling to make the experiment possible, he proposed teaching in
Irish schools nothing but those subjects which would conduce to the
understanding of the *philosophia perennis*, or otherwise discipline and
strengthen the mind; and he proposed to set the mass of the people
free from the farce of a compulsory education they did not desire and
which merely sapped their capacity for traditional belief.[68] Returned
to the status of 'irreplaceable individuals' in a 'hierarchical society', he
thought they would rediscover the 'priceless gifts' of the spirit, 'clair-
voyance, prevision' and other visionary faculties, for which the Irish
peasantry had long been renowned.[69]

Purgatory very obviously takes up some of these arguments and
presents them in poetic form. The Old Man and the Boy in Yeats's
play are representative of the old and the new Ireland, and Yeats is at
great pains to show us the principles for which they stand. Thus the
Old Man is shown to be still in contact with 'ancient wisdom', and
Yeats sketches in the nature and extent of his education: though robbed
of his inheritance, he has been able to make contact with the classical
culture:

> A gamekeeper's wife taught me to read,
> A Catholic curate taught me Latin.
> There were old books and books made fine

> By eighteenth-century French binding, books
> Modern and ancient, books by the ton.

The Old Man is well-read both in philosophy and in the arts: he knows
the Platonic theory of the aerial and celestial vehicles, and refers to
Tertullian's treatise on the mixed nature of the soul, *de Anima*:[70] he has
also read the more mystical of the modern English poets, for he quotes
Rossetti's *Eden Bower*:[71]

> 'Then the bridesleep fell upon Adam':
> Where did I read those words?

The Boy, on the other hand, has neither acquired nor felt the lack of
learning: he has had

> . . . the education that befits
> A bastard that a pedlar got
> Upon a tinker's daughter in a ditch.

He has no values beyond the material—'grand clothes, And maybe a
grand horse to ride'—and he has no moral sense at all:

> What's right and wrong?
> My grand-dad got the girl and the money.

At the climax of the play, he turns aside from a visionary experience
to steal a bag of money, Yeats's simple symbolic comment on the crass
materialism of the younger generation growing up in Ireland, and as
the gyres moved on towards the moment of reversal, everywhere in
the world.

Purgatory, then, is on one plane a comment on the progressive
degeneration of humanity, and it is a more searching one than might at
first appear. Yeats does not merely proceed by the simple juxtaposition
of two generations, the good and the bad, as in the passages I have
quoted: beyond this there is a deeper symbolical undercurrent, and the
problem is how far to take the interpretation of the play as a historical
allegory, for it is possible to read ulterior meaning into almost
every incident. What is at stake will appear from a close study of the
plot.

IV

Purgatory describes the ruin of a single Irish family, which began when the daughter of the house married a 'drunken groom'. This parvenu wasted the estates, to 'pay what he had lost on cards' or 'spent on horses, drink and women', and finally 'burned down the house when drunk'. The Old Man of the play, who is the son of this disastrous marriage, came on his father in the ruins and 'stuck him with a knife': then he became a pedlar and took to the roads, wandering between the 'half-doors' of the peasantry and the 'hall-doors' of the local gentry. The play begins with his return to the scene of his crime, which is now haunted by his mother's ghost:

> She never knew the worst, because
> She died in giving birth to me,
> But now she knows it all, being dead.

To rescue his mother's soul from its remorse at the consequences of her marriage, the Old Man now kills his son and ends the family line, 'my father and my son on the same jack-knife', in Yeats's brutal phrase:

> I killed that lad because had he grown up
> He would have struck a woman's fancy,
> Begot, and passed pollution on.

As I have said, the play ends with his recognition of the inadequacy of his own action: only by her own exertions can his mother escape from the Dreaming Back.

All this has already been given its widest interpretation by John Heath-Stubbs:

The last owner of the house, the heiress of an aristocratic family, has debased herself by marrying a drunken groom. This symbolises the corruption of the old Anglo-Irish aristocracy, which allowed itself to become contaminated by contact with the rising bourgeoisie. The old man, who represents the revolutionary generation or Yeats himself, is the child of this union, now dispossessed of his heritage. His own son, who typifies the younger generation of the new Ireland, has his father's violence, but knows nothing of the

traditions of the past for which Yeats himself cared so much.
The play concludes with the killing of the younger man by his
father.[72]

If we read the play in this way, it becomes a historical allegory, beginning from a moment in time when unity of culture was possible.
Yeats's symbol for this momentary efflorescence is the house itself:

> Great people lived and died in this house;
> Magistrates, colonels, members of Parliament,
> Captains and Governors, and long ago
> Men that had fought at Aughrim and the Boyne.
> Some that had gone on government work
> To London or to India came home to die,
> Or came from London every spring
> To look at the May-blossom in the park. . . .

Mirrored here is the condition of social equipoise that Yeats's philosophy of history makes possible for a brief period within every cycle,
and from it *Purgatory* leads us down, through three successive generations, to the final aimless violence he associates with a reversal of the
gyres.

Mr. Heath-Stubbs's interpretation can be elaborated at some length.
If he is right, then the 'ruined house' against which the action is played
out, under a cloud 'and that's symbolical', becomes not merely the
symbol of the deterioration of the aristocratic tradition within a single
family, but the emblem of Ireland itself. This seems quite feasible: in
'Meditations in Time of Civil War', Yeats had made his own 'loosening
wall' and house the symbol of national ruin, and a similar extension of
meaning is implicit in his poems on Coole Park.[73] Further, if the whole
action images the progressive deterioration of a democracy, the
'mother' of the play may symbolise the spirit of ancient Ireland, which
was typically represented by a woman figure, as in Yeats's own *Cathleen Ní Houlihan* and the poem 'I am of Ireland' in *Words For Music
Perhaps*.[74] The murder of the Boy, which is presented as a morally
desirable but ultimately unavailing act, will presumably reflect a deep
conviction of Yeats's: that the individual could do little to halt the
deterioration of society, which would continue until a new cycle
began.

What may particularly incline us to this reading is Yeats's insistence,
quite irrelevant to the plot, on the Boy's exact age:

But that is my age, sixteen years old
At the Puck Fair.

Since the play was written and performed in 1938, this can, if we wish, be taken as a device for dating back the final stage in the deterioration of Ireland to 1922, the year of the adoption of the constitution and of the outbreak of civil war. Modern democratic Ireland dates from this time, and from democracy, in Yeats's view, came 'the sort now growing up', whom he despised. Though it is equally possible that the detail is mere local colour, I think it at least conceivable that this argument should be read into the play.

For all this, I am sure Mr. Heath-Stubbs misinterprets *Purgatory*, or at least reads the play with wrong emphasis. It is not really possible to take it as we take, say, *Cathleen Ní Houlihan*. Yeats does not intend simple allegory, for he is at as much pains to individualise his characters as he is to stress the symbolic significance of their destiny:

Old Man: This night is the anniversary
Of my mother's wedding night,
Or of the night wherein I was begotten.
My father is riding from the public house,
A whiskey-bottle under his arm.
[*A window is lit showing a young girl.*]
Look at the window; she stands there
Listening, the servants are all in bed,
She is alone, he has stayed late
Bragging and drinking in the public house.
Boy: There's nothing but an empty gap in the wall.

This is not a generalisation about Ireland; it is in fact the application of Swedenborg's theory that the 'minute particulars' of life remain present to the ghost, and it serves admirably to convince us that we are in contact with a particular individual memory, so that all expectation of allegory dies as we listen to the speech which follows:

It's louder now because he rides
Upon a gravelled avenue
All grass today. The hoofbeat stops,
He has gone to the other side of the house,
Gone to the stable, put the horse up,
She has gone down to open the door.

> This night she is no better than her man
> And does not mind that he is half drunk,
> She is mad about him.

In speeches like this, where the rapidity of the rhythm and the vivid colloquialisms in the style mask a classical selectiveness and economy, Yeats orientates us finally away from the abstract. *Purgatory* is a symbolist play, and we have a right to expect that the characters shall be truly representative, microcosms of the great historical process which is the background to all they say and do: we glimpse for a moment that this is so, but the argument is not allowed to stray far from the concrete. Yeats had a horror of allegory, which he sharply differentiated from symbolism, and the skill with which he brings *Purgatory* back from the very brink is, I think, a technical triumph.

For the remainder of the play we are not allowed to forget that Yeats's theme is the supernatural, and the sociological argument recedes into the background, to be taken up in recollection only: when we remember the description of the house, perhaps, which is made a deliberate generalisation:

> Great people lived and died in this house;
> Magistrates, colonels, members of Parliament,
> Captains and Governors, and long ago
> Men that had fought at Aughrim and the Boyne.

With this style, so different for instance from the exact statement of the second part of 'The Tower', we may contrast the incisive particularisation of the conclusion:

> The window is lit up because my father
> Has come to find a glass for his whiskey.
> He leans there like some tired beast.

The success of *Purgatory* is largely due to the alternation of two contrasting techniques.

Perhaps the closest analogy with *Purgatory*, from the point of view of its characterisation, lies in Yeats's play *On Baile's Strand*.[75] There, as I have quoted his note to show, he had at first intended to make all his characters, Cuchulain, Conchubar, Fool and Blind Man, symbolic; and he deprecates his intention by saying that his weakness as a playwright was to be persecuted by 'abstract images': he had always to resist this tendency and fight hard to keep his *dramatis personae* flesh and blood.[76] In the case of *On Baile's Strand*, it cost him years of revision to make his play fit for the stage, but by the time he wrote *Purgatory* he had learned the tact that comes with much experience. I am sure the play would have been much weaker if it had been the kind of direct allegory Mr. Heath-Stubbs suggests: it would in fact have fallen between two stools, wavering between politics and ghosts. As it is, Yeats individualises, and this gives the play its strength and dramatic impact.

V

Once we have understood the level at which to read *Purgatory* we have understood the play, for the symbolism itself is quite straightforward. Yeats uses the simplest properties: the play is acted in almost total darkness, and this is symbolic of evil, as light is of good; faint moonlight leads the two beggars up the path to their ancestral house, by which Yeats perhaps indicates that they are brought there by a dim perception of the divine will. All the symbolic properties of the play are as simple and as naturally introduced, and this economy of means Yeats learned from his models, for it is typically Japanese.

The play opens on an almost bare stage. Yeats requires no more of the designer than 'a ruined house and a bare tree in the background', and we are reminded of the 'single pine tree' that is invariably painted on the back-wall in the performance of the Noh plays.[77] Another feature of the Noh drama to which Yeats gave much attention was the habit of 'playing upon a single metaphor, as delicate as the echoing rhythm of line in Chinese and Japanese painting',[78] and he adopts a similar technique in *Purgatory*, as in all his dance plays: in *The Dreaming Of The Bones*, for example, he returns again and again to the symbolic crowing of a cock.[79] Here, the tree on the back-wall is the central symbol: it is described at the beginning of the play in words meant to bring out Yeats's familiar green-tree dry-tree antithesis:

Old Man: Study that tree.
          What is it like?
    Boy: A silly old man.
Old Man: It's like—no matter what it's like.
          I saw it a year ago stripped bare as now,
          So I chose a better trade.
          I saw it fifty years ago
          Before the thunderbolt had riven it,

> Green leaves, ripe leaves, leaves thick as butter,
> Fat, greasy life.

This is Julian's tree, with its 'superabundance' of sensual foliage, and it
is the tree of life of the 'Raya Mehemna' and Yeats's other Kabbalistic
books:[80] it is the tree Yeats describes in his essay on William Morris,
in whom he detects a consistent, half-conscious use of the symbol. As
he says there,[81] the Green Tree represents 'natural abundance', and the
Dry Tree, which he calls the 'image of the ruined land', spiritual
disaster. In *Purgatory* the dry tree is the symbol of individual and family
ruin and beyond this of the ruin of all culture and order throughout
the world, at the end of a cycle, when civilisation is riven by the
thunderbolt of the divine will.

Later in the play, following Japanese models, Yeats reverts to this
symbol and imagines the dry tree converted to a new purity and
beauty: it is now the symbol of the soul of man, purified of all suffering,
as the Old Man imagines his mother's soul now is, by the expiatory
process after death:

> Study that tree.
> It stands there like a purified soul,
> All cold, sweet, glistening light.
> Dear mother, the window is dark again,
> But you are in the light because
> I finished all that consequence.

It is a characteristic of Yeats's mature thought that he should use this
kind of imagery, and lead us beyond the dry tree of disaffection and
despair to this new, spiritualised vision: his image here is the natural
development of Attracta's prayer that, 'all foliage gone', she may
'shoot' into her joy.[82] I should add that blinding light, as Yeats quotes
Shelley and medieval philosophy to show,[83] is a traditional symbol for
'pure corporeality', or for the celestial body, as notably in his own
'Ribh at the Tomb of Baile and Aillinn'.[84] There, the radiance shed
from the bodies of two 'purified' lovers in heaven falls in the divine
form of a perfect circle to the grass, and Ribh makes it clear that this
is the light of the world:

> Though somewhat broken by the leaves, that light
> Lies in a circle on the grass; therein
> I turn the pages of my holy book.

The simple and moving lines I have quoted from *Purgatory* do not perhaps require such profound analysis, but it is worth pointing out Yeats's care to make them valid, at any level the reader may wish, as imagery of the real nature of heaven.

Although Yeats sets off the dark atmosphere of his play with this symbol of human perfectibility, the action of *Purgatory* is played out against the background of the dry tree, the sinister emblem of ruin. In front of this tree the two perfectly individualised figures who are Yeats's actors stand, and the old beggar tells his son the story of the decline of their family; suddenly the window is miraculously illuminated, and they are in the presence of his mother's ghost. In this way Yeats conjoins his images of the beggar and the lit house, as I have shown him doing in *The King Of The Great Clock Tower*, as he did also in the lyric of the period called 'The Curse of Cromwell', where an old beggar comes upon a vision of 'a great house' in the middle of the night, 'its windows all alight', and sees his dead friends merrymaking within it.[85] Always in Yeats's poetry, the lit house is the symbol for the supernatural world, and the beggar represents fallen humanity, sustained by this vision of its source.

This is particularly so in *Purgatory*, where the character of the Old Man is referred to a specific original by so unusual a device as the inflection of the verse. There is a deliberate reminiscence of Lear:[86]

> I am a wretched foul old man
> And therefore harmless.

When Yeats echoes a phrase and rhythm of Shakespeare in this way, he does so with a definite intention, here to enhance the stature of his hero, and to make the audience see him in a grimmer and more terrible light. Yeats thought of Shakespeare as a poet who, though he did not knowingly build on them, was subconsciously in contact with the archetypes,[87] and the Lear he refers to in his own *Last Poems* has behind him not merely the Gaelic poetic convention of the spiritual beggar, but the great Platonic symbol of man, dressed in the 'muddy vesture of decay', lost in the wilderness of the world.[88] For Yeats, Lear's heath was in a special sense the symbol of the fallen universe, and his storm of the torrent of human misfortune, and by sketching in this symbolism behind the figure of his hero, he adds a dimension to the character of the Old Man. The analogy with Shakespeare, though not elsewhere breaking surface so cleanly, is consistently pursued: the alternation of brutal language and pathos at the climax of the play is clearly reminiscent

of Lear, and the self-dramatisation of the old man's final speeches
is also Shakespearian. No educated audience could fail to recognise
some of these allusions, or miss the association Yeats wishes us to make.

The use of Shakespeare in *Purgatory* is an excellent example of Yeats's
indebtedness to the techniques of the Noh theatre, where allusions to
classical literature are consistently employed to lend depth to a play.
Yeats had of course used a precisely similar technique in each of his
previous dance-plays—referring us to *Othello* in *The King Of The Great
Clock Tower* and to *Julius Caesar* in *The Herne's Egg*—but never, perhaps, to such purpose as at the *dénouement* of the present play, which
is Elizabethan even in its psychology. Goaded to the verge of madness,
the Old Man kills his son, soliloquising as he does so in words terrible
in their irrelevance:

> 'Hush-a-bye baby, thy father's a knight,
> Thy mother a lady, lovely and bright.'
> No, that is something that I read in a book,
> And if I sing it must be to my mother,
> And I lack rhyme.[89]

But he cannot hold up his mother's dream; the hoofbeats return and
she is returned to the scene of her self-abandonment and shame; and
the play ends on a note Japanese in its resignation, and with the traditional Noh formula of prayer.[90]

What is perhaps most immediately striking in the conclusion is the
epigrammatic violence of statement Yeats permits himself: one remembers the old man's laconic and terrible comments on his act, 'twice a
murderer and all for nothing', 'my father and my son on the same
jack-knife', and more even than this the way in which Yeats's style
deliberately courts the sordid:

> I am a wretched foul old man
> And therefore harmless. When I have stuck
> This old jack-knife into a sod
> And pulled it out all bright again,
> And picked up all the money that he dropped,
> I'll to a distant place, and there
> Tell my old jokes among new men.

Yeats attributes the same ugliness to the memories of the impure dead,
for the properties of the woman's dream are whiskey, crude lust 'on a

mattress', 'bragging and drinking in the public house'; and even the past of his own country, when unity of culture was possible, is given no better appellation than 'fat, greasy life'. Here at least Yeats is building upon his practice in *The Herne's Egg*, for the squalor of these images, and sometimes the crude and violent colloquialisms of the language, is made to reflect the condition of the fallen world. *Purgatory* is a play of several tensions, but the most important is the contrast between heaven and generation:

> Dear mother, the window is dark again,
> But you are in the light because
> I finished all that consequence.

Whatever his hopes for Ireland in a new cycle, Yeats did not forget that, for the individual soul, there is only one escape.

CHAPTER FIVE

THE DEATH OF CUCHULAIN

I

THE LETTERS IN which Yeats discusses the theme of his last play are important, for they give a vital clue to its full meaning. The most significant was written to Ethel Mannin:

> I am writing a play on the death of Cuchulain, an episode or two from the old epic. My 'private philosophy' is there but there must be no sign of it; all must be like an old fairy tale. It guides me to certain conclusions and gives me precision but I do not write it.[1]

Yeats goes on to explain the root-proposition on which he has founded himself, and it turns out to be a very Platonic one:

> To me all things are made of the conflict of two states of consciousness, beings or persons which die each other's life, live each other's death. This is true of life and death themselves.[2]

These sentences are interesting quite apart from the light they throw on Yeats's dramatic technique, where the philosophical premise on which a work is based is always implied, never directly stated. Beyond this, they give us a key to what is notoriously a difficult play.

Though it may superficially seem otherwise, *The Death of Cuchulain*[3] is nothing if not Platonic, and I will begin by reconstructing something of the climate of feeling against which it has to be read. A useful starting point is the text Yeats refers to in Heraclitus. When Heraclitus says that 'men and gods die each other's life, live each other's death',[4] he means in the first place that the human and the divine are opposites, and that men understand nothing of life in the divine world, just as Cuchulain in Yeats's play is unable to see the Morrigu, or even to believe in her presence in a room. But if the human and the divine are mutually exclusive, the text in Heraclitus indicates also that they are in some sense complementary, and if we are to approach *The Death of*

Cuchulain profitably, it is necessary to know something of the relation between his two worlds.

Greek philosophy called the divine world *reality*, and the material world was thought of as *unreal*.[5] This cliché of Platonism Yeats takes over into his own mature verse and prose, in which my card index gives no single instance of his using the word 'reality' in any other sense. 'Lead us from the unreal to the real', he writes,[6] and again 'Seek out reality, leave things that seem',[7] in both cases emphasising the distinction between the world of becoming and that of being; he also writes that 'Parmenides thought of reality as a motionless sphere',[8] and gives his idiom a Berkleian twist in *The Herne's Egg*, where he implies that nothing exists save in the mind of God:

> There is no reality but the Great Herne.[9]

If I have now established the meaning the word 'reality' had for Yeats, I have made one point essential to understanding his play; and it will next be as well to provide some indication of the spirit in which Platonism thought of the divine world, which brings us close to the atmosphere of Yeats's own verse at its most mystical. Perhaps the best way may be to condense Plotinus: here is one of the most immediately moving passages in his prose, a description of the landscape of reality:

> For all things there are heaven, and there the earth is heaven, as also are the sea, animals, plants and men. And all things there are diaphanous; and nothing is dark and resisting, but every thing is apparent to every one internally and throughout. And the splendour there is infinite, since even that which is small is great. The sun too which is there is all the stars: and again each star is the sun and all the stars. Motion likewise there is pure; for the motion is not confounded by a mover different from it. Permanency also suffers no change of its nature, because it is not mingled with the unstable. But the life there is wisdom; a wisdom not obtained from the reasoning process, but the first wisdom, not derived from another.[10]

Yeats's poem 'There'[11] is a single instance of his indebtedness to passages such as this; and the relevance to his play is very obvious, and follows from the fact that this is the world which Cuchulain enters with death. The play, a play of rejoicing, centres about his transfiguration.

I have said that Greek philosophy spoke of the divine and the human as complementary, and the precise relation between the two worlds can be illustrated from Yeats's poem 'Ribh denounces Patrick':[12]

Natural and supernatural with the self-same ring are wed.
As man, as beast, as an ephemeral fly begets, Godhead begets Godhead.
For things below are copies, the Great Smaragdine Tablet said.

Platonism thought of the divine world as a reality of which the temporal world is an exact copy, or shadow, so that every object in the heavenly world has its (necessarily imperfect and unstable) replica on earth; and no object in the material world is allowed any reality save as a copy of the eternal.[13] Thus in Yeats's poem human wedlock is a 'copy' of the divine union: Yeats founds himself upon an inscription attributed to Hermes Trismegistus,[14] but he might equally well have referred us to any other Platonic philosopher, or to Shelley or Blake; there is nothing recondite in his arguments. And it should be added that if the physical world is a poor shadow of the eternal, it is not the less beautiful for this: even the 'ephemeral fly' is an image of the divine beauty, as Plotinus continues the passage I have been quoting to make clear:

For what more beautiful image of it [reality] could have been generated? What other fire can be a better image of the fire which is there, than the fire which is here? Or what other earth than this, of the earth which is there? What sphere also could be more accurate and venerable, or more orderly in its motion, than that of this sensible universe? And what other sun after the intelligible sun, can be prior to this which is the object of sight?[15]

To all this Yeats subscribes, notably in *Words For Music Perhaps*:

Things out of perfection sail,
And all their swelling canvas wear.[16]

Everything in the material world, then, is reminiscent of perfection, and in the same context he tells us that among 'birds or beasts or men' there is always one who is the exact image of the 'perfect'.[17] So also in his play, humanity is presented as completely oblivious of the divine, but it is not the less dignified or heroic for this. Yeats's philosophy allowed him to combine a passionate conviction of the unreality of the physical world with passionate belief in the essential goodness and nobility of its inhabitants, and this belief *The Death of Cuchulain* faithfully reflects.

The Death of Cuchulain is in fact an odd fusion of the Platonic and the Gaelic, and Yeats takes the Irish deities of the Sidhe to represent the inhabitants of the divine world; the Morrigu in the narrative itself, and a whole hosting in the final song after Cuchulain's death and transfiguration to that company:

> Conall, Cuchulain, Usna's boys,
> All that most ancient race.

After 'Supernatural Songs'[18] Yeats wrote little about God as a single being, but much of the Sidhe, in *The King Of The Great Clock Tower*, for example,[19] and in 'Under Ben Bulben',[20] and he justified himself by a prose argument of great interest. His drift is at first sight peculiarly obscure:

> I think that two conceptions, that of reality as a congeries of beings, that of reality as a single being, alternate in our emotion and in history, and must always remain something that human reason, because subject always to one or the other, cannot reconcile . . . I think that there are historical cycles when one or the other predominates, and that a cycle approaches when all shall be as particular and concrete as human intensity allows. Again and again I have tried to sing that approach, 'The Hosting of the Sidhe', 'O sweet everlasting voices', and those lines about 'The lonely majestical multitude', and have almost understood my intention. Again and again with remorse, a sense of defeat, I have failed when I would write of God, written coldly and conventionally.[21]

Here I feel sure that Yeats is remembering a text in Plato's *Sophist,* where Plato discusses whether divinity appears to human eyes as 'many or one' and gives Empedocles as his authority for supposing that it is seen as 'first one . . . and then many'.[22] The argument connects closely with Empedocles' cyclic theory of history, on which Yeats so largely founded himself: in one phase of civilisation men worship a single god, and in the next a plurality. So in the passage from Yeats I have quoted, we are asked to believe that 'a cycle approaches' when men will revert to the worship of a multiplicity of gods:[23] it was of course one of Yeats's oldest beliefs that Ireland under a new cycle would return to paganism and 'sacrifice a mullet to Artemis' or revert to its local deities.[24] Yeats goes on to imagine himself as the Virgil to this new cycle, its vatic singer; and justifies the assumption by saying that he has always failed when writing of God as unity, but has succeeded when conceiving of him as multiplicity. These arguments seem to have been of great importance to his verse, for after them he represents Godhead almost exclusively by that 'congeries of beings', the Sidhe.

The Death of Cuchulain is an odd play, Irish in its narrative and some of its symbolism, but in its essence as Platonic as any of Yeats's work. The real point is, I think, that Yeats interpreted Irish myth through the Platonic philosophy; this is clearly shown in his theory of the origin of the Sidhe. If I understand 'Under Ben Bulben' rightly, Yeats thought that the great Irish heroes underwent, with their deaths, the elaborate process of purification he derives from Neoplatonism, passing through all the purgatorial states, after which, 'completeness of their passions won', they made up the number of the gods.[25] This idea of man's gradual transmutation into the superhuman Yeats will have derived from Plutarch;[26]* and it is a single instance of that habit of juxtaposition and assimilation which is characteristic of his last play. *The Death of Cuchulain* is a study of the relation between Man and reality, and though I will now digress into a study of Yeats's sources, the present arguments are central to his meaning, and will have to be resumed.

II

The comic prologue to Yeats's play makes it clear that it will be unintelligible without some knowledge of 'the old epics and Mr. Yeats's plays about them', and since the common reader often has not the knowledge of Gaelic legend necessary, this is an additional reason for its having remained obscure. The play is in fact a subtle rearrangement of the relevant part of the Cuchulain cycle, not so complete a reorganisation of legend as *The Only Jealousy of Emer*, but as ingenious a set of insertions and emendations as *The Green Helmet*,[27] and it will serve to illustrate the skill with which Yeats developed his source material to the ends of drama.

The point of the narrative is of course that the Morrigu, one of the three Irish war-goddesses, brings about Cuchulain's death; she bewitches Eithne Inguba into giving him a false message which leads him out to fight, and after his death reappears to dominate the stage and explain that she has engineered the whole action. Yeats, in a characteristically urbane and insolent phrase, even makes her the choreographer for Emer's following dance:

* It is equally, of course, a traditional Indian belief, as Yeats will have known from Madame Blavatsky.

The Morrigu: The dead can hear me, and to the dead I speak.
This head is great Cuchulain's, these other six
Gave him six mortal wounds. This man came
· first;
Youth lingered though the years ran on, that season
A woman loves the best. Maeve's latest lover,
This man, had given him the second wound,
He had possessed her once; these were her sons,
Two valiant men that gave the third and fourth.
These other men were men of no account,
They saw that he was weakening and crept in;
One gave him the sixth wound and one the fifth;
Conall avenged him. I arranged the dance.

Here the Morrigu speaks of the men who killed Cuchulain in terms which make it very clear that they are her mere tools (though she is not contemptuous; humanity is allowed its tragic dignity), and by holding up Cuchulain's head demonstrates that he is in effect her own victim. She addresses her speech 'to the dead', and this is in deference to Yeats's convictions as to the nature of reality. Humanity will be oblivious to the presences of the divine world.

There are a number of Gaelic legends to the effect that the Morrigu held sway over Cuchulain's life and death.[28] In one of them, Cuchulain meets a woman, quarrels with her about a cow, and attacks her; then the woman is transformed into a crow, the conventional symbol for the Morrigu:

'If I had only known that it was you,' said Cuchulain, 'we should not have parted thus.' 'Whatever you have done,' said she, 'will bring you ill-luck.' 'You cannot harm me,' said he. 'Certainly I can,' said the woman, 'I am guarding your deathbed, and I shall be guarding it henceforth.'[29]

In this story, the Morrigu tells Cuchulain that he will live as long as the calf of her cow 'shall be a yearling'. He does not believe her, but the intimation is that the prophecy will be fulfilled.

This legend, with those I give below, suggests a tradition that the Morrigu presided over Cuchulain's destiny, and Yeats may well have had it in mind in his play. His main sources, however, are beyond doubt the last two legends in the Cuchulain cycle: Cuchulain's sojourn in the Valley of the Dumb and the narrative of his death. I will take my quotations from the compendium of translations collected by Eleanor Hull,[30] since this will be most convenient for reference.

As a young man, one of Cuchulain's major exploits had been to kill a monster called Calatin. After Calatin's death his wife gave birth to three daughters, deformed, each having one eye in the middle of her forehead; a detail remembered in the description of the Morrigu in Yeats's play:

> A woman that has an eye in the middle of her forehead!
> A woman that is headed like a crow.

These three daughters were the Morrigu, Badb, and Macha, the three Irish goddesses of war, and they were adopted soon after birth by Cuchulain's inveterate enemy Maeve, who recognised their supernatural powers and made herself responsible for their upbringing. Maeve sent them to Babylon and even to Hell to acquire magical arts. In all this her motive was to educate them in hatred for Cuchulain, so that she could rely upon them to bring about his death.

Yeats's play takes up the Gaelic narrative (though he does not explicitly say so) at the point where Cuchulain has been sent by his wife Emer to the Valley of the Dumb;[31] Maeve has invaded the land with a great army, and there is a legend current that to oppose her will bring about Cuchulain's death, so that it is necessary to confine him to a place where he can obtain no news of the progress of events. To make sure that he does not leave the Valley, Emer sends a girl named Niamh to be his bedfellow; in Yeats's version, no doubt to make the play harmonise with the rest of his own Cuchulain cycle, it is Eithne Inguba who is sent. Meanwhile Maeve calls up the three daughters of Calatin to scout for her enemy; taking the form of black birds, the conventional symbol for supernatural evil in Irish mythology, they go in search of him:

> up then they rose birdlike, airily soaring with the magic moaning wind of their own making.[32]

When his whereabouts are discovered, it is necessary to tempt him out to battle so that he may be slain; and in the Gaelic legend this task is allotted to Badb, though in *The Death of Cuchulain* it is the province of the Morrigu. Yeats may have been seizing his opportunity to integrate all the legends of the Gaelic cycle, but I think his central consideration in making the change was one of dramatic economy. Three war-goddesses no doubt seemed superfluous.

In the original, Badb has recourse to her magical powers:

Now then she took on her Niamh's shape, and being come where
Cuchullin was, bade him attack the hosts, saying: 'My soul, my
hero, and my warrior! dún Delgan is burnt, the plain of Conaille,
Muirthemne's plain and the whole province, ravaged, for that in
place of letting thee out to check this army I e'en have hindered and
withheld thee.' Cuchullin said: 'Alas, after that 'tis hard to trust in
women! I thought that for all gold of the globe and for the whole
world's wealth never would'st thou have granted me this leave. Yet
since 'tis thou that sufferest me to affront battle and dire combat with
all Erin's men, verily I will go to it.'[33]

Yeats prefers a more prosaic device: the Morrigu bewitches Eithne
Inguba and makes her misrepresent a message which Emer has given
her:

Eithne: I am your wife's messenger, she has bid me say
       You must not linger here in sloth, for Maeve
       With all those Connacht ruffians at her back
       Burns barns and houses up at Emain Macha. . . .

What Emer in fact wrote was that Cuchulain was on no account to
leave the house:

Cuchulain: This letter is from Emer.
       It tells a different story. I am not to move
       Until tomorrow morning, for, if now,
       I must face odds no man can face and live.
       Tomorrow morning Conall Caernach comes
       With a great host.

Here Yeats pares down and simplifies his source: possibly he felt that
this seemingly more realistic version would impose less strain on an
audience's credulity, and so would be more amenable to the needs of
the modern stage.

In the Gaelic legend, Badb's machinations are discovered when the
real Niamh appears:

Next, Niamh overtook him and 'Alas, my little Cú,' she cried,
'Not for the globe's gold, not for the whole world's wealth, had I

e'er given thee that leave; neither was it I that licensed thee, but Calatin's daughter Badb in my shape taken upon her to deceive thee. Abide with me then, my friend, my gentle loving darling.' But he believing nought of what she said commanded Laegh to harness the horses.[34]

In Yeats, Cuchulain himself uncovers the deception when he opens Emer's letter and finds that Eithne has inverted her message; Eithne, confused as to whether Maeve or some goddess has been practising upon her, protests her innocence, but he will not listen to her:

> . . . she that put those words into your mouth
> Had nothing monstrous: you put them there yourself;
> You need a younger man, a friendlier man,
> But, fearing what my violence might do,
> Thought out these words to send me to my death.

He treats her with heroic gentleness, telling his servants to give her to Conall Caernach after his death 'because the women Have called him a good lover'; but nothing now can dissuade him from going out to the battle. Partly because of his bitterness at what seems to him Eithne's defection, and partly because the death-wish has come upon him, he has no further desire to live.

Yeats's sources are very elaborate in describing the further magical practices by which Badb and her sister decoy Cuchulain to his death: they waylay him on the way to the battle, and by witchcraft rob him of his strength.[35] All this Yeats omits, taking us at once from the scene with Eithne Inguba to the final episode of Cuchulain's death against the pillar. There, in a trance-state, he is visited by a vision in which the principal *personae* of his life, Aoife and the Blind Man of *On Baile's Strand*, reappear to him, a device by which Yeats imparts unity to his own cycle of Cuchulain plays; it may have been suggested by a similar episode in the Gaelic, where the soul of Cuchulain appears 'to the thrice fifty queens who had loved him', though this is after his death.[36] The incident of Cuchulain's stand at the pillar-stone is, as is well known, traditional:

> He went to the pillar stone that was on the plain; and he put his breast-girdle round it so that he might not die seated nor lying down, but that he might die standing up. Then came the men around him, but they durst not go up to him, for they thought he was still alive.

Then came to Cúchulainn the Grey of Macha to protect him, so long as his soul was in him. . . .

Then came the birds and settled on his shoulder.

'There were not wont to be birds about that pillar', said Erc, son of Cairpré. Then Lugaid arranged Cúchulainn's hair over his shoulder and cut off his head.[37]

In Gaelic legend, black birds are as much symbols of supernatural evil as white birds are of the purified spirit, and Eleanor Hull adds a note to make clear that 'it was Calatin's daughter Badb who hovered over him in the form of a crow'.[38] This incident Yeats develops into the entry of the Morrigu with Cuchulain's severed head.

Such are the sources of the narrative part of Yeats's play, and their reconstruction should serve to make his plot quite clear. Yeats alters, inserts, omits, in order to shape his play for the stage and to round off his own Cuchulain cycle: there is a certain amount of by-play to underline man's remoteness from the supernatural world, but broadly he does not stray far from the original. On the other hand, I do not think that we can read the play as narrative for narrative's sake; Yeats was nothing if not a didactic poet. The narrative of *The Death of Cuchulain* is a means rather than an end; it is used to carry certain ideas of Yeats's own, and it will be useful to disentangle them.

III

Yeats had perhaps two main motives in writing his narrative. In the first place, he wanted to give a definitive portrait of the heroic character, and he is at pains to sketch in Cuchulain's courage, simplicity, honour, single-mindedness, the curious gentleness he brought to his women and, characteristically, his sexual prowess. At the same time, he had a more philosophical object, for *The Death of Cuchulain* is a play about the death-wish. We are shown in considerable detail both how the fact that a doom was upon him affected Cuchulain's behaviour, and, what for Yeats was equally important, how it affected the attitudes of those around him. A central didactic strain in the play's argument follows from this: Yeats wishes to show us the psychology of a man predestined to die.

When he decided to develop this side of his theme, Yeats was no more than following his original. The Gaelic is much concerned with the death-wish; while Cuchulain is giving his reasons for going out to the battle, it comes upon him and transfigures him:

Moreover, loath as ye be to dismiss me into danger and against my foes, even so cheerful am I that now go to have my side bored and my body mangled, neither knowest thou better than I myself know that in this onset I must fall. No more then hinder my path and course; for whether I stay I am devoted to death, or whether I go my life's span is run out.[39]

In a passage which must be a late Christian interpolation, and which Yeats will have translated back into terms of the old pagan deities, he has a vision of angels:

The one Almighty God whom they that are up there adore, Him I do worship, and in the King Supreme that made Heaven and Earth I do believe. Now, henceforth and forevermore welcome Death.[40]

I think it is fair to say that Cuchulain is so transfigured by the presence of death as to appear almost a holy man, and that this gives the Gaelic legend much of its cathartic power.

All this is certainly remembered in Yeats's play, where very great stress is laid on the fact of Cuchulain's transfiguration. At the beginning of the play, he is quite himself: Yeats characterises him as the calm, confident hero:

> Eithne: No matter what's the odds, no matter though
> Your death may come of it, ride out and fight.
> The scene is set and you must out and fight.
> Cuchulain: You have told me nothing. I am already armed,
> I have sent a messenger to gather men
> And wait for his return.

The turning-point in the action is Eithne's supposed defection; when he is confronted by that, by some strange interior process of the soul Cuchulain loses 'the passion necessary to life'. He understands now that death is very near to him, accepts it completely, and desires nothing else; and the consequence is that events in the material world around him lose all importance, while the supernatural world seems very near. Thus he falls into a trance-state at the pillar-stone, and we are told that he 'cannot understand' the sequence of past events in his own memory; the visionary presences of Aoife and the Blind Man are real enough to him, but his simple, almost naïve statements as he talks to them show that the world is far away. I imagine Yeats wishes us to think of a man transfigured, in life but not of it, unable now to differentiate between the important and the inconsequential, because his own past life no longer seems to him quite real:

> There was no reason so to spoil your veil . . .
> Then I went mad, I fought against the sea . . .

We should, I think, take it that Cuchulain has had a premonition of the nature of reality, which leads him to accept his fate; he is favoured with a vision which, if not of angels, is at least of the progress of the soul after death:

> There floats out there
> The shape that I shall take when I am dead,
> My soul's first shape, a soft feathery shape.
> And is not that a strange shape for the soul
> Of a great fighting man?

Cuchulain has now become as much a holy man as in the Gaelic, and the main distinction is that Yeats prefers traditional imagery. The bird is, as I have said, a symbol for the purified soul in Egyptian theurgy, in Platonism, in Kabbalism and in Irish myth itself.

Yeats's treatment of this side of his theme is many-sided; he goes far beyond his original. We are not merely shown Cuchulain's own reaction to the nearness of death; we are shown also how those around him are affected by his transfiguration. All react in the same way, with mingled fascination and 'loathing'. This is well shown by Eithne Inguba's speech when Cuchulain forgives her for her treachery; she does not herself rightly know what has led her seemingly to betray him; and she cannot understand how he can be so resigned:

> You're not the man I loved.
> That violent man forgave no treachery.
> If, thinking what you think, you can forgive,
> It is because you are about to die.

There is hatred in these words—'you're not the man I loved'—and Cuchulain's reply makes it clear that there is also fascination:

> Speak low if you would speak about my death,
> Or not in that strange voice exulting in it.

The words 'you are about to die' are several times repeated of Cuchulain, by Eithne once more and by Aoife, and in every case with the
same mingled emotions. In this way Yeats underlines the importance
of the *motif* to his play.

The crux of the action comes when Emer dances before the severed
heads, and we are told in the prologue that the dance must convey
both 'love and loathing'. Yeats simplifies his argument for dramatic
purposes, and we can take it if we like that Emer feels 'loathing' for
Cuchulain's slain enemies and unmixed love for her husband; but I do
not think that a great dancer would play the scene in this way. Emer,
I think, feels both ecstasy and disgust as she dances before her husband's
head; her dance is identical with the Queen's in *A Full Moon In March*
and should therefore convey the same emotions:

> She moves as if to prostrate herself before it [the head], in adoration
> or triumph. She is about to prostrate herself before it, perhaps does
> so, then rises, looking up as if listening; she seems to hesitate between
> the head and what she hears. Then she stands motionless. There is
> silence, and in the silence a few faint bird-notes.

The ecstasy, I feel sure, is of a very mixed nature, and I shall show
later in this essay that Yeats was basing himself on a Platonic source.
As he saw it, the fact of death aroused two polar emotions in the spec-
tator: adoration, because death is the beginning of reality; and horror
because it is life's opposite, something alien to flesh and blood. Emer
prostrates herself before Cuchulain's head as the symbol of his transfiguration, listening as she does so to the 'bird-notes' which symbolise
his entry upon reality, and both these emotions are implicit in her
dance.

Yeats skilfully adapts his Gaelic sources to build his play around the
death-wish; and in giving his arguments a Platonic bias he clearly goes
beyond them; he makes use of a certain amount of his private erudition, but hardly enough to make the whole obscure. On the other
hand, *The Death of Cuchulain* finishes by being a very learned play,
though the erudition is packed into very small compass: it is condensed,
largely, into the last thirty lines, to which I am therefore compelled to
give disproportionate space. It is not in the narrative that *The Death of
Cuchulain* is difficult, it is in the prologue and finale, and by means of
them Yeats expands very greatly the significance of all that lies
between.

IV

Yeats begins his play with a prologue which (I am told) strongly resembles the Kyogen or comic interludes in the Japanese Noh plays.[41] It is functional, in that it prepares us for the atmosphere of what is to follow, as when Yeats tells us what to expect from Emer's dance: she is to be

the tragi-comedian dancer, the tragic dancer, upon the same neck love and loathing, life and death.

He advises us bitterly that the play is made of such 'antiquated stuff' as this, now 'out of fashion', and that we are not to look to it for what he thought of as arid modernity; his dancer is to look 'timeless, Rameses the Great', and will have nothing in common with the dancers of modern art:

I spit three times. I spit upon the dancers painted by Degas. I spit upon their short bodices, their stiff stays, their toes whereon they spin like peg-tops, above all upon that chambermaid face.

Yeats also prepares us in another sense for what is to come: he refers to his cyclic theory of history in order to explain the deterioration of contemporary taste. I think we have to assume all the arguments of *Purgatory* if we are fully to understand his prologue; history is moving towards a reversal of the gyres, and the world to which he offers his play is, as he says in 'A Bronze Head', 'in its decline and fall'.[42] In 'this vile age', Yeats's prologue tells us, the average audience has no sense of tragedy, being composed of 'people who are educating themselves out of book societies and the like, sciolists all, pickpockets and opinionated bitches'; a phrase in which he possibly remembers a favourite epigram of Synge's, 'the sciolist is never sad'.[43] Yeats's prologue, then, has a double function: to align us emotionally to the tragic scene that is to follow, and to remind us that his play has been written out of period, and that a civilisation in process of lapsing into 'intellectual barbarism' will be incapable of appreciating it.

The prologue also introduces us to Yeats's musicians, who play such an important role in the symbolism of the play:

There is a singer, a piper, and a drummer. I have picked them up here and there about the streets, and I will teach them, if I live, the music of the beggar-man, Homer's music.

The singer in fact turns out to be a 'harlot' and the other musicians 'beggars': she sings the final chorus of the play 'to the beggar man', and to accompaniment on 'pipe and drum'. Here at once one of the functions of the finale suggests itself, for it is obviously a product of Yeats's interest in popular ballads, 'the music of the streets';[44] but we have to determine whether there is any significance in the character-isation beyond this. Yeats's final choruses are always infinitely sugges-tive, and (as Miss Ishibashi has so excellently demonstrated in her work on the subject)[45] their function is to lead the audience on beyond the mere exact statement of the narrative into a world of philosophical speculation; to indicate the lines on which Yeats wishes us, on leaving the theatre, to meditate; and, in short, to add a dimension to the play. As she has also shown, the opening chorus (here the prologue) and the finale are always interdependent. These considerations make it quite certain to me that there is ulterior significance in the conclusion of Yeats's play.

What we have first to determine is the symbolic meaning, for Yeats, of the harlot, and to do so is to break new ground in Yeats criticism. There is a passage in *Wheels and Butterflies* which is so immediately relevant that it cannot be ignored; it explains, if we are able to under-stand it, the precise meaning of Yeats's harlot symbol, and relates it to his cyclic theory of history, his views on reality, and his thesis that God-head appears to human eyes as alternately 'one and many'.[46] In its context it is autobiographical: Yeats is describing the development of his own early art:

Presently Oisin and his islands faded and the sort of images that came into *Rosa Alchemica* and *The Adoration of the Magi* took their place. Our civilisation was about to reverse itself, or some new civilisation to be born from all that our age had rejected, from all that my stories symbolised as a harlot, and take after its mother; because we had worshipped a single god it would worship many or receive from Joachim de Flora's holy spirit a multitudinous influx.[47]

Here Yeats makes it clear that the harlot is his symbol for the matrix from which a new masculine, 'harsh, surgical' dispensation[48] will pro-ceed, and that the new civilisation will revert to paganism, or to the worship of divinity in all its multitudinous forms; he draws an analogy with the cyclic theory of history of Joachim de Flora, which I have discussed. The continuation of this passage is also relevant to the arguments which the present essay is to make; Yeats goes on to discuss the meaning of his play *The Player Queen*, and he does not imply (as critics seem to have thought) that he *abandoned* the arguments of *The Adoration of the Magi* when he wrote that play, but that he *combined* them with something new:

> Then after some years came the thought that a man always tried to become his opposite, to become what he would abhor if he did not desire it [Yeats means that his thought attached itself to the theory he has previously been outlining, not that it replaced it]. I wasted some three summers and some part of each winter before I had banished the ghost and turned what I had meant for tragedy into a farce: *The Player Queen*.[49]

Yeats's theory of opposites is important to *The Player Queen*, but it is not really central to it, as all commentators have imagined; if the play is 'about' anything it is about his 'harlot' and his cyclic theory of history, as I shall show. As Yeats goes on to say in his prose essay referred to, he wanted 'to display the conflict in all its forms'; to combine, that is, the theory of opposite phases of civilisation with his theory of man desiring his opposite.[50] This is what *The Player Queen* sets out to do, and it is precisely the complexity of its argument which has made it so easy to misunderstand.

Before entering the deep waters which this argument opens before us, it will be best to see exactly what Yeats meant when he called the harlot his symbol for the matrix of a new Civilisation. From his earliest period, Yeats had thought kindly of the harlot figure, not merely because of the influence of Dowson and the 'nineties generally, though this may have played its part. His interest in eastern philosophy reinforced whatever the climate of feeling of the decadence may have brought to him, and taught him to look at the harlot from a standpoint beyond all conventional concepts of good and evil, as he himself points out:

> There are Indian courtesans that meditate many hours a day awaiting without sense of sin their moment, perhaps many lives hence, to leave man for God. For the present they are efficient courtesans. Ascetics . . . have lived in their houses and received pilgrims there. Kings, princes, soldiers, beggars, courtesans and the fool by the

wayside are all equal to the eye of sanctity, for everybody's road is different, everybody awaits his moment.[51]

We should also bear in mind that the Noh dramatists thought kindly of the harlot: Zeami, the famous Japanese critic, records that only four kinds of women should be represented in tragedy, for only four are capable of inducing a feeling of *yugen* or 'mysterious calm': the aristocrat, the *femme spirituelle*, the madwoman, and the courtesan.[52] Yeats's own attitude was conditioned by such authorities as this, and it is certain that, while the harlot denominated a type of civilisation quite different from the Christian, he did not associate the figure with vice or imply that the civilisation for which it stood would be vicious or corrupt.

These are important factors, but Yeats's central authority for giving the importance he did to the harlot figure was beyond doubt Blake. Blake so hated the concept of virginity, which seemed to him cold and negative, and had such sympathy with the sufferings of humanity, that he could not conceive that the Christian era could have manifested itself through a virgin: Mary, he suggests, might better have been a harlot:

> Was Jesus born of a virgin pure
> With narrow soul and looks demure?
> If He intended to take on sin
> His mother should an harlot have been,
> Just such an one as Magdalen
> With seven devils in her pen.
> Or were Jew virgins still more cursed
> And with more suckling devils nursed?
> Or what was it that He took on
> That he might bring Salvation?
> A body subject to be tempted,
> From neither pain nor grief exempted—
> Or such a body as might not feel
> The passions with which sinners deal?[53]

The argument of these beautiful lines (which Yeats chose for his own short Blake anthology) so captured Blake's imagination that in *Jerusalem* he has the Virgin Mary openly admit: 'I am indeed a Harlot':

> O Forgiveness and Pity and Compassion! If I were Pure I should never

Have known thee: If I were Unpolluted, I should never have
Glorified thy Holiness or rejoiced in thy great Salvation.[54]

Behind these lines is Blake's Platonic theory that the opposites are
basically one and that true religion consists of their reconciliation: a
thesis which *Jerusalem* magnificently expounds:

What is a Wife and what is a Harlot? What is a Church, and What
Is a Theatre? Are they Two and not One? Can they Exist Separate?
Are not Religion and Politics the Same Thing? Brotherhood *is*
Religion.
O Demonstrations of Reason dividing Families in Cruelty and
Pride.[55]

These are arguments which Yeats, as a young man, had by heart, and
their influence on his own symbolism was naturally great.

It is demonstrable that, even in his early work, Yeats used the harlot
figure in a very Blakean sense. If he could not rationally trace back the
Christian civilisation to such a source, and he differed from Blake in
that he did not find this feasible, at least it was a tenable proposition
that the next dispensation might lead to a reversal of values. In the
passage from *Wheels and Butterflies* on which I am basing myself, he
speaks of his early 'stories' as making this point, and what he has
principally in mind is no doubt *The Adoration of the Magi*, set in the
brothel quarter of Paris. There an old woman, dying, is presented as
the prophetess of a new era about to dawn; the pagan gods of Greece
and of Ireland are about to return into the world, and:

When they are about to overthrow the things that are today and
bring again the things that are yesterday, they have no one to help
them but one whom the things that are today have cast out. Bow
down and very low, for they have chosen for their priestess this
woman in whose heart all follies have gathered, and in whose body
all desires have awakened.[56]

Another relevant story is 'Red Hanrahan's Song About Ireland'. Here
Hanrahan looks forward to the overthrow of the present cycle, when
'the Grey Winds' of absolute destruction will blow up:[57] he sings a
prophetic song to celebrate the restoration of Ireland to her ancient
dignity. Yeats carefully prepares a tableau by which Hanrahan sings to
an audience of beggars and prostitutes, the elect in the new era; for

Margaret Rooney, his heroine, is a 'notorious' woman, 'hunted out' of her parish by the priest:

> While he sang he became greatly moved and a tear rolled down his cheek and Margaret Rooney put her face upon her hands and wept too. Then a blind beggar by the fire shook his rags with a sob, and after that every one wept.[58]

That the tableau in this small but moving story is precisely the same as that in *The Death of Cuchulain* seems to me a very strong indication of what Yeats had in mind when he wrote his play.

Perhaps I have now said enough to demonstrate the significance of Yeats's harlot figure, who represents all that is cast out in this era, all that will be justified in the era to come. In Yeats's play, however, the harlot does not stand alone; she is made love to by all the horsemen of the Sidhe. The meaning of this detail is extremely important, and can easily be demonstrated; but to explain it, it is first necessary to know something of the esoteric meaning of *The Player Queen*.

V

In *The Death of Cuchulain*, Yeats's prostitute tells how she is visited by all the gods of ancient Ireland; Yeats describes her feelings for them in poetry which strangely combines the brutal and the urbane, playing upon the fashionable slang meaning of the word 'adore':

> Maeve had three in an hour, they say.
> I adore those clever eyes,
> Those muscular bodies, but can get
> No grip upon their thighs.

In *The Player Queen*, the Queen cohabits with a white unicorn, and the implication is that when Decima becomes queen the unicorn will transfer its affections to her. These two bizarre episodes may seem to have nothing in common, but they are demonstrably variations on a single theme.

The Player Queen[59] seems to me a splendid play, in which Yeats completely realises his symbolism. The play centres upon a contrast between the two Queens: the legitimate ruler, and Decima, an actress in a troupe of strolling players, who makes use of a palace revolution to usurp her place. The Queen herself is a pious but shabby figure, preoccupied with the negative virtues:

Queen: I am almost certain that I am ready for martyrdom . . . I
have now attained to the age of my patroness, Holy Saint
Octema, when she was martyred at Antioch . . . I wish I
could resemble Holy Saint Octema in everything.

Decima, on the other hand, is 'a brazen, bragging baggage', and Yeats
uses beautiful subtlety in suggesting her exact function, which is as a
counterpart to the harlot figure of his early prose:

Decima: Do you know what song I was singing just now?
Nona: It is that song you're always singing. Septimus made it up.
Decima: It is the song of the mad singing daughter of a harlot. The
only song she had. Her father was a drunken sailor waiting
for the full tide, and yet she thought her mother had fore-
told that she would marry a prince and become a great
queen. [*Singing*]

'When she was got,' my mother sang,
'I heard a seamew cry.
I saw a flake of yellow foam
That dropped upon my thigh.'

How therefore could she help but braid
The gold upon my hair
And dream that I should carry
The golden top of care?

The moment ago as I lay here I thought I could play a queen's part,
a great queen's part; the only part in the world I can play is a great
queen's part.

The bird-woman sexual symbolism here connects with Yeats's common
image for the annunciation at the beginning of a new era, and Decima
goes on to compare herself explicitly with Leda. She dances, and her
dance is used to make clear that her function in the play is that of the
harlot, for it is a dance of universal sexual invitation:

Any bird or beast may rest
An empty head upon my breast.

But it is not a question of *human* sexual invitation, for in the course of
her dance Decima relates herself both to Leda and to Pasiphae (though
I think Yeats was thinking of Europa rather than Pasiphae, especially

in view of his later allusion to this myth,[60] and that this is an instance of his inexact classical scholarship):

> Shall I fancy beast or fowl?
> Queen Pasiphae chose a bull,
> While a passion for a swan
> Made Queen Leda stretch and yawn,
> Wherefore spin ye, whirl ye, dance ye,
> Till Queen Decima's found her fancy.

The point of this scene is that Decima does not want a man, but a beast:

> Spring and straddle, stride and strut,
> Shall I choose a bird or brute?
> Name the feather or the fur
> For my single comforter?

The 'bird' and 'brute' as Yeats is using them are very obviously symbols for the divine, since Decima builds her song round instances of divine sexual communication in classical mythology, and under the symbolism of the dance of the players, she is in fact making a sexual invitation to Godhead. We are left to infer that the form in which divinity is to descend to Decima is that of the unicorn, the disguise under which it manifests in this palace.

To understand this, it is necessary to know something of the traditional symbolic significance of the unicorn, which is perhaps the most celebrated of all emblems of alchemy as an image for the divinity, and was taken over into more orthodox medieval symbology, where it became an image of Christ.[61] Yeats indicates his meaning in the play itself, where he derives his symbol from 'the Great Beastery of Paris'; there is also a glance back to his earlier play, *The Unicorn from the Stars*,[62] where (as the title indicates) the image, *monoceros de astris*, represents Godhead. The symbol was in fact known to Yeats from the Order of the Golden Dawn, in which the novice was awarded the title of *Monocris de astris* when he was thought to be sufficiently purified to be in contact with the divine will.[63] In *The Player Queen* it is certainly suggested that the harlot Decima is to copulate with the unicorn and so, a new cycle arriving, propagate a new race; we are told of the Unicorn that 'he alone can be the new Adam' but that the difficulty is that 'he is chaste': that is, the new cycle is slow in eventuating. Septimus expresses all this in words that admit of no doubt:

I will rail upon the unicorn for his chastity. I will bid him trample mankind to death and beget a new race.

In the present order of things at the palace, furthermore, the unicorn couples by night with the legitimate queen, though he begets on her nothing but a sense of shame and a desire to retire from the world. By all this I think Yeats completely establishes his meaning: that his Queen is a symbol for the Christian dispensation, now 'almost ready for martyrdom', and Decima for woman in a new era, from whom divinity will beget a new race of men, pagan but heroic, incontinent, virile and proud.

Yeats reinforces his central argument most ingeniously by the incidental symbolism of his play. The Prime Minister, for example, is a farce character, a mere buffoon, but his favourite oath is 'bridesleep of Adam', an epithet in which Yeats remembers the line from Rossetti's *Eden Bower*, 'then the bridesleep fell upon Adam', which he used also in *Purgatory*.[64] At the climax of the play, in recognising Decima as the new queen, the Prime Minister uses words which suggest that he fancies himself as the Adam in the new dispensation, and proposes to usurp the function of Godhead:

> Sleep of Adam, I must have this woman for wife.

Again (and this is central) the Players have come to the palace to act in 'The Tragical Comedy of Noah's Deluge'; and this is most certainly an ingenious piece of symbolism, in which Yeats remembers Blake. No one who has read the Quaritch edition could fail to remember, as one of Yeats's most successful pieces of exegesis, those pages in which he relates Blake's image of Noah's Ark to his author's cyclic theory of history, and explains that 'the destruction of all things by the flood' is a symbol for the disaster that overtakes humanity at the end of a cycle.[65] He also explains the significance of Noah himself, as the symbolism is used by Blake:

> After the flood, three methods of conversing with Paradise, the beautiful internal world, remain to men, poetry, painting and music, typified by Noah, Shem and Japhet.[66]

In *The Player Queen* the disaster at a reversal of the gyres is symbolised by the palace revolution, which 'The Tragical Comedy' is used subtly to associate with Noah's flood, and Septimus, Yeats's poet and actor-dramatist, is the player who takes the part of Noah, while Decima is allotted the part of Noah's wife. By this Yeats infers that Decima, before the revolution enables her to meet her destiny as the bride of Godhead, has to *pose* as Noah's wife (the beloved of the artist): he is referring to the special relation between poetry and harlotry, and to the fact that the artist can see beauty in the harlot figure which (for Yeats) is truly there, but which bourgeois morality cannot recognise. With the revolution, Septimus abandons Decima to her fate, thus symbolically renouncing his marriage and setting her free to fulfil her destiny as the bride of God. He takes nothing with him but Noah's hat:

> I will save this noble, high-crowned hat of Noah. I will carry it thus with dignity. I will go slowly that they may see I am not afraid.

In the symbolism of this passage, Septimus abandons the idea of an impossible marriage (with what is really God's) which can bring him nothing but pain, and he accepts his own true destiny, the 'hat of Noah', symbol for the dignity of poetry, which alone can survive the destruction at a reversal of the gyres. After the revolution, Decima puts on the mask of Noah's sister; she will now be the friend and protectress of the artist but (being God's) can no longer accept his sexual love.

If the reader is not yet convinced as to the esoteric meaning of *The Player Queen*, one further instance may be enough to persuade him. At the climax of the play, when the crown changes hands, there is the grotesque comic detail, introduced with great levity, of an old man who is possessed by the spirit of an ass:

> Old Man: When I bray like a donkey, the crown changes. . . . It is the donkey that carried Christ into Jerusalem, and that is why he is so proud; and that is why he knows the hour when there is to be a new King or a new Queen.

This, I have no doubt, is Yeats's symbol for the moment of reversal of the gyres, and it is a comic burlesque of a detail in *The Adoration of the Magi*, a fact which may serve to connect the two works. In the early story, the moment when divinity descends to the harlot is commemorated by an old man's crowing like a cock: a voice issuing from his mouth informs us of the reason:

> I am Hermes the Shepherd of the Dead, and you have heard my sign that has been my sign from the old days.[67]

The cock is indeed the symbol of *Hermes psychopompus*, and it is a rein-carnation symbol,[68] here representing the rebirth of divinity into the world. Yeats found it used in this special sense in G. R. S. Mead's book on Hermes Trismegistus, where 'the crowing of the cock' 'which plays so important a part in the crucifixion story in the Gospels' is traced back to Egyptian theurgy as a symbol for the beginning of a new Platonic year and for the hour at which 'the Virgin gives birth to the Aeon' (Godhead).[69] In *The Player Queen* Yeats parodies this detail for the purposes of farcical comedy, and is no more serious than when he burlesques de Sade[70] by having Septimus write love-poems to one woman on another's back, but the braying of Christ's donkey has no doubt a real significance, and symbolises the moment of cyclical change.

The Player Queen is a play much overlaid by Yeats's theory of opposites and his 'doctrine of the mask', and it is full also of fanciful imagery which cannot be too closely interrogated, but I doubt whether it will in future be possible to discuss it apart from the concept of the gyres.[71] The parallel in *The Death of Cuchulain* is exact. Here, Yeats's mature practice makes his symbolism as bare and unornamented as, in his earlier play, it had been complicated and ornate; but the harlot who is made love to by all the horsemen of the Sidhe has precisely the significance of Decima: she is symbolic of all that is most pagan and subjective in the feminine principle, to which divinity (now seen as 'many') will descend, and on which it will beget the heroes of a new age. The image in Yeats's last play is spare and terrible, and (in that Yeats is able convincingly to elevate a small-town harlot to this essenti-ally noble function), I find it compassionate and curiously moving.

VI

We are now able to take the meaning of Yeats's final chorus line by line. Possibly because he died soon after the completion of his draft and had no opportunity for revision, it has all the appearance of being unfinished work.[72]* With the finale to *The Only Jealousy of Emer*[73] it is perhaps the most difficult piece of verse Yeats wrote, and criticism cannot avoid the task of exegesis.

The obscurity is largely in the first verse:

> The harlot sang to the beggar-man:
> I meet them face to face,

---

*This does not affect the fact that it is, even as it stands, very fine poetry.

Conall, Cuchulain, Usna's boys,
All that most ancient race;
Maeve had three in an hour, they say.
I adore those clever eyes,
Those muscular bodies, but can get
No grip upon their thighs.
I meet those long pale faces,
Hear their great horses, then
Recall what centuries have passed
Since they were living men.
That there are still some living
That do my limbs unclothe,
But that the flesh my flesh has gripped
I both adore and loathe.

We must understand, first, that Cuchulain has died; Emer has adored his severed head as the symbol that he has entered upon reality; now he has joined the company of the Irish Gods, and the scene has changed 'to some Irish fair of our own day'. Here in her rags the harlot appears, and describes how Conall, Cuchulain, Naoise, all the heroes who are now among the 'pale, long-visaged company' of the Irish Gods, come to make love to her, but cannot consummate the sexual act (if they could, a new civilisation would have begun from their embraces): their bodies and hers are disparate and she can get no purchase on their thighs. Here, as I have shown him doing in *The Herne's Egg*, Yeats remembers Plutarch's dictum that the divine body is of 'thin air', and that humanity cannot cohabit with it. The harlot goes on to explain how she 'adores' the Sidhe (using the word with double meaning, in its full and equally in its slang sense), and gives us the first of those oddly vivid and concrete descriptions of their physical appearance, to which Yeats returns in 'Under Ben Bulben'; then the passage concludes with a very difficult and obscure proposition in the antithesis of the last four lines. This could have at first sight either of two meanings: that the harlot adores and loathes only the living (because, with them, she is able to consummate the sexual act); or that her adoration and loathing are reserved for the Sidhe (reading into Yeats's phrase 'the flesh my flesh has gripped' the implication 'tried to grip'). This would make the harlot mean that mere sexuality with human beings is worthless beside the ecstasy derived from the sexual act, even if unfulfilled, when it is performed with one's opposite.

I am convinced that the latter reading is the correct one, and that the lines can be paraphrased as follows: 'there are some human beings who still make love to me, but I do not love them with the intensity I feel for the disparate and evasive (and therefore also loathsome) bodies of the Sidhe'. There does not, in fact, seem much doubt of Yeats's meaning for a reader who comes to him with a knowledge of Platonism. Love, for Yeats, is at its strongest when it contains within itself an element of hate, and this *odi et amo* motif he found also in Hermes Trismegistus, especially in G. R. S. Mead's essay on him called 'The Hating Of The Body', from which I think Yeats's own theory of opposites, in part, derives.[74] Hermes teaches that man can love nothing but his own opposite, that which is possessed of qualities precisely contrary to his own, and which, if he were not compelled by the sense of his own lack to love it, he would reject as alien:

Such are the things which men call good and beautiful, Asclepius—things which we cannot flee or hate.[75]

This is presented as true on the sexual plane as on all others, and Yeats remembers it in a number of passages, two of which I will quote.

Young, we discover an opposite through our love; old, we discover our love through some opposite neither hate nor despair can destroy . . .[76]

When a man loves a girl it should be because her face and character offer what he lacks, the more profound his nature the more should he realise his lack and the greater be the difference. It is as though he wanted to take his own death into his arms, and beget a stronger life upon that death . . .[77]

Now *The Death of Cuchulain*, as Yeats explained for Ethel Mannin, is a play concerned with the conflict of two absolutely opposite states of consciousness, the human and the divine; and if these opposites could be fused in the sexual act, it follows (for Yeats's Platonic authorities) that the ecstasy engendered must be greater than any other conceivable. This, I think, confirms the interpretation we must give to the present lines; but there is also a parallel within the play itself, in Emer's dance before the severed heads. There, as Yeats explains, the dancer must try to convey both 'love and loathing', for Emer is dancing before her opposite; like the Queen in *A Full Moon In March*, she is dancing in mingled adoration and revulsion before the fact of death. Where Emer's 'passionate intensity' has such a cause, it follows that the harlot's

must be similar: that the surrender of her body to the embraces of the
dead lies at the root of her ecstasy, with which no merely human
pleasure can compete.

Having established his argument, Yeats at once develops it with
ingenuity:

> Are those things that men adore and loathe
> Their sole reality?
> What stood in the Post Office
> With Pearse and Connolly?
> What comes out of the mountain
> Where men first shed their blood?
> Who thought Cuchulain till it seemed
> He stood where they had stood?

If it is the property of reality that men must both adore and loathe it
when they meet with it, may not the converse of this be true also: may
it not be that those moments in life which fill men with adoration and
loathing bring them in contact with reality? When Pearse and Con-
nolly fought in the Dublin Post Office during the Easter Rebellion,
did it not seem as if the shade of Cuchulain (as Yeats had also suggested
in 'The Statues') rose from the dead to stand beside them? When
young men first shed their blood in battle, does it not seem as if their
dead ancestors are with them, rising from their traditional burying
places on the mountain-side to bring them spiritual succour? And when
a poet or a sculptor (Oliver Sheppard, who made the statue of Cuchulain in the Dublin Post Office, or even Yeats himself) meditates upon
the scene of that heroic stand, does not his mingled exultation and
horror have the effect of making the image of Cuchulain seem to
materialise before his eyes once more? These are the great moments in
life, Yeats is saying, beside which nothing else matters; they are the
only moments in which man transcends his limitations and sees himself
as complete. He is certainly using the word 'reality' here in the sense
of those moments when man completely realises himself, but I think
the Platonic meaning persists together with this. For a Platonist, the
vision of reality awakens ecstasy in the beholder, the kind of ecstasy
which Plotinus feels in those passages from his prose with which I have
prefaced this essay; and in ecstasy, for a Platonist, the emotions of love
and hatred are fused and co-exist. Does not Yeats mean that the
moment of heroism is such a moment, when, as with Cuchulain
fastened to his pillar at the moment of death, the visionary and the
merely human seem equally real; when man is able to accept the

existence of spiritual presences and to integrate them into his merely human life?

Whatever their meaning, these magnificent lines succeed in evoking in the reader the emotion of exultation which is our central response to the play as a whole; the emotion implicit in Cuchulain himself when he is conscious of the death-wish and goes out to meet his fate. Yeats ends his final chorus on this note, the lines which remain serving merely to point a contrast between arid modernity and the physical image of Cuchulain which his words almost serve to bring before our eyes:

> No body like his body
> Has modern woman borne,
> But an old man looking on life
> Imagines it in scorn.

Here we are returned to the theme of the reversal of the gyres, and to Yeats's belief in the progressive degeneration of humanity, physical as well as mental, which he felt to be the order of things as unity of being became impossible.[78] His final chorus, and indeed the play as a whole, has been conceived 'in scorn' of modern man and everything he stands for, though as the 'harlot' ends her song 'to the beggar-man' we should be conscious that we are in the presence of a symbol that things will not always be so, and that an upheaval in civilisation will bring redress.

VII

To leave *The Death of Cuchulain* here would be to be guilty of false emphasis. We can say, if we like, that the narrative and choreographic part of any of Yeats's dance-plays constitutes a picture, and the lyrics which begin and end it a kind of frame; the frame sets off and enhances the picture itself, but it is no more than an embellishment. When we return to the narrative part of *The Death of Cuchulain* with full understanding of the lyrical, we see it in a different light; no longer as a mere 'fairy tale', but as a deliberate attempt to oppose the standards of a collapsing civilisation with those of the heroic age; a proposal of values from which western man has fallen and to which, in Yeats's judgment, he is about to return. It will perhaps be best to close this essay on a consideration of what Yeats made of these values.

The heroic age, for Yeats, was a thing of the immediate future as much as of the past, and his play has consequently to convey its nearness as well as its golden age remoteness. At the same time he has

to underline its utter incompatibility with the values and manners of
'this vile age', and this he does in his prologue; by presenting us with
the 'pickpockets and opinionated bitches' of the modern intelligentsia,
and then by juxtaposing his simple and noble hero. The contrast, I
think, is completely successful, but it does not resolve the central
dramatic problem: the heroic age can be made to seem infinitely
desirable, but it does not follow that it will seem infinitely near at hand.
The problem Yeats had before him was thus very highly complex,
perhaps insoluble; and it is interesting to see how he sets about resolving
it.

He had to choose, fundamentally, between free and blank verse: the
style of *Purgatory* and *The Herne's Egg* and that of all his earlier drama.
The blank verse of his plays had evolved over a long period, and Yeats
had set before himself certain fixed rules of composition: his verse was
spare, deliberately 'unpoetic' in imagery, and it had a considerable
dignity and a certain adaptability and 'pace'. On the other hand, the
blank verse of *The King Of The Great Clock Tower* had seemed to
Yeats wooden and conventional; he had valued the play only for its
lyrics; and he had then deliberately thrown the style away and evolved
a newer, more contemporary manner. This free verse style had been
at once more vital and more personal than the earlier; it had immediacy
of impact, a colloquial texture, and, at least in *The Herne's Egg*, a
certain coarseness of fibre. For his last play, Yeats had to choose between the two, and he chose to revert to his blank verse style; that is to
say, to sacrifice nearness to distance in the presentation. Perhaps because
the simplicity and dignity of what he had to convey seemed to demand
it, he chose the more formal and more essentially serious medium of
expression. The high seriousness of the theme had to manifest itself at
all costs.

The result of all this is, I think, a very uneven play, where the writing
may be on any of several distinct planes. I have said that the Morrigu's
climactic speech attracts me:

> These other men were men of no account;
> They saw that he was weakening and crept in;
> One gave him the sixth wound and one the fifth;
> Conall avenged him. I arranged the dance.

Here the blank verse is energetic and concise; Yeats runs through a
whole gamut of emotions in the course of the speech, and this proves
the style to be workmanlike; but what distinguishes it for me above

most else in the play is the sardonic humour of the presentation, by which the Morrigu appears as a mistress of the ballet. In general, Yeats found it necessary to eschew humour of this kind, which he perhaps felt would detract from the heroic dignity of his story. Here is a characteristic passage, written, I would say, on the next plane below that of the. Morrigu's speech. Cuchulain is telling Aoife how he killed the son she bore him:

> Aoife: I have been told you did not know his name
> And wanted, because he had a look of me,
> To be his friend, but Conchubar forbade it.
> Cuchulain: Forbade it and commanded me to fight.
> That very day I had sworn to do his will,
> Yet refused him, and spoke about a look;
> But somebody spoke of witchcraft and I said
> Witchcraft had made the look, and fought and killed
> him.
> Then I went mad, I fought against the sea.

The episode of Cuchulain's fight with the waves was clearly much in Yeats's mind in his last period, and he made fine verse of it in 'The Circus Animals' Desertion':

> And when the Fool and Blind Man stole the bread,
> Cuchulain fought the ungovernable sea. . . .[79]

Moving as this poetry is, however, I do not think it is superior to that simple last line given to Cuchulain in the play:

> Then I went mad, I fought against the sea.

This seems to me the best Yeats ever made of his symbolic detail; it conveys all that he could have wished of man's helplessness and his essential nobility; presented as a memory glimpsed from the threshold of reality, there is a peculiar poignancy in its understatement. Writing of this kind seems eminently satisfactory, even though one misses Yeats's characteristic *wit*, and the least one can say is that he measures up to his Gaelic sources.

More frequently he falls below them, and my personal feeling is that he falls below the standards of *The Herne's Egg* also. Here is the Blind Man in Cuchulain's vision, coming to kill him with a jack-knife:

Blind Man: I have been fumbling with my stick since dawn.
           And then heard many voices. I began to beg.
           Somebody said that I was in Maeve's tent,
           And somebody else, a big man by his voice,
           That if I brought Cuchulain's head in a bag
           I would be given twelve pennies; I had the bag
           To carry what I get at kitchen doors.
           Somebody told me how to find the place;
           I thought it would have taken till the night,
           But this has been my lucky day.
Cuchulain: Twelve pennies!

Here, for contrast, is Tom Fool from *The Herne's Egg* describing what
brought him out to kill Congal:

Congal: What is your name, boy?
Fool: Poor Tom Fool.
        Everybody knows Tom Fool.
Congal: I saw something in the mist,
        There lower down upon the slope,
        I went up close to it, and saw
        A donkey, somebody's stray donkey,
        A donkey and a fool—I don't like it at all.
Fool: I won't be Tom the Fool after tonight.
      I have made a level patch out there,
      Clearing away the stones, and there
      I shall fight a man and kill a man
      And get great glory.
Congal: Where did you get
        The cauldron lid, the pot and the spit?
Fool: I sat in Widow Rooney's kitchen,
      Somebody said 'King Congal's on the mountain
      Cursed to die at the hands of a fool.'
      Somebody else said, 'Kill him, Tom,'
      And everybody began to laugh
      And said I should kill him at the full moon
      And that is tonight.
Congal: I too have heard
        That Congal is to die tonight.
        Take a drink.

I realise that not all critics find the highly personal rhythms of Yeats's free verse satisfying, but I am sure it is obvious that Tom Fool's speech is more *alive* than the Blind Man's: the statement in each case is condensed, simplified, and in the method of presentation almost naïve, but the rhythms in *The Herne's Egg* are far closer to modern speech, and the language has much more impact simply because it has more salt: 'I don't like it at all', 'I won't be Tom the Fool after tonight', 'Take a drink'. In *The Death of Cuchulain* Yeats presents us with a very simple, even a stylised dramatic situation (and this is not necessarily a fault), but he does so in a blank verse which is eclectic rather than contemporary, at least in rhythm, and is not very noticeably an improvement on that of early work like *On Baile's Strand*. It has a certain vigour, but it is somehow a literary, contrived vigour, the kind of *energia* that can be obtained from following rules of composition; I do not think it has that joyous vitality which comes from the mimesis of contemporary speech. The ultimate inadequacy of Yeats's dramatic blank verse has often been noted, and it is primarily for this reason that parts of his play's narrative fail to grip me; as a model for imitation I find it as much a dead end as *Sohrab and Rustum*, though it is a failure of a very different kind.

If the communication is inadequate, this does not mean that the world of Yeats's play is in itself spurious and 'literary'; the atmosphere is in fact highly individual, and we are often conscious of personal feeling beneath the verse. This is well illustrated by the imagery of the fallen world which intrudes into the play; however dignified and noble life in the heroic age may be, Yeats does not forget that it is a poor copy of the ideal. Thus the vision of his death which manifests itself to Cuchulain connects closely with the squalid imagery of the last scene of *The Herne's Egg*, while it also reminds us of *Purgatory*:

> Cuchulain: Twelve pennies! What better reason for killing a
>   man?
>   You have a knife, but have you sharpened it?
> Blind Man: I keep it sharp because it cuts my food.

Cuchulain may be a great man, but death is none the less a sordid fact; the Morrigu may finally lift the veil and show us that his death is as noble and heroic as anything in his life, but this is not how it appears to the hero himself. Similar imagery occurs in that speech of Eithne Inguba where, having betrayed her lover, she asks nothing more than to die:

> When you are gone
> I shall denounce myself to all your cooks,
> Scullions, armourers, bedmakers and messengers,
> Until they hammer me with a ladle, cut me with a knife,
> Impale me upon a spit, put me to death
> By what foul way best please their fancy. . . .

We may contrast this horrifying passage with some of the eclectic rhetoric in the play:

> Age makes more skilful but not better men . . .

> Servant: Is her confession true?
> Cuchulain: I make the truth!

Perhaps it will thus be seen for what it is: the voice of the whole man speaking, a liberty Yeats does not often allow himself in this play.

The sexual detail of the play is also highly personal, and, I think, more characteristic of Yeats's own position than of the manners of the heroic age. The Gaelic provides a source for the incident of Cuchulain's wife sending a girl to sleep with him,[80] but Yeats puts matters very bluntly:

> And there is something more to make it certain
> I shall not stir till morning: you are sent
> To be my bedfellow.

He omits everything of the affectionate detail of his original—'Alas, my little Cú [hound], my friend, my gentle loving darling'[81]—which might serve to gild this pill. There is also the incident of Cuchulain's disposal of his mistress, which may in the last resort be moving and justified, but is at least equally blunt:

> . . . and should I not return
> Give her to Conall Caernach because the women
> Have called him a good lover.

This sexual directness, then, is a very definite characteristic of the narrative, and it is remembered, like much else, in the finale. There, Yeats is returned to a lyric measure, and so is able to express himself in more brutal, and also more vital terms:

Maeve had three in an hour, they say.
I adore those clever eyes.

As a love-poet, Yeats seems to me a very modern writer (though he accepts much more of the traditional attitude to love than any other poet of our times). Like Baudelaire, or his successors, he is not averse to mingling *les noms les plus tendres et les noms les plus effroyablement grossiers* in his lovers' mouths, and his adherence to this characteristic in *The Death of Cuchulain* makes it a typically candid and I suppose to some critics an unpalatable play.

Finally, *The Death of Cuchulain* is a living and a highly individual play in its central argument: the transfiguration of Cuchulain as the death-wish comes upon him. This also is there in Yeats's original, but in relating it to his own philosophy of reality he makes it different from anything the Gaelic can have intended. Yeats communicates the change in Cuchulain indirectly, by a technique of suggestion: the characters merely hint at what they feel, but we are left in no doubt:

> Speak low if you would speak about my death,
> Or not in that strange voice exulting in it.

This seems to me the dominant emotion of the play, in narrative and lyrics alike, and it is for the communication of this emotion that I imagine it will continue to be read.

PART THREE

THE RELATED LYRICS

CHAPTER SIX

FIVE PLATONIC POEMS

IN THE PRECEDING chapters I have had much to say of Yeats's use of the symbolism of Neoplatonism, and in this essay I will entrench my arguments by explaining five of his poems which, perhaps more obviously than any others, derive from Platonic sources. Almost all Yeats's work could be said to do this in point of *thought*, but I am concerned here less with philosophy than with the Platonic symbology itself.

Perhaps I may begin with a certain amount of recapitulation. The symbolic system of Neoplatonism was fixed and one might even say rigid: the sea, for example, symbolised always 'the waters of emotion and passion', or simply life; man was consistently thought of as the beggar, dressed in the rags of mortality; the tomb, the forest and the cave were all symbols of the material world; after death, the soul, often accompanied by a mystic escort of dolphins, crossed the sea to heaven, the Isles of the Blessed.[1] Yeats knew this system of symbolism from several sources: from Madame Blavatsky, in his formative years; then from Taylor's translations of the commentators on Plato, and especially from Porphyry's essay on 'The Cave of the Nymphs'; also from Plato himself, Plotinus, Proclus, Julian, Philoponus, and the other Platonic philosophers he had read, and from the seventeenth-century Cambridge Platonists. He took it over into his verse in the confidence that it would prevent his own symbolism from being arbitrary or unintelligible; it was traditional, for it had persisted throughout the middle ages, where it influenced among others Dante, and, later, Spenser; and, as the symbolism of a religious system which he himself was largely able to accept, it is clear that he thought of it as profound. In using it, again, he had precedent in the work of two English poets he particularly admired: Blake is full of Platonic symbolism, and in fact painted a picture of Porphyry's cave;* while Shelley's *Prometheus Unbound* can hardly be fully understood without a knowledge of the tradition. The symbolism of Neoplatonism is, for me, curiously moving, in that it is essentially the product of deep religious conviction, and it is hardly

*'The Sea of Time and Space' (identified by Kathleen Raine).

surprising that Blake, Shelley and Yeats, three students of 'heterodox mysticism', should have adopted it.

THE GOATHERD'S SONG FROM 'SHEPHERD AND GOATHERD'.

In the winter of 1914-15, as I have said, Yeats was busy relating the Platonic theory of the fate of the soul after death to the teachings of such visionaries as Boehme and Swedenborg, and comparing what he found there with the traditions of folklore and the superstitions of popular occultism. Not long after, Major Robert Gregory was killed in action, and Yeats rehearsed the death of his 'dear friend's dear son' in several poems. 'Shepherd And Goatherd'[2] is one of these and it connects closely with the occult researches that were occupying Yeats at the period.

The shepherd and goatherd of Yeats's poem sing antithetical songs, in the Greek pastoral convention,[3] to express the sympathy of the Irish villagers with Lady Gregory in her bereavement. The sources of the poem are in fact complex; there may be an influence from Spenser's *Shepherd's Calendar*, and (since Yeats thought of Coole Park as an Irish Urbino), of Castiglione's famous saying 'Would that I were a shepherd that I might look down daily upon Urbino':[4] there is almost certainly an allusion to the Platonic use of sheep and goats as symbols for young and old souls respectively, but this it will be best to take up later. In any case, Yeats leaves us in no doubt that his poem has occult significance: the shepherd's grief is that of the ordinary man, and we are told explicitly that he knows nothing beyond the 'natural life', but the goatherd is a man of very different cast. Dark things are said of him:

> They say that on your barren mountain ridge
> You have measured out the road that the soul treads
> When it has vanished from our natural eyes.

This is of course precisely what Yeats was himself at the time occupied in doing; and the goatherd assents to the characterisation here made of him in words which make it clear that his song has a profound meaning:

> Indeed
> My daily thoughts since the first stupor of youth
> Have found the path my goats' feet cannot find.

With this cryptic remark he begins his elegy, and his central theme is that, after death, Robert Gregory will grow 'younger every second'.

Jaunting, journeying
To his own dayspring
He unpacks the loaded pern
Of all 'twas pain or joy to learn.

With these words we are taken at once to the heart of the Platonic theology.

Yeats probably made early acquaintance with the tradition that the soul, after death, lives backwards through time, for he will have read of it in the section on Dionysus in Taylor's *Dissertation*:

> According to the Orphic theology, souls, while under the government of Saturn, who is pure intellect, instead of progressing, as now, from youth to age, advance in retrograde progression from age to youth.[5]

The intellectual world is of course heaven, and in the Orphic mysteries, Taylor goes on to say, the soul in heaven was represented as a child: this, he explains, is why Dionysus before his fall is presented as the *puer aeternus*, for before his dismemberment he lived in perpetual youth, having no connection with the material world.[6] If such a theory was a part of the Orphic religion, it was clearly in existence long before Plato, but Plato adopted it. In a famous myth, from which Yeats derived also the Platonic authority he claimed for his theory of the gyres, Plato says that there are two 'cycles': the cycle of Jupiter (which the Neoplatonist commentators, known to Yeats from Taylor's *Plato*, interpret as meaning the physical world), and the cycle of Saturn, or the intellectual world, the pre-natal condition from which the soul descends at birth and to which it returns after death.[7] In the Kingdom of Saturn:

> [man] is no longer seen advancing to old age, but is again changed to the contrary and naturally becomes, as it were, younger and more delicate.[8]

In the previous cycle of civilisation, Plato goes on, the world was an earthly paradise which resembled the intellectual condition: men seemed to live backwards in time even before their deaths:

> The white hairs of those more advanced in years became black, and the cheeks of those that had beards became smooth, and thus each

was restored to the past flower of his age. The bodies, likewise, of
such as were in the bloom of youth returned to the nature of a child
recently born . . . [and people] were assimilated to this nature, both
in soul and body.[9]

By this Plato probably means to describe both the nature of life in
heaven and (symbolically) the nature of life in the material world
when men live in concord and according to the rules of pure intellect;
or so the commentary of Proclus[10] interprets him.

What Yeats made of this myth is fortunately quite clear; for, although he has left no direct commentary on it, we have his analysis
of a famous passage in Shelley which derives from it. The text in
Plato I have quoted is almost certainly the source of Asia's song in
Prometheus Unbound; Yeats had no doubt of the fact. Music, Shelley's
song tells us, can give the soul a fragmentary perception of the real
nature of heaven; the listener seems, momentarily, to embark on that
journey which we must take after death, over the sea of emotion and
passion to the Isles of the Blessed. So it is that, while the music lasts,
Asia seems to move backward through time:

> We have passed Age's icy caves,
> And Manhood's dark and tossing waves,
> And Youth's smooth ocean, smiling to betray:
> Beyond the glassy gulfs we flee
> Of shadow-peopled Infancy,
> Through Death and Birth, to a diviner day;
> A paradise of vaulted bowers
> Lit by downward-gazing flowers,
> And watery paths that wind between
> Wildernesses calm and green,
> Peopled by Shapes too bright to see,
> And rest, having beheld; somewhat like thee;
> Which walk upon the sea, and chant melodiously.[11]

According to Yeats's commentary on these lines 'Asia sails against the
current from age to youth, from youth to infancy, and so to the pre-
natal condition "peopled by Shapes too bright to see" '.[12] In the fourth
act of Prometheus Unbound, he goes on, 'this condition, man's first happiness and his last, sings its ecstatic song'. The last act of Prometheus
Unbound has, ostensibly, a sociological meaning; but it is clear that
Yeats interpreted it through Plato: that when the gyres brought round

a moment of concord and the 'golden years' returned, the world would become an image of the pre-natal state, an earthly paradise.

If Yeats had Plato for his authority and Shelley for his model in 'Shepherd And Goatherd', he also had heterodox mysticism and the beliefs of folklore behind him. He had noted the parallelism in *Visions and Beliefs*:

> In the west of Ireland the country people say that after death the process of life is reversed, and Swedenborg's angels move always towards 'the springtime of their life' and grow more and more beautiful 'the more thousand years they live'.[13]

In fact Swedenborg's angels move towards the 'dayspring of their youth',[14] so that when Yeats uses the word in 'Shepherd And Goatherd' it is no doubt a conscious reminiscence. Beyond this concurrence of the authorities, there was also the myth of Tir-nan-Oge, the country of the young; and on another plane the whole widespread symbolism of Godhead as the *puer aeternus*. All these traditions are no doubt remembered by Yeats in his own philosophy of life after death:

> [The dead] examine their past if undisturbed by our importunity, tracing events to their source, and as they take the form their thought suggests, seem to live backwards through time.[15]

In Yeats's purgatorial condition of the Return, the ghost relives the events of its life in reverse order, working always from effect to cause, in order to purify itself of good and evil, thought and emotion. By this means he explains the whole complex of his authorities, Platonic and visionary alike.

The goatherd's song will now be seen to be peculiarly Platonic in symbolism and general tone. Robert Gregory, after death, will grow 'younger every second'. In life, he had been 'solemn and reserved' because of his 'dreams' and 'ambitions', but now he will revert joyously 'to his own dayspring' or to the pre-natal condition, after having purified himself during the purgatorial process of 'all 'twas pain or joy to learn'. Yeats compares this process of the Return to the unwinding of a 'loaded pern', an image which, as I have said, takes us back to the 'spindle of necessity' at the end of Plato's *Republic*, on which the destinies of men are wound. As the Return continues, the dead man will learn to dismiss all his adult memories, forget every occurrence of his manhood, the 'outrageous war' in which he died, and even the works of art which during life he created. Then he will enter upon a second adolescence in the intellectual world.

The imagery Yeats uses to describe this second adolescence may need some further elucidation. It is perfectly in keeping with the pastoral tone of the whole, but it is strangely archaic in so far as it is applied to Robert Gregory.

> At some old winding whitethorn root
> He'll practise on the shepherd's flute,
> Or on the close-cropped grass
> Court his shepherd lass,
> Or put his heart into some game
> Till daytime, playtime, seem the same.

At first sight these lines suggest nothing so much as some seventeenth- or eighteenth-century rural scene, an English or French landscape painting of the period, perhaps: my personal association is with Watteau's 'Embarkation For Cythera', though I have no real reason to suppose that Yeats had this painting in mind. The imagery, however, probably remembers in the first place Plato, who continues the passage I have been quoting to describe the intellectual world as a simple pastoral landscape:

And when they are distributed about Saturn, and live the life which is there, he says fruits are produced in abundance from the trees, and many other things spring spontaneously from the earth. The inhabitants also are naked and without beds, and for the most part are fed dwelling in the open air. The grass likewise springing abundantly from the earth supplies them with soft couches.[16]

These are the Elysian fields, but a similar imagery, Yeats noted, came to the visionaries and visionary artists of the eighteenth century: we must remember that, in his system, certain perceptions of reality are only possible at particular periods within a culture. Swedenborg's heaven, for example, was of precisely this genre:

Swedenborg, because he belongs to an eighteenth century not yet touched by the romantic reverie, finds horror amid rocky, uninhabited places, and so believes that the evil are in such places, while the good are amid smooth grass and garden walks and the clear sunlight of Claude Lorraine.[17]

Yeats read a parallel visionary significance into the paintings of Blake and his followers, whether they were always fully conscious of it or no:

> Always in his [Blake's] boys and girls dancing on smooth grass and in golden light, as on pastoral scenes cut upon wood by his disciples Palmer and Calvert, one notices the peaceful Swedenborgian heaven.[18]

We must remember that Yeats believed that the visionary artist, and especially perhaps the visionary painter, was in direct contact with reality: there might be a significance in his imagery of which he was not consciously aware. That is why Yeats wrote, many years later:

> Calvert and Wilson, Blake and Claude,
> Prepared a rest for the people of God.[19]

They did so in a quite literal sense, even Claude: for the real theme of their painting was the delineation of the prenatal condition, the 'rest' to which the 'good' finally attain. With this idiosyncrasy of Yeats's art criticism in mind, it is clear that the lines in question may derive from one of many eighteenth-century landscapes.

The goatherd's song concludes with a very Platonic image. The soul does not remain in the condition of adolescence; when it has purified itself of all mere information such as it may have acquired during life, and is left bare of all 'knowledge' except knowledge of the Self, it will return to the cradle, and to a dream-like state of infancy in the intellectual world:

> All knowledge lost in trance
> Of sweeter ignorance.

Here there are strong echoes both of Plato—who says that the inhabitant of the intellectual world partakes of a child's nature 'both in soul and body'[20]—and of Asia's song in Shelley, where the soul returns to 'infancy' and so to 'a diviner day'. Yeats's poem in fact follows Shelley's so closely in all its details that I feel sure he had *Prometheus Unbound* in mind when he composed it.

'CHOSEN'

Yeats wrote this poem as a technical exercise and, as he tells us himself, as an experiment in the metre of Donne's 'Nocturnall Upon St. Lucie's Day'.[21] There are in fact strong resemblances in imagery as in form—the 'Nocturnall' may have suggested to Yeats the idea of using zodiacal imagery—but we cannot take the works as complementary. Yeats's poem is in fact an answer to Donne's; one might almost say a refutation of what is after all one of the most pessimistic of his lyrics:

> Study me then, you who shall lovers bee
> At the next world, that is, at the next Spring:
>   For I am every dead thing,
>   In whom love wrought new Alchimie. . . .
> He ruined me, and I am re-begot
> Of absence, darkness, death; things which are not.[22]

Yeats, it is clear, intended his poem to state the counter-truth to this catalogue of love's 'privations'; and to make it as full an 'answer' as possible he drew on the full weight of his Platonic learning.

When we read 'Chosen',[23] we have therefore to take into consideration all Yeats's philosophical knowledge, especially those texts which he was reading at the time he wrote it: the Enneads of Plotinus and Plato's myth of Er.[24] The poem, in fact, is probably more heavily overlaid with traditional learning than any other of his works, for there are three distinct strains of Platonic thought in it. I am primarily concerned with Yeats's use of the symbol of the Milky Way, which he had evidently assimilated before 1903, since in Ideas of Good And Evil he rebukes Tintoretto for having painted a picture on the subject while in ignorance of the tradition:

> Tintoretto's 'Origin Of The Milky Way', which is Allegory without any Symbolism, is, apart from its fine painting, but a moment's amusement for our fancy.[25]

If I am to make sense of Yeats's symbolism of the Milky Way, however (and it is the 'miraculous stream' of his poem), I must first consider the general meaning of the whole.

The first strain of Platonic thought in 'Chosen' follows from its title. 'The lot of love is chosen', the woman who is the speaker tells us, and again:

> I struggled with the horror of daybreak,
> I chose it for my lot!

This does not of course mean anything so trite as that the lover passively accepts the necessity of suffering; she deliberately and heroically chooses her own destiny, and what she actually chooses is the endless, agonising cycle of love in the material world, night followed by day, union by separation: the wheel of human existence ceaselessly turning, and providing no possibility of final stasis or of continued peace. Yeats reinforces this side of his theme by comparing her lover, the male principle of the poem, to the sun, his great principle of creative energy:

> Scarce did he my body touch,
> Scarce sank he from the west
> Or found a subterranean rest
> On the maternal midnight of my breast,
> Before I had marked him on his northern way,
> And seemed to stand although in bed I lay.

Love's incapacity to find rest, the woman tells us, is symbolised both in the sun's remorseless apparent progress through the signs of the 'whirling zodiac', and in its diurnal course through the sky between sunrise and sunset, sunset and sunrise. Her torment in this absence of all stasis is communicated in the last line given: the compulsions of time will not allow her lover to rest on the 'maternal midnight' of her breast, and she seems to stand in her agonised determination to follow him, her sun, as he rises towards the zenith of their separation.

It may not be easy to see why the lover should have 'chosen' so terrible a destiny as that Yeats here sets out, but this is made clear in the second verse. His heroine does so because of the compensatory advantages to be derived from 'pleasure with a man', though I should stress that only his great frankness and honesty make Yeats give 'pleasure' as her motive, and that the kind of pleasure he has in mind is very far from being sensual. By holding back the explanation of her motivation until the last line of the poem, Yeats imparts a dramatic tension to the whole; but if his first verse does not give us this information it does answer two other important questions that will arise in the reader's mind, for it tells us both when the choice was made, and why the lover's destiny should be as it is. Love's bargains, in Yeats's philosophy, are commonly transacted outside of time,[26] and in this case I feel sure that he wishes us to remember Plato's myth of Er, where the souls of men, in heaven, between incarnations, 'choose' the 'lots' that represent their destinies in their future lives.[27] The verbal reminiscence is unmistakable, and I feel sure that this extension of the meaning is inherent in the poem for any reader who is familiar with Plato, as Yeats of course wished his audience to be. Similarly, since he compares the lover to the sun in its diurnal and annual circuit of the heavens, I think it is highly probable that the philosophic basis of the whole is to be found in Plotinus' essay 'The Heavenly Circuit' which Yeats often refers to elsewhere; in the poem 'Veronica's Napkin', for instance, where it is the 'symbolical glory' of the 'air', and in the letters to Sturge Moore; both references being made at the period when 'Chosen' was composed.[28] In this essay Plotinus accounts for the circular rotation of the heavenly bodies by applying his symbol of the perfect circle of which God is the centre. The planets circle about God because they are separated from Him, because they can approach no closer than they are placed, and they do not wish to increase the distance of their separation. The soul's own cyclic destiny, the endless reiterative recurrence of days and seasons, births and rebirths, which it learns to accept, is symbolised in the motion of the spheres.

> The Soul exists in revolution around God to whom it clings in love, holding itself to the utmost of its power near to Him as the Being on which all depends; and since it cannot coincide with God it circles about him.[29]

Plotinus tells us that the soul circles because it cannot find peace at any point within its cycle, for 'everywhere it finds something else besides the Soul':[30] it desires nothing save to be alone with itself, in absolute self-possession, for that is to find God. If we apply the religious meaning behind the symbolism, it is clear that the lover is driven to the restlessness that is his fate, both because of his aching consciousness of his separation from God, and because of the ultimate inadequacy of all possible experience, however passionate or kathartic, that may come to him in the material world.

The second verse resolves the poem's tension by means of another Platonic symbol, this time the sphere.

> I struggled with the horror of daybreak,
> I chose it for my lot! If questioned on
> My utmost pleasure with a man
> By some new-married bride, I take
> That stillness for a theme
> Where his heart my heart did seem
> And both adrift on the miraculous stream
> Where—wrote a learned astrologer—
> The Zodiac is changed into a sphere.

The function of the sphere in Yeats's poetry as a symbol for perfection, and as a mature equivalent for the rose-imagery of his early verse, has often been noticed, but I have not seen it traced to its proper origin. The symbol is current in pre-Socratic philosophy, and finds its fullest exegesis in the fragments which remain to us of Parmenides' treatise *The Way of Truth*.[31] This is the 'great treatise of Parmenides' which Yeats imagines, in his poem 'The Gift Of Harun Al-Rashid', as surviving in its entirety in the Caliph's library, and as providing a complete schematisation of the 'gyres and cubes and midnight things' that make up the geometry of his own system.[32] In the fragments we in fact have, Parmenides postulates that 'reality' is best considered under the symbol of a 'motionless three-dimensional sphere', and proceeds to demonstrate by what is almost a geometrical proof that the sphere is the image of perfect harmony, every point on its surface standing equidistant from its centre. To appreciate the symbol fully, I imagine that some sympathy with the Platonic conception of the divine as perfect harmony is necessary; at all events it was adopted by Plato, in his *Parmenides* and elsewhere, and by the Neoplatonists generally (though Plotinus prefers the symbol of the circle), after which it became a favourite symbol in the tradition of alchemy and remains a commonplace of occultism. Yeats of course knew it from all these sources, and he adopts it, often, as a symbol of the fragmentary perception of reality made possible by sexual love, as in 'Among School Children':

> . . . it seemed that our two natures blent
> Into a sphere from youthful sympathy.[33]

Here the allusion is to Aristophanes' fable in the *Symposium*,[34] and beyond it (or rather together with it, for the fable has at bottom the same significance) to the spiritual elevation of the lover. In its context in 'Chosen' the sphere is used to stand for the single consolation that makes all the torment of love endurable, and causes the protagonist of the poem to 'choose' it: the peace of the moment after love, when the lovers have, for a moment, insight into perfection, and escape, while the stillness lasts, from the 'common round' of material existence.

This hardly seems very obscure; and Yeats himself has provided a note[35] to explain the identity of the 'learned astrologer' he refers to. His authority is Macrobius, and the passage he reproduces he had seen both in Taylor's *Porphyry* and in his *Dissertation*.[36] Yeats's note in fact slightly misrepresents Macrobius' text, so I will reproduce the original here. It is concerned with the descent of the soul:

Since those who are about to descend are yet in Cancer, and have not left the Milky Way, they rank in the order of the gods . . . From the confine, therefore, in which the zodiac and galaxy touch one another, the soul, descending from a round figure which is the only divine form, is produced into a cone.[37]

This difficult passage introduces us to a highly complex set of symbols, far more recondite than the zodiacal imagery Donne uses in his 'Nocturnall', and very pertinent to Yeats's poem.

In Platonism, the soul has a pre-natal existence in heaven, after which it descends through a series of stages into the material world, acquiring during its descent the attributes of personality it will have in its future life. The symbol used for the soul's abode before birth, as Yeats knew from Taylor's *Porphyry*, was the Milky Way.[38] From there, the soul descended, and the Platonists used the signs of the zodiac to symbolise the stages of the descent. Cancer is 'the confine in which the zodiac and galaxy touch one another', or where Milky Way and zodiac meet, and Cancer is therefore known as 'the gate'. The soul passes through this gate, and descends through the signs that follow Cancer: in Leo it is given its sensitive and imaginative nature; in Virgo, the power to interpret perception; in Libra, desire; in Scorpio, its assertive and masculine characteristics; in Sagittarius, practical ability; and so on. After death, as we have seen, the soul lives backwards through time: it returns through the gate of Capricorn (from which it follows that a wise soul might be symbolised by a goat),* and sheds its attributes in passing through the succeeding zodiacal signs, after which it is free to return to its source. Between Cancer and Leo is the constellation known to Platonism as 'the winecup of Bacchus', and before its descent the soul drinks from this 'cold intoxicating cup' (often referred to by Yeats) with the result that its pre-natal memory is destroyed. The harmony of its being is now shattered, and it loses its spherical shape; it is important to realise that since 'the primordial shape of everything manifested' is spheroidal, the harmonious soul both is a sphere, and descends from a sphere.[39]

Yeats's poem refers directly to this group of symbols. He is not concerned with the fate of the soul before birth, but he is concerned with the fleeting vision of reality made possible by love; then, for a moment, the lovers' souls seem to be back at their starting-point on

---

*Thus in 'Shepherd And Goatherd'. There, Yeats uses sheep as symbols for unwise souls: for Aries was his symbol for reincarnation and descent into the ignorance of generation.

the Milky Way, 'both adrift on the miraculous stream' of the galaxy, or perhaps of the river of heaven which is situated at its edge. There, in the 'confine' of Cancer, the spiritual and material worlds intersect and the imperfect is transformed into the perfect, 'changed into a sphere'. But apart from that moment, human beings are:

> on the track
> Of the whirling Zodiac.

They are caught in the unending circuit of birth, death and rebirth: the descent from Cancer and the return through Capricorn endlessly repeated until by cultivation of the 'intellectual life' they win liberation from time.

'THE DELPHIC ORACLE UPON PLOTINUS'

This poem,[40] which a critic has called a 'gay and preposterous' joke,[41] and which is in fact one of the most profoundly serious of all Yeats's works, can best be seen for what it is by a reader acquainted with Porphyry's essay 'The Cave Of The Nymphs'.[42] Yeats felt that the influence of this essay on modern European art was considerable, maintaining (perhaps rightly) that Shelley's 'The Witch Of Atlas' and Botticelli's 'Nativity' were examples of works composed under its influence;[43] and he makes copious use of it in his own verse.

'The Cave Of The Nymphs' is ostensibly a commentary on the symbolism inherent in part of the *Odyssey*; though its value does not lie in the field of Homeric studies, but in the complete exegesis it affords of the Platonic system of symbolism. In Homer's poem, the wanderings of Odysseus end with his arrival at Phaeacia, a holy city exempt from war and the tyranny of the seasons; from there he sails home, crossing the sea in a Phaeacian boat, until he is brought to a cave on the coast of Ithaca. The cave is full of honey-bees and honey is stored there; it is dedicated to the nymphs. This narrative[44] Porphyry interprets as a myth of the return of the soul, a parallel to the zodiacal symbolism I have referred to; and the starting point in his interpretation is the symbolic meaning attached to the sea-voyage. Platonism symbolises the birth of the soul as its journey from the Isles of the Blessed in a celestial boat (the 'vehicle' in which the soul was thought to be contained); during life the soul is tossed about on the sea of emotion and passion; after death, living backwards through time, it recrosses the sea and returns to the island paradise from which it set out. All this symbolism can be read into the *Odyssey*, where the fruitless wanderings of Odysseus over the hostile sea are taken to symbolise the life of the unregenerate soul; his arrival at the holy city of Phaeacia, where it is perpetual spring, is read to mean the conversion of the soul to the intellectual life; and his return to Ithaca, to symbolise the soul's restoration to heaven, its native land, which can only be accomplished by virtue of the intellectual life.[45] With this in mind, Porphyry considers the significance of the cave at which Odysseus lands on what, for Platonism, is his return to the Isles of the Blessed; he takes it to be a symbol for the womb, or the matrix of generation, the threshold of the world. Through this gate the soul first descends into the material universe, and through it it must reascend: its garment of flesh is woven on the looms the cave contains; the honey which is there is semen, or 'the pleasure arising from generation';[46] the honey-bees and the nymphs who reside there are symbols for the two kinds of souls who are born into the world. All generated souls are nymphs, for a nymph is a water-spirit, and thus a spirit in love with the sea of generation; but the honey-bees are the souls of the just, for as Porphyry beautifully says 'this insect loves to return to the place from whence it came, and is eminently just and sober'.[47] Porphyry goes on to examine many other details of Homer's text, such as the amphorae and mixing-bowls which are in the cave; he interprets them all from the Platonic tradition, but I omit what is not relevant to Yeats.

Yeats knew and loved this once-famous essay, and he used many of its symbols in his own verse. 'Honey of generation' occurs in 'Among School Children' and is referred to Porphyry by a note,[48] and where this is so we are justified in interpreting 'The Stare's Nest At My Window' from the same source:

> We have fed the heart on fantasies,
> The heart's grown brutal from the fare,
> More substance in our enmities
> Than in our love: O honey-bees
> Come build in the empty house of the stare.[49]

The honey-bees, I take it, are the souls of the just, and Yeats is praying for the return of justice to an Ireland ravaged by civil war. His poetry is equally full of the symbolism of the sea-voyage to and from perfection: 'things out of perfection sail',[50] 'Swift has sailed into his rest',[51] and the poet himself has 'crossed the seas' and come to 'the holy city of Byzantium',[52] a city which is surely reminiscent of Phaeacia. In the present poem, the symbolism of the sea-voyage is the link with 'The Cave Of The Nymphs', but in Yeats's sequel, 'News For The Delphic Oracle', the whole of Porphyry's essay is relevant, and this is why I have reconstructed it at length here.

'The Delphic Oracle Upon Plotinus' is an original poem based upon the verse-oracle delivered to Amelius after the death of Plotinus, which as it happens is preserved, with a commentary, in Porphyry's *Life*.[53] The Greek original of this poem has always been much loved by Platonists, and Yeats knew the translations by Taylor and MacKenna, as he did the additional commentary by Henry More.[54] The oracle is addressed to Plotinus himself, and describes his journey over the sea of life to the Isles of the Blessed; after death Plotinus does not have to recross the sea by expiating his memories, for his life has had the purity of a saint's. Living as he did 'in the sleepless vision within and without',[55] he had nothing to expiate. On his death, then, he is free to 'enter at once the heavenly consort': but he has had to struggle against the sea during life, when he was sustained by visionary experience:

'Oft-times as you strove to rise above the bitter waves of this blood-drenched life, above the sickening whirl, toiling in the midmost of the rushing flood and the unimaginable turmoil, oft-times, from the Ever Blessed, there was shown to you the term still close at hand. . . .

But now that you have cast the screen aside, quitted the tomb that held your lofty soul, you enter at once the heavenly consort:

Where fragrant breezes play, where all is unison and winning tenderness and guileless joy, and the place is lavish of the nectar-streams the unfailing Gods bestow, with the blandishments of the loves, and delicious airs, and tranquil sky.

Where Minos and Rhadamanthus dwell, great brethren of the golden race of mighty Zeus; where dwells the just Aeacus, and Plato, consecrated power, and stately Pythagoras and all else that form the choir of immortal love, there where the heart is ever lifted in joyous festival.'[56]

While Plotinus lived, he was in visionary contact with reality, 'the term still close at hand', and after death he was admitted at once to the company of philosophers, musicians and lovers who make up, with the immortals, and the three judges of the dead, the number of 'the golden race'. His death was instant transfiguration: 'then the term ever near was vouchsafed to Plotinus', as Porphyry beautifully says.[57]

It may not be apparent why the company of heaven should consist so exclusively of philosophers, musicians and lovers; and it is worth clarifying this point, for to do so will explain why Yeats used his poem as he did, to serve as the end-paper to *Words For Music Perhaps*. I will quote Henry More's commentary, which was favourite reading for Yeats. In heaven, More says, the soul's occupation consists:

> 'not only in rational discourses, which is so agreeable to the Philosophical Ingeny, but innocent Pastimes, in which the Musical and Amorous propension may be also recreated. For these Three dispositions are the flowr of all the rest, as Plotinus has somewhere noted.'[58]

In fact Plotinus wrote a long essay to show that the metaphysician, musician and lover are the three kinds of men most capable of visionary experience, and thus of cultivating the intellectual life and obtaining release from the cycle of material existence, 'the metaphysician taking to the path by instinct, the musician and the nature peculiarly susceptible to love needing outside guidance'.[59] Yeats knew the text in Plotinus, of course, as well as he did More's interpretation of the oracle, and it made his poem peculiarly apposite to the theme of *Words For Music Perhaps*. In his song-cycle, Yeats's beggar-woman and journeyman are tragically conscious that their love is something outside time, and must wait until they themselves are outside time for its consummation:

> What can be shown?
> What true love be?
> All could be known or shown
> If time were but gone.
> '*That's certainly the case*,' said he.[60]

Plotinus, as Houghton points out,[61] had given Yeats precedent for believing that the soul continued its individual existence in heaven; and the authorities I have quoted gave him Platonic authority that it would consummate its love there. Yeats ends all his song-cycles with a classical text in paraphrase that will bear out his main arguments in the cycle as a whole, and he does so here: the heaven so much desired by Plotinus is also that desired by Jack the Journeyman and Crazy Jane, where they will consummate their spiritual union:

> There stately Pythagoras
> And all the choir of love.

I see nothing inept in this treatment, which is for me a mark of the nobility of Yeats's thought: 'everything that lives is holy', and the soul of his ragged beggar-woman is as much a 'beautiful lofty thing' as that of Plotinus. Through love, she has the same vision of her source.

In Yeats's poem, the soul of man, under the figure of Plotinus, is seen proceeding to its consummation, the consummation which has been glimpsed in visionary experience by Jack and Crazy Jane. Yeats begins with an image of characteristic levity, but it is levity of the kind Goethe characterises as *holder Leichtsinn*, tragic levity not meant to detract from the essential seriousness of the whole:

> Behold that great Plotinus swim,
> Buffeted by such seas;

This is an unexpected development of an earlier prose passage, where Yeats, talking of the Platonic sea, had characterised man as 'a swimmer, or rather the waves themselves';[62] and it startles, even shocks; but it gives Yeats the dynamic impact his poem needs (and which Mac-Kenna's translation of the original Greek perhaps lacks). Yeats pares down his Greek text for the sake of concision, and proceeds at once to the heart of his theme, balancing his levity against his tragic purpose. The faint insolence of the following 'bland', and the sharp impact of the verse's close, are merged, now, into the growing dignity of the whole:

> Bland Rhadamanthus beckons him,
> But the Golden Race looks dim,
> Salt blood blocks his eyes.

We have to remember that Plotinus is travelling across the sea of life, and has no knowledge of his destination save what he can glimpse from visionary experience; he has, for a moment, a fragmentary perception of his goal, but it vanishes; the contaminating salt of material concerns, the property of his blood as also of the sea, half blinds him to what he has perceived. This is a development of part of the oracle I have not quoted, which describes how, during life, Plotinus' eyes sometimes grew 'dim' to visions, and his mind was 'rapt down unsanctioned paths'.[63] Rhadamanthus is one of the three judges of the dead, and there may be significance in the fact that he, and not Aeacus or Minos, is Plotinus' guide. We are told in Plato's *Gorgias*[64] that Rhadamanthus judges the souls who come from Asia, and Plotinus can be thought of, if we choose, as in a sense Asiatic: he is a product of the Christian dispensation, which in Yeats's system is an Asiatic influx, and determines the essential nature of all the souls born into it.[65] I do not think it is necessary to take this reading; but I would not care to say outright that Yeats did not intend it.

The remainder of the poem needs no further commentary; its function as argument is to people Yeats's heaven. Plato is given as the type of the philosopher; Pythagoras, surrounded by his 'immortal choir', appears in the character of master-musician; and Yeats completes More's argument by making it clear that the singers are 'the choir of love':

> Scattered on the level grass
> Or winding through the grove
> Plato there and Minos pass,
> There stately Pythagoras
> And all the choir of love.

All that I need do is to notice the simplicity and dignity of the presentation, the quiet opening lines rising to a pitch of some excitement with the exclamatory 'there' of the fourth line, where Yeats varies his rhythm, only to restore it in the calm composure of his conclusion, with its air of confident hope. I find 'The Delphic Oracle Upon Plotinus' peculiarly moving, and I think it is technically one of the most perfect of Yeats's lyrics.

'NEWS FOR THE DELPHIC ORACLE'

In 'The Delphic Oracle Upon Plotinus' Yeats refers only generally to Porphyry's symbolic system, but in its sequel[66] he draws upon his source much more freely, and his argument becomes much more intricate. I think it should be remembered that he believed he had precedent in using Porphyry as a source, not only in the Florentine Platonism that may have influenced Botticelli, but in so readily accessible a poem as Shelley's *The Witch of Atlas*; he could not have seen Blake's painting of the Cave of the Nymphs, which was discovered after his death. If we try to reconstruct the Yeatsian interpretation of *The Witch of Atlas*[67] (and to do so will help us to understand 'News For The Delphic Oracle'), we shall arrive at something like the following reading: I do not say it is necessarily the correct reading, or that a coherent philosophical argument can be forced on Shelley's charming fantasy, but it is what

Yeats will have made of his text. The Witch of Atlas, who is 'a sea-nymph and was born from one of the Atlantides', is a personification of beauty.[68]* She is shown dwelling in a cave, by which Shelley symbolises the descent of absolute beauty into the material world. While there she is wooed by the dryads and hamadryads, symbols for the creatures of time and space, but rejects their love with the words 'I know I cannot die'; for absolute beauty is essentially something out-side time, a property of reality. Then she creates her own lover by breathing life into a 'repugnant mass' of 'fire and snow'; that is, the love of beauty instils intellectual life into humanity, previously a mere battle-ground of the opposites, and the lover (who lives in a trance-state) becomes sensible of the visionary world. With her purified, 'sex-less' lover, like Asia in her enchanted boat, she sails everywhere over the sea of life, playing practical jokes on solemnity and redressing wrongs; for those who die after lives of great purity, she unwinds 'the woven imagery' of 'second childhood's swaddling bands': a clear sym-bol for the return to the intellectual condition. Some of this symbolism is so clearly traditional that it must have been part of Shelley's purpose, and what is most relevant is of course the cave, where Yeats finds all the detail of Porphyry's essay, honey, honey-bees, mixing-bowls, looms, 'the raiment of purple stain' and the Witch's own 'spinning and embroidering'. Yeats wrote an essay to explain his interpretation of the cave,[69] which is essentially a study of Porphyry and reconstructs the Platonic symbolism, so that he himself had made Porphyry available to the modern reader, and can hardly be accused of drawing on a private or remote source.

'News For The Delphic Oracle' is as charming and inconsequential a poem as 'The Delphic Oracle Upon Plotinus' is dignified and serious. It is 'news' in the sense that a picture-postcard is news, a message sent to the oracle from the resort of perfection. Yeats gives a complete sketch of the panorama of the Platonic heaven, but he has no serious purpose at all, or rather, the serious purpose is there, but is kept beneath the surface of the verse, and the poem allowed to make its initial impact as landscape. Critics have supposed that it is mocking in tone, but the mockery is not directed against Platonism; we should not read derision into the poem's gay levity, the easy familiarity of 'there all the golden codgers lay', 'man-picker Niamh' and the other slang phrases. The colloquialisms are there *pour épater*, as they admirably do all those critics who suppose that a poet must lose his sense of humour in face of something in which he believes; and, beyond this, they give the

*Yeats's own interpretation.

poem that toughness and resilience which comes from contact with common speech. 'I like "The Shells" ', Yeats wrote of one of Dorothy Wellesley's poems at this time. 'It is charming and profound and full of good words—eyebright, Pangloss, formality, copulate':[70] and his own poem, which contains some of the same words, subordinates profundity to poetry in much the same spirit. It is possible, since there are certain parallel reminiscences in his later work,* that Yeats was trying to emulate a much-loved Anglo-Irish poem, 'The Groves Of Blarney':[71]

> There's statues gracing
> This noble place in—
> All heathen gods
> And nymphs so fair,
> Bold Neptune, Plutarch
> And Nicodemus,
> All standing naked
> In the open air.

Certainly a part of the amusement of 'News For The Delphic Oracle' is that he mixes his mythologies. He also mixes his symbols, drawing on Kabbalism and the tradition of alchemy as well as on Platonism, but all the component parts are triumphantly blended, and we are left with a sense of unity in a poem where the unities are mischievously flouted, which is perhaps a mark of his success.

Yeats collects authorities for his poem from far and wide, and he does this especially in his first verse. Heaven is still the province of the philosopher, lover and musician; Pythagoras is there as the choirmaster and Plotinus, stretching and yawning after his swim, joins him; but the lovers, Niamh and Oisin, come from a different mythology, though *Wheels and Butterflies* had interpreted their journey to fairyland as a voyage to the Isles of the Blessed.[72] Oisin's 'faery bride' is now 'man-picker Niamh', and the precise shade of levity intended is seen from the fact that, on the only other occasion when Yeats uses this odd compound, he refers it to a barmaid.[73] All the inhabitants of Yeats's island paradise are sighing 'for love', and here he is probably bringing Dante into his argument; for, in the circle of limbo to which Dante consigns the Platonists, their only punishment is to sigh, in their frustrated desire for closer contact with God.

---

*'John Kinsella's Lament' parodies the Anglo-Irish 'Lament of Morian Shehone for Miss Mary Bourke' and 'Three Songs To The One Burden' remembers Charles Kickham's 'Patrick Sheehan'.

> Non avea pianto, ma' che di sospiri
> Che l'aura eterna facevan tremare.

'Here was no plaint that could be heard, except of sighs, which caused the eternal air to tremble.'[74]

Yeats, I think, designedly inverts Dante's argument, for the sighs of his Platonists come less from frustration than from content.

This is the broad meaning of the first verse, but the incidental detail is so ingenious that I must explain it here. There is a fascinating complex of symbols in the first four lines:

> There all the golden codgers lay,
> There the silver dew,
> And the great water sighed for love,
> And the wind sighed too.

The 'golden codgers' are of course the golden race of the immortals, but in the gold-silver antithesis which the image is made to introduce, Yeats uses a favourite symbol from alchemy: fused gold and silver, the solar and lunar principles indissolubly knit, is an alchemical emblem of perfection he had often turned to effect in his early poetry, in 'The Man Who Dreamed Of Faeryland'[75] for example. A parallel device is provided in the water-wind antithesis which follows. Yeats's 'great water' is the sea of life, now becalmed as it laps round the Isles of the Blessed; but water and wind are also Kabbalistic symbols for the masculine and feminine principles,[76] which are here presented as being in perfect harmony, their opposition resolved. Yeats's 'silver dew' is a most complicated image. It is, I think, an indirect allusion to the 'nectar' mentioned in the Greek oracle; More's commentary makes much of this detail and suggests that there may be a real philosophical basis for supposing that the soul in heaven, by some 'graceful motions analogical to our Tast', takes in 'delicate refection'.[77] Dew is indeed a symbol for the food of heaven, but it is so in the quite different tradition of the Kabbala, where it is 'the manna that is prepared for the just in the world to come', and the nourishment of 'the holy supernal ones'.[78] At the period when Yeats was most interested in the Kabbala, he had described Fand in heaven as walking through 'flaming dew'.[79]

The end of the verse is almost equally ingenious. After presenting to us his choir, who stand in a ring round 'tall Pythagoras', and sketching in his lovers reclining on the grass, Yeats introduces his philosopher:

Plotinus came and looked about,
The salt-flakes on his breast,
And having stretched and yawned awhile
Lay sighing like the rest.

There is insolence, of course, in this 'came and looked about', but I think the lines are essentially a moving tribute to Plotinus. We know from the earlier poem on the subject that the 'salt-flakes' are the symbol of the contaminating contact of the material world, but here they are no longer blocking the philosopher's eyes and half-blinding him to visionary experience; they are worn proudly on his breast, and now serve as the symbol of the particular defilement which Plotinus endured, and transcended, during life. I think, then, that this is an allusion to Plotinus' leprosy:[80] Yeats, possibly with *The Ancient Mariner* in mind, had been preoccupied with the whiteness of leprosy when he wrote his play *The King's Threshold*.[81] Again, Plotinus yawns and stretches before he accommodates himself to the ecstatic happiness of the blessed, and since stretching and yawning is Yeats's consistent euphemism for the lassitude after the sexual act (as in *The Player Queen* and 'Three Things'),[82] I take it that the beatitude of the soul in heaven is being compared to the peace after love. In this way Yeats gives his subtlest expression to a comparison which had much occupied him in his mature verse.

In the second verse, we are shown the destiny of those souls, less fortunate than Plotinus, who have had to recross the sea of emotion and passion in the expiation of their memories after death. Since the purified spirit, in Platonism, is 'assimilated to the nature of a child, both in soul and body', they are represented as children, but here as in 'Byzantium' what Yeats really has in mind is a concrete image from sculpture, a statue which I have not been able to identify, but which he describes to Sturge Moore:

'Do you know Raphael's statue of the Dolphin carrying one of the Holy Innocents to Heaven?'[83]

This statue Yeats gives as the source of his image, in 'Byzantium', of spirits 'astraddle on the dolphin's mire and blood';[84] and since he generalises from his source there, making 'one of the Holy Innocents' a symbol for any purified spirit, we may assume a similar generalisation in the present poem. As they recross the sea of life during the process of the dreaming back, the spirits 'relive their death' and 'their wounds open again': an image applicable both to the massacre of the innocents and to any soul, after death, expiating its past life. As for the dolphin, it is a very ancient image, which can be traced back before Eleusis, and entered Platonism from an earlier philosophic tradition: it was a symbol in the Pythagorean doctrine of metempsychosis, and Yeats had read of it both in Hermes Trismegistus[85] and, as has often been said, in Eugenie Strong:

'dolphins . . . form a mystic escort of the dead to the Islands of the Blest'.[86]

It was also the love-beast, and this is perhaps remembered in Yeats's symbol. It is apt that the intuitions of love should guide the soul across the sea of life, and when Yeats says that 'the brute dolphins plunge' into the sea, his adjective is probably applied to stress the carnal aspect of love, and his whole image to describe how (according to his system) a man's ruling love may cause him to be fixated at a certain point in the dreaming back, and lead him to refuse to discard memories which are particularly dear or deeply felt. Thus the dolphins turn aside, sometimes, from their course for heaven, and plunge into the sea of remembered emotion.

The Innocents are also distracted by their 'ancestral patterns', the memories which recur of the whole cycle of their past incarnations, from which they are now gaining liberation. The ancestral patterns 'dance' like sunlight (or waves) on the sea, and this brings home to us the vastness of Yeats's ocean, on which a whole cycle of man's incarnations is a mere speck. We must think of the sea as representing the entirety of life, past, present and to come, and so in some ways the image of Anima Mundi, as Henry More gave Yeats precedent in supposing:[87] it is in fact a symbol for the world of time. Circumventing all these obstacles, the purified souls are borne in to a 'cliff-sheltered bay', and the choir of immortal love wade out to welcome them to heaven, where they 'pitch their burdens off'. The whole verse is curiously moving, but there is a suggested colloquialism in the strong word 'pitch'; and this, like the unexplained and apparently inconsequential reference to Raphael, is clearly *pour épater*.

In the last verse, as Henn has shown, Yeats balances his image from sculpture with a set of allusions to Poussin's 'Marriage of Peleus and Thetis'.[88] I see no more reason to suppose that Poussin should have known the occult tradition than that Tintoretto had done so; but Yeats would have thought of him as falling within the period, between the

Renaissance preoccupation with the self and the 'romantic reverie', when the artist had an intuitive perception of the landscape of reality. Peleus was a mortal who married an immortal, and the marriage was celebrated in the presence of all 'the golden race'; the introduction of the nuptials into the poem goes to underline the argument Yeats took over from More: that love may be consummated in heaven. Peleus and Thetis are strongly contrasted and their marriage is in fact a union of 'opposites': love has 'blinded' Peleus with tears, and he is the type of the spiritual lover; but Thetis half-turns from him, distracted by the commotion behind her:

> From where Pan's cavern is
> Intolerable music falls.
> Foul goat-head, brutal arm appear,
> Belly, shoulder, bum,
> Flash fishlike; nymphs and satyrs
> Copulate in the foam.

The cavern is Porphyry's cave, which Yeats very properly situates on the edge of heaven, facing the foam of life: in Porphyry it is on the coast of Ithaca, which symbolises the Isles of the Blessed, and he makes it clear that one of its mouths gives on the fields of heaven:

> The cave should have a twofold entrance; one made for the descent of men, but the other for the ascent of Gods.[89]

Since the cave represents 'generation', it is natural that Pan should be its local deity. As early as the rituals of the Golden Dawn, Yeats had known him as the patron of carnal licence,[90] and, though he does not appear in Porphyry, he is one of the presences in the Witch of Atlas' cave.[91] The nymphs and satyrs who dance orgiastically in the foam also derive from Porphyry: they are the symbols of souls, as yet in heaven, but about to be born into the world, and they dance because, as Porphyry says, 'the lapse into generation is delightful'.[92] By the introduction of this detail Yeats completes his account of the geography of heaven: in the second verse he has shown us the path by which souls arrive at the Isles of the Blessed: now he shows us the road by which they return to the world.

I have left until now the explanation of why Thetis turns away from Peleus to listen to the ecstatic cries of the souls awaiting generation, because it involves arguments of some importance in the canon of

Yeats criticism. Almost every critic who has approached this poem has deprecated the last verse as showing the 'sexual abandon' of Yeats's heaven; and nothing could be further from the truth. One salient reason for the introduction of the Peleus-Thetis detail is to contrast the love of heaven with the mere sexuality Yeats ascribes to the physical world. Peleus is the type of the heavenly lover, and his love, if not asexual, is innocent and pure:

> Slim adolescence that a nymph has stripped,
> Peleus on Thetis stares.
> Her limbs are delicate as an eyelid,
> Love has blinded him with tears.

These beautiful lines are concerned with the ideal love which Yeats believed was only possible after death: the juxtaposition of the 'foul' dance of the nymphs and satyrs points a bitter moral. Thetis serves as the bridge between the two worlds: she is the object of Peleus' devotion, but she is also half in love with generation. This follows from the fact that she is a sea-nymph; Yeats would have thought of her as he did of the Witch of Atlas, 'born of one of the Atlantides' and compelled to descend into the material world. He would have regarded her as half-divine, half an inhabitant of the fallen universe; and this is after all mythologically accurate, for, though herself divine, she bore a mortal son. In Yeats's poem we are told that 'Thetis' belly listens' to Pan's music, and this I imagine is a reference to her divided nature. Her son, Achilles, is already conceived, and though she is by nature an inhabitant of heaven, her maternal instincts bind her to time.

'THE BLACK TOWER'

'The Black Tower'[93] is a poem much like 'News For The Delphic Oracle' in that its symbolism is mixed; much that is Platonic rubs shoulders with much that is not. Where this happens in Yeats, the poem is usually one of a series, and the earlier poems on the theme present the symbolism in more orthodox, 'purer' terms. This is certainly the case with 'The Black Tower', which can only be considered as a unit in a larger pattern.

The poem is based on Heraclitus' theory of life as a conflict between opposites, a theory we have seen applied, on the sexual plane, in *A Full Moon In March*. There, the Queen and Swineherd are the opposites, and are made symbols of the war of the sexes, a tension which cannot be resolved while man is subject to time. Heraclitus saw the whole of life as being made up of such tensions, and Yeats of course followed him in this, though he sometimes prefers the Kantian term 'antinomies' in describing the conflict:

> All those antinomies
> Of day and night.

As a result of his theory, Heraclitus' symbol for life is warfare: 'war is the father of all and king of all', he writes, and the symbol came to be associated with his name:

> The ancients used to hint at a kind of divine war, and Heraclitus spoke as follows: one must know that war is everywhere and the normal order of things is strife and all things occur by the law of strife and necessity.[94]

The symbol was taken over by others; by Empedocles, whose cyclic theory is based on the supposition of unending 'warfare' between two opposite principles;[95] and by Plotinus, whose image for life is a battle. Because of its 'imperfections', he says, life in the physical world is no more than 'a conflict of part against part . . . at war with itself', and if it seems unified at all, this is only 'the unity or harmony of a drama torn with struggle'.[96] In Plotinus' system, nothing in life is exempt from this warfare save the intellective soul, which he symbolises as 'an old watch-tower beaten by storms',[97] and by means of which men are directed always away from life and towards the Good, or absolute beauty. Here at once we have an analogy with Yeats's poem 'Symbols',[98] where the religious life is imaged as 'a storm-beaten old watchtower', while beneath it the 'all-destroying sword-blade' flashes, and the opposites, power and folly, beauty and mere virility, are seen in interaction.

It is not hard to find directer references than this in Yeats, as when he speaks of the 'war of opposites' as 'a slow-moving thing'. Another, very important instance is the long autobiographical preface to *The Resurrection*, in the course of which he relates his cyclic philosophy of history to the theory, as Empedocles also did, and like him again presents the cosmic pattern as a conflict between two opposite principles, which alternately gain predominance: 'in turn they conquer as the cycles roll' as Empedocles puts it.[99] Yeats begins from an argument I have already referred to, quoting Heraclitus to bear him out: that the opposites inherent in the Great Year are the subjective and the objective principle, symbolised in his play by the Greek and the Hebrew:

Whatever its length it [the Great Year] divided, and so did every unit whose multiple it was, into waxing and waning, day and night, or summer and winter. There was everywhere a conflict like that of my play, between two principles, or elemental forms of the mind, each 'dying the other's life, living the other's death'.[100]

Even as a boy, Yeats goes on, he had sensed that the antagonism between these two principles was absolute and interminable, and had reacted away from the Victorian idea of progress by conceiving 'an aversion to that myth'. He had expressed his antipathy in his poem 'The Wanderings Of Oisin' where among other things the hero had come to 'an island of endless battle for an object never achieved'.[101] Now, in mature life, he was returning to the subject in his play, which had for theme the conflict between pagan, subjective man and objective Christianity; and, in *The Resurrection*, he had taken no steps to conceal where his own sympathies lay. He took his stand with the Greek, the type of subjective man, even if everything the Greek stood for had been, at the beginning of the present cycle, subverted by Christianity:

Why must I think the victorious cause the better? Why should Mommsen think the less of Cicero because Caesar beat him? I am satisfied, the Platonic Year in my head, to find but drama. I prefer that the defeated cause should be more vividly described than that which has the advertisement of victory. No battle has been finally won or lost.[102]

For the wheel would eventually come full circle, and subjective man regain his past dominance: the pattern of history was cyclic, and the present objective phase was drawing to an end.

This argument is resumed in the minor poem 'What Was Lost?'[103] where Yeats continues his metaphor of the endless battle; not a perfect, stylised battle as in *The Herne's Egg*, but an interminable conflict where there is winning and losing without the possibility of final victory:

I sing what was lost and dread what was won,
I walk in a battle fought over again,
My king a lost king, and lost soldiers my men.

In these lines, Yeats identifies himself with the subjective cause, with its belief in the essential purity of the human soul, and its proud self-sufficiency and 'joy': this is what he sings, and he dreads the present predominance of the objective, Christian principle, modern man's insistence on the impurity of the personality, and his tendencies towards self-immolation and the merely passive virtues. Yeats's 'king' is the principle of pure subjectivity, and here he is perhaps thinking of Plato's *Statesman*. Each of Plato's cycles has its 'king', who is in the last resort either Jupiter or Saturn.[104] Expressions such as 'Saturno rege' are conventional in classical literature, and persist into Latin lyric poetry.[105]

The final couplet of the poem drives home Yeats's antipathy to the Victorian myth of progress, and counters it with Heraclitus' theory that the tension between the opposites cannot be resolved:

> Feet to the Rising and Setting may run,
> They always beat on the same small stone.

Here the symbols of the rising and setting sun stand for subjectivity and objectivity respectively, brightness and darkness, as always in Yeats's system. At any given moment in history, men will take up their positions according to the principle with which they are in affinity; but progress in history is merely apparent. They will never arrive at their goal, which is either a condition of pure subjectivity, or of pure objectivity, according to their temperamental alignment; for the antinomies cannot be resolved while man is subject to time.

In the last years of his life, the pattern of events in the world around him moved Yeats to return to this theme, and he does so in 'The Black Tower', where the soldiers represent subjective humanity, fighting for survival in a world where the principle of subjectivity is in eclipse. Several passages in the letters bring us close to the poem's argument; I will quote a diatribe against the communists, the propagandists of pity as Yeats contemptuously calls them,[106] for he saw communism as a last manifestation of objectivity: the worshippers godless now, as the gyres ran down, but still as incapable of joy or of self-sufficient contemplation as objective man had always been. In this letter, he is answering Dorothy Wellesley, who had said that his attitude to humanity was deficient in 'love':

> A Dutch mystic has said, 'I must rejoyce, I must rejoyce without ceasing though the whole world shudder at my joy'. Joy is the salvation of the soul. You say we must love, yes but love is not pity. It does not desire to change its object. It is a form of the eternal contemplation of what is. When I take a woman in my arms I do not

want to change her. If I saw her in rags I would get her better clothes that I might resume my contemplation. But these communists put their heads in the rags and smother.[107]

'The Black Tower' has been called 'a poem about propaganda',[108] largely on the strength of the second verse, where the enemies of Yeats's subjective soldiers come with 'banners' to 'bribe or threaten', hoping to wean the defenders away from their allegiance to their king. I feel sure that what Yeats has in mind here is the insidious spiritual propaganda of communism, with its insistence on the weakness of the individual personality and its passion for reform and change.

In 'The Black Tower', Yeats's soldiers are in a state of famine, perhaps of siege, 'their money spent, their wine gone sour': they 'feed as the goatherd feeds', which is possibly a reference back to the subjective philosophy of 'Shepherd And Goatherd'. Under this symbolism Yeats presents the sufferings which the adherents of the *philosophia perennis* undergo in the godless modern world, but his soldiers do not think of capitulation: 'those banners come not in'. They remain faithful to their 'old black tower', which is of course Plotinus' 'old watchtower beaten by storms', the intellective soul, by which man perceives the infinite. Other related sources suggest themselves here: for minor details of imagery, perhaps Browning's *Childe Roland*, and more certainly, the ruined tower of Shelley's *Laon And Cythna* where the old hermit pursues his subjective philosophy in oblivion of the world.[109] But the imagery and feeling of the poem are so clearly medieval that I think we must look for a primary source in that tradition; and this is not hard to find. Much of the symbolism of Neoplatonism was kept alive by the alchemists, and later by their heirs the Rosicrucians, and since the persecution of subjective religion began in this period, we find the image of the ruined tower being taken up, one cannot say from what source. I quote a bitter passage from *Secret Symbols Of The Rosicrucians*:

Our, the true believers', dwelling place is a dark, grey and sinister castle, bewitched, surrounded by a very thick cloud, so that no one may come near it.[110]

As a member of a Rosicrucian order it is impossible for Yeats not to have known this imagery, and I imagine that he has it in mind in his preface to *Axel*, where he commends as traditional the symbol of the lonely castle in that Rosicrucian play.[111] 'The Black Tower' is a visionary poem, whose symbolism came to Yeats in meditation,[112] and it seems likely that the castle-image came first, and that the sub-sidiary medieval detail then attached itself to it.

Behind this Rosicrucian element in the poem, there are other examples of what I have called mixed symbolism. Though the atmos-phere of the whole is thoroughly medieval, the refrain brings before us the ancient pagan dead:

> There in the tomb stand the dead upright,
> But winds come up from the shore:
> They shake when the winds roar,
> Old bones upon the mountain shake.

Here Yeats is, I think, glancing at the ancient Gaelic custom of burying the dead standing and armed as if for battle,[113] and the purpose of the refrain is to suggest that his subjective soldiers are sustained in adversity by their sense of kinship with the heroic dead. The objective cycle has not yet ended, for 'the dark grows blacker' as it progresses towards its last phase, but 'faint moonlight' drops into the tomb, in token that the degeneration of humanity will not continue for ever, and that a new subjective cycle, for which Yeats's symbol is always the moon, is about to begin. With this restoration, as Yeats tells us elsewhere, he felt that men would return to the beliefs of their ancestors, 'overthrow the things that are today and bring the things that were yesterday',[114] and he felt that Ireland would return to the worship of its ancient gods, so that the pagan dead might expect to be justified in a new dispensation and would be in sympathy with it. Thus in this poem 'the winds roar', and as they do so the 'old bones upon the mountain shake' as if they were about to be reanimated into new life. This wind intimates that the end of a cycle is near at hand, for this is Yeats's symbol for the destructive bouleversement that takes place at a reversal of the gyres; it is the apocalyptic 'great wind of love and hate' which destroys the established world order in 'The Secret Rose',[115] and the 'sudden blast of dusty wind' which (together with Yeats's equally apocalyptic horse-men) presages the final overthrow of civilisation in 'Nineteen Hundred And Nineteen'.[116] The idea of the destruction of the world by wind is biblical, of course, and can be met with in Daniel and Ezekiel as well as in Revelation;[117] but Yeats remembers equally the Irish symbol of wind as the great destroyer; the imagery in 'Nineteen Hundred And Nine-teen', for example, is very Irish, for the medieval Irish peasantry called 'whirling wind' 'the dance of the daughters of Herodias';[118] and Yeats so uses this picturesque detail as to make it an unequivocal symbol for 'the moment before revelation'. So in 'The Black Tower' also the super-natural wind blows, perhaps from the 'shore' of the Platonic sea of life, and the dead seem to prepare themselves for life in a new heroic age, while the tower's beleaguered defenders are left equally confident that their siege is soon to be lifted, and that a new cycle will soon restore subjective man to his ancient pre-eminence and dignity. On this note of promise the poem ends.

We are left with the difficult symbol of the cook, where Yeats's visual image may well be eclectic:

> The tower's old cook that must climb and clamber
> Catching small birds in the dew of the morn
> While we hale men lie stretched in slumber
> Swears that he hears the king's great horn.
> But he's a lying hound:
> Stand we on guard oath-bound!

Here the absent 'king' whose return is awaited so eagerly is self-evidently a Platonic symbol representing the principle of pure sub-jectivity soon to be reborn by a new annunciation into the world; he is not dead, as the tower's godless enemies have suggested, for true religion can never be superannuated. When he returns, he will be preceded by the winding of a horn, and we remember that Yeats has an early reference to God 'winding his lonely horn';[119] the symbol here also embraces the annunciatory trumpets of Revelation, to which Yeats had found a parallel in the classical tradition.* The image of the cook, on the other hand, must be medieval, though I do not know Yeats's source; but even without it the meaning seems quite clear. We have only to read Malory's story of Beaumains and Kay to know that the cook was the most servile functionary in a castle,[120] and Yeats makes it a symbol of all that is grossest in man, both here and in his early lyric 'The Hawk'.[121] In that anecdotal poem Yeats explains his inability to find arguments to confute a 'knave' by saying that the 'yellow-eyed hawk of the mind' is only happy in the 'air' of pure intellect, and will not descend with titbits of prey for the 'scullion' and 'old cook' who wait for it beneath; the cook here obviously represents the merely natural man, with whose needs the pure intellect is not concerned. So in 'The Black Tower' the cook no doubt stands for the merely natural man, and goes out at sunrise (the hour at which, from

---

*Cicero, he says, thought that a new era would be preceded by the sounding of visionary trumpets in middle air, and based his belief on Etruscan myth.

the association with pure subjectivity I have explained, the king's return may be expected) to scout for titbits of information; the soldiers themselves, who have learned to discipline their hopes, are not convinced by his report. Though the natural man might hope for immediate liberation from the 'terror' at the end of a cycle, subjective philosophy taught that the end had not yet arrived; first must come the great wind of universal chaos, 'destroyer and preserver', and only then could civilisation be renewed.

CHAPTER SEVEN

'BYZANTIUM'

WITH THE FINDINGS of my previous appendix before us, we are in an excellent position for the exegesis of 'Byzantium',[1] and since there are numerous scattered references to the poem in the preceding pages, it may make for completeness if I take it up here. I would not say that 'Byzantium' could be called a Platonic poem, for it contains allusions to the Noh plays and even the rituals of the Golden Dawn as well as to the tradition, but it is certainly best understood if we approach it with a knowledge of the Platonic symbolism. If past analyses have fallen down (and I think they have) I believe that this is largely because they have lacked such knowledge.

Yeats gives two reasons for having written his poem at all. One, which we shall discover to be of very great consequence, is contained in the dedicatory letter to *The Winding Stair*, in which he says that he wrote the poem after an illness to 'warm myself back into life'.[2] He told Sturge Moore, on the other hand, that the poem was written to elucidate the symbolism of its companion-piece, 'Sailing To Byzantium';[3] he felt that the 'idea' of that poem 'needed exposition'.[4] This I think is an unhelpful and in some ways a misleading remark, for while it is true that 'Byzantium' takes up the symbolism of the earlier poem and expands it in very great detail, the two are very different in one significant respect. In the earlier poem, Byzantium itself is a symbol for the world of intellect and the spirit, as opposed to the world of the senses; but in the present text it represents the intellectual world in a very special sense, for (as I shall show) Yeats makes it a symbol of the life after death. As the point of fusion of two cultures, a theocratic community where the orient and the occident merged into one, Byzantium was a very apt symbol for the Platonic heaven, pure intellect, where the opposites are reconciled; and it is important to recognise that it does now represent 'the artifice of eternity' upon which man enters when 'out of nature'. In making it so, Yeats merely reverted to his original intention, as this is reflected by the form 'Sailing To Byzantium' took in the first drafts:

231

Here all is young; the chapel walls display
A sleeping infant on his mother's knee.
Weary with toil Teigue sleeps till break of day. . . .[5]

Byzantium, then, is Elysium, the 'country of the young'; the land to
which Teigue, the visionary fool of *The Hourglass*, goes nightly in his
dreams. The city's symbol is the 'sleeping infant', a detail in which
Yeats remembers the *puer aeternus*, but which serves also, as in 'Shepherd And Goatherd', as his consistent image for the perfected human
soul.[6]

The action of 'Byzantium' thus takes place in the heavenly world;
but the crux of the poem, so far as exegesis is concerned, occurs in the
introductory first verse:

> The unpurged images of day recede;
> The Emperor's drunken soldiery are abed;
> Night resonance recedes, night-walkers' song
> After great cathedral gong.

It is crucial, I think, that we take these lines as fully symbolic; a
curfew sounds, after which the 'images' of day and the 'resonance' of
night alike recede, and nothing remains in view but the 'dome' of the
great cathedral of St. Sophia, looming up above deserted streets; and
since Yeats did not write long stretches of mere imagery, all this has
to be assigned some meaning beyond the merely literal. We may perhaps begin with the cathedral of St. Sophia itself, which Yeats has
referred to in his prose as an image for the 'Holy Wisdom',[7] so that it
is reasonable to give it this meaning here. If this is so, then the 'cathedral gong', which sounds its menacing curfew, must represent some
form of emanation from the Holy Wisdom, a signal from the divinity,
and it must be a warning sign, since its effect is to clear the streets. It
will help exegesis to know that Yeats uses the word 'gong' here as
synonymous with 'bell', since (as he explained to Sturge Moore)[8] gongs
were used instead of bells in the Byzantine church. The sound of a bell
is Yeats's consistent symbol for the divine; the stroke of midnight
means for him the moment of death:

> At stroke of midnight God shall win . . .[9]
> At stroke of midnight soul cannot endure
> A bodily or mental furniture . . .[10]

In *The King Of The Great Clock Tower*, the mere 'beating of a bell', not necessarily striking midnight, signifies an intimation from the spiritual world, as I have shown.[11] I think, therefore, that we should understand Yeats's warning gong here to mean a warning signal from the other world, an intimation of the nearness of death. It is significant that he wrote the poem 'to warm myself back into life' after a serious illness, for I imagine his poem to refer to just such a momentary lapse of consciousness and presentiment of death as might occur during a crisis of disease.

When the gong is sounded, the effect is to clear the streets of all 'images' both of 'day' and night; and to take the meaning here it is necessary to know the function of the day-night antithesis in Yeats's symbolism. I think we could fairly say that 'day' represents the conscious mind, and 'night' the subconscious; we have to remember that, for Yeats, the subconscious mind was in contact with Anima Mundi, and so with realities beyond the grave, so that its 'fathomless wisdom'[12] would be thought of as far purer than the mere 'unpurged' imagery of the conscious waking psyche. 'Night' may even mean for Yeats the life after death itself, a usage he perhaps derived from *Oedipus At Colonus*:

And I call upon the ancestral night, I, the blind man, to gather you into itself.[13]

Here Oedipus is praying that Polyneices may die, and be gathered up into the dark world beyond the grave. Yeats uses the phrase in the same sense in 'A Dialogue Of Self And Soul'.

Think of ancestral night that can . . .
Deliver from the crime of death and birth.[14]

The life after death, if the human spirit is properly aligned to it, can deliver from the wheel of reincarnation. If 'night' means the life after death in 'Byzantium', then 'night resonance' is a peculiarly appropriate phrase for the imagery of the subconscious mind, in contact with Anima Mundi or the collective unconscious. 'Day' on the other hand means always the waking world; as also in 'A Dialogue Of Self And Soul', where Yeats associates it with the concepts of 'love and war'. With this in mind, I think we can now paraphrase 'Byzantium's' first four lines: 'on an intimation of death, both the conscious and subconscious mind are evacuated of all imagery.' I will add two glosses from Platonism:

the moment of the soul's descent into Hades was symbolised, in the Orphic mysteries, by the beating of a gong;[15] and war, as I have already shown, was the symbol for the waking world, which may explain Yeats's 'drunken soldiery'.

The meaning of these lines is thus precise, though the 'night-walkers' song' (and perhaps the 'soldiery' too) are largely decoration to prevent the argument from seeming excessively abstract; and Yeats's drift is identical with that of 'Ribh Considers Christian Love Insufficient':[16]

> At stroke of midnight soul cannot endure
> A bodily or mental furniture.

Yeats had precedent in several cultures for supposing that the mind must be emptied of all imagery on the approach of death. I have already quoted one relevant commentary of his own:

> The Indian ascetic passing into his deathlike trance knows that if his mind is not pure, if there is anything there but the symbol of his God, some passion, ambition, desire or phantasy will confer on him its shape or purpose, for he is entering upon a state where thought and existence are the same.[17]

Yeats also had authority for his belief in Western culture, in the precepts of St. John of the Cross:

> The understanding [of the mystic] must be pure and empty of all sensible objects, all clear intellectual perceptions, resting on faith.[18]

This maxim Yeats read in Von Hügel's book on St. Catherine of Genoa, where it is prominently quoted.

'Byzantium' goes on to make clear that Yeats's mind, as he enters upon his 'deathlike trance', is vacant of all imagery save the symbol of his God; after the curfew nothing remains to be seen but the soaring dome of 'The Holy Wisdom', which 'disdains' 'all that man is' and in its massive simplicity rebukes:

> All mere complexities,
> The fury and the mire of human veins.

With this detail Yeats introduces his first undeniably Platonic image, for 'mire or mud', as Plotinus says, is a very ancient symbol for the corruptibility of matter.[19] The meaning here is quite clear: the fact of the nearness of death awakens in the poet's mind a very lively idea of the majesty and omnipotence of God, beside which all material concerns are seen for what they are; worthless, beneath contempt.

Yeats's 'deathlike trance' now takes him beyond the confines of the physical world, into the other world beyond the grave, and to travel in this new world he needs a Virgil, a guide:

> Before me floats an image, man or shade,
> Shade more than man, more image than a shade.

I think it is very likely that, during his illness, Yeats really did imagine himself as travelling in the spiritual world, for he had a great deal of previous experience of this nature. The adepts of the Golden Dawn used meditation to enable them to 'travel in the Spirit Medium', and much stress was laid on the need to obtain a disembodied spirit as a guide:

> Under no circumstances should the Seer wander alone; he should always wait until one of these elemental beings or 'guides' appears, and he should continue vibrating the names until one does appear, or until he obtains the sense that one is present.[20]

Whatever we may make of all this, it is no doubt Yeats's meaning; and it remains to establish what he intends by his differentiation between 'image' and 'shade'. This (Platonic) distinction has its root in Egyptian theurgy, to a knowledge of which Yeats lays claim in *A Vision*,[21] and which makes its presence felt in his poem with the word 'mummy-cloth'. He may have derived his knowledge from Madame Blavatsky or from her friend Isaac Myer; I will quote from Myer, whose views (I am told) are in the light of present knowledge scholarly and sound. The distinction is at root between two kinds of apparition, known to all classical cultures, and which the Egyptians called man's *Khaibit* and his *Ka*:

> The Ka ... was a spiritual double, a second perfect exemplar or copy of the flesh, blood, body, etc., but of a matter less dense than corporeal matter, having however all its shape and features, being child, man or woman as the living had been. It had power to enter or leave the tomb when it pleased. The Ka corresponded somewhat to the Latin *genius*. Its original meaning may have been *image*; it was like the Greek *Eidolon*.

The shadow or shade was called Khaibit. The Greeks had a *skia* and the Romans an *umbra*. This shade preserved the individuality of the deceased, and was an important part of the personality having an independent existence. There was a valley in the netherworld in which the shades were.[22]

Briefly, the distinction is that the image is a lifeless automaton, projected by the spirit in its own likeness into the physical world, while the shade is a substantial personality, the purgatorial ghost. Yeats's own philosophy of the ghost accepted this distinction, notably in *Wheels And Butterflies*, where it is discussed at length.[23]

The very difficult and strange second verse of Yeats's poem continues to define the exact nature of Yeats's spirit-guide, which is said to be an odd compound: 'Hades' bobbin wrapped in mummy-cloth.' The phrase 'Hades' bobbin' takes us back to the spool on which, in Plato's *Republic*, the destiny of man is wound; but I doubt if we should look to Yeats's words for any very precise symbolism: the line seems to me to be imagery; and Yeats's purpose is no doubt to suggest, by a horrifying image, the essential *lifelessness* of his automaton, a mere thing. It also helps him to establish the undercurrent of an Ariadne motif in the lines, since the bobbin can 'unwind the winding path'; here we remember Shelley's image for the return to the intellectual condition, to enter which, living backwards through time, is to 'unwind the woven imagery/Of second childhood's swaddling bands'.[24] The Ariadne motif gives us also a link with Blake (though Yeats inverts him):

> I give you the end of a golden string:
> Only wind it into a ball—
> It will lead you in at Heaven's gate,
> Built in Jerusalem's wall.[25]

The phrase, then, is suggestive rather than meaningful, and so also no doubt is Yeats's 'mummy-cloth': as in 'All Souls' Night',[26] this detail seems largely decoration, intended to make Yeats's mentor seem ancient, repellent, remote from life. Here, however, there is an esoteric meaning also, if we care to take it. In Yeats's philosophy of the ghost, the purified spirit wears always a celestial body, clothing or 'cloak' for its protection,[27] a belief almost orthodox, and remembered in the Christian belief in the 'raiment' of angels, but nevertheless essentially a Platonic concept and thence traceable back to Egyptian theurgy. In ancient Egypt, the 'intellectual part of man's spirit' was symbolised by the mummy, and its cloak or celestial body by the mummy-cloth, which in Myer's phrase had 'mystical meanings' and was 'considered to protect the spirits of the dead and assist them in their journey to the abode of the eternal blessed'.[28] This, then, is a possible extension of the meaning: whether we choose to think of Yeats's lifeless guide as swathed in mummy-cloth merely or as dressed in the celestial clothing properly pertaining to an angel, depends, I imagine, on which concept we find more repellent. Yeats's purpose is certainly to disquieten the reader.

The key word 'Hades' now enables Yeats to shift his imagery into a different sphere of symbolism, and to refer us to the Homeric Book of the Dead:

> A mouth that has no moisture and no breath
> Breathless months may summon.

This, as I have elsewhere explained, I take as an indirect allusion to Tiresias, Homer's summoner of the shades.[29] Like him, Yeats's guide may be able to introduce the traveller to the inhabitants of the Spirit world; to the unpurified dead, that is, for Hades is the symbol of the purgatorial condition, the region of air. Yeats does not develop this side of his theme, however; he leaves it as mere suggestion, or 'atmosphere', and the verse concludes with a reference to Heraclitus' epigram: 'Men and gods die each others' life, live each others' death':[30]

> I hail the superhuman;
> I call it death-in-life and life-in-death.

In these lines Yeats salutes his guide, recognising it as completely dissimilar to himself, for the shade and the living human being are by their nature opposites.

Yeats's spirit mentor now takes him on a kind of conducted tour of the world beyond the grave, symbolised by the city of Byzantium; and he is first shown the state of those souls who have passed through the purgatorial process and attained to paradise: though Yeats represents this diagrammatically rather than in realistic terms. All that we actually see is a single tree, the emperor's tree of his previous poem, with a single artificial bird singing in its upper branches:

> Miracle, bird or golden handiwork,
> More miracle than bird or handiwork,
> Planted on the star-lit golden bough,
> Can like the cocks of Hades crow,

Or, by the moon embittered, scorn aloud
In glory of changeless metal
Common bird or petal
And all complex ties of mire and blood.

This tree can be shown to represent the tree of life, and the bird singing in its topmost branches symbolises the purified soul, which has risen to the summit of existence or (if I may revert to Yeats's own earlier metaphor) completed the ascent of the winding purgatorial stair. Yeats gives a similar, if very much more ornate, version of the symbol in his early prose, where he speaks of 'the Tree of Life with ever-sighing souls moving in its branches instead of sap, and among its leaves all the fowl of the air, and on its highest bough one white fowl bearing a crown'.[31] Here the 'fowl of the air' are purified souls, or angels, and the 'fowl bearing a crown' is God; Yeats's source for birds and tree alike (as he himself indicates)[32] is a text in the Kabbala. As he does, the Kabbalistic writers symbolise the whole of life by the diagram of a single tree, at whose apex the purified soul is placed, and beneath which the bestial shapes of the rebel angels stalk through the forest of generation:

> In the branches of the Tree the birds lodge and build their nests; that is, the souls or angels have their place: and beneath it those animals which have power seek the shade; [that is, the fallen angels promote the ends of evil]; for in it [the shade of the tree] every beast of the forest doth walk.[33]

'Planted' on the topmost bough of the tree, Yeats's bird 'can like the cocks of Hades crow', and this detail enables me to confirm my interpretation of his tree image, though it is in itself almost a private symbol. It is a reminiscence of a detail in the ritual of the Golden Dawn, in which the 'bird of Hermes' (that is, the cock of Hades; the symbol of Hermes *psychopompus*, the shepherd of the dead) was represented as perched at the very summit of the Kabbalistic tree of life.[34] The cock of Hermes, as I have said, was a rebirth symbol, and so the Golden Dawn emblem indicates that the soul, even when it has reached the summit of existence, even during its temporary sojourn in heaven, accepts the necessity of rebirth in the world.* So also in 'Byzantium', the soul, even when it arrives at the 'starlit golden bough' of its ultimate destiny,

---

*The archetype behind the Golden Dawn's emblem was no doubt the phoenix of Osiris. The phoenix, to the Egyptians a symbol of rebirth, was often depicted perching in the branches of a tree (*v.* Erich Neumann, *The Origins and History of Consciousness*, London, 1954, p. 237).

can, and sometimes does, accept the necessity of reincarnation. Alternatively, it may 'scorn' material existence altogether, and deride 'all complexities of mire and blood': avail itself of its opportunity for final escape from the physical world. It will do this, Yeats tells us, if it is 'embittered' by the moon: and here I think we have to give the moon, which Yeats himself calls the most changeable of his symbols, its Platonic and Dantesque meaning as the governor of generation;[35] though I imagine Yeats also wishes us to remember it as his symbol for the feminine principle in nature. We can thus paraphrase the whole verse as follows: 'the soul (symbolised as a mechanical golden bird; golden since this is the alchemical emblem for the perfect; metal so as to be as far as possible removed from mere physical life; hammered into shape on the anvils of the purgatorial process) can, when it has reached the summit of perfection, accept at will the lot of another incarnation; or, if it is embittered by women or life generally, renounce for ever the material world.'

I should perhaps add a note on the moon-star antithesis in this verse. The moon is Yeats's symbol for woman's beauty or for the principle of generation, as in 'A Man Young And Old'[36] and 'The Crazed Moon'[37] respectively; and the star is his emblem for divinity. We see this well from the winding stair imagery in 'A Dialogue Of Self And Soul':

> Set all your mind upon the steep ascent,
> Upon the broken, crumbling battlement,
> Upon the breathless, starlit air,
> Upon the star that marks the hidden pole.[38]

Here, where the general meaning is similar to that of the present verse in 'Byzantium', the word 'starlit' means, roughly, 'blessed', for it denominates the pure air into which man emerges after climbing the purgatorial stair; and the 'star that marks the hidden pole' represents that portion of divinity which is disclosed to the visionary after his ascent; the essence of divinity is 'hidden' from human eyes. Yeats's 'starlit golden bough' must be similarly understood; and when the first verse of 'Byzantium' describes the Holy Wisdom as 'a starlit or a moon-lit dome', this may be another parallel, and mean that man may glimpse God either purely or imperfectly, through the mists of generation. I think, however, that this phrase is decoration rather than symbol.

It may add something to Yeats's scholarship if I go on to gloss the verse's last few lines, where the bird sings its extraordinarily bitter song in rebuke of 'common bird or petal', no doubt from its vantage-point

among what Yeats followed Dante in calling the petals of the Supernal
Rose.[39] It has learned to see the material world as it does, of course,
on the anvils of its purgation, which are, one feels, akin to the furnaces
of Blake's Los: he is the creative and visionary spirit in humanity,
stripping from man's eyes the cloths of generation which blind him
to the spiritual world:

> . . . the integuments of his Eye
> And Ear unbinding in dire pain, with many blows.[40]

The bird is thus in the very Platonic position of being able to see, and
mock, the grossness of material existence, and one feels intuitively that
one knows what authority Yeats has in mind; in so eclectic a passage,
the words of the bird's song are not beyond all conjecture. I have said
that Yeats's symbol of 'mire and blood' is a borrowing from Plotinus,
and the whole passage may very possibly echo those lines in 'The
Impassivity of the Unembodied' (which Yeats called the most beautiful
of the Enneads,[41] and which is so important in his own theory of the
soul) where Plotinus turns from the contemplation of the spiritual
world to rebuke the 'mire' of physical life, inveigh against the intractability of matter:

> The Intellective Soul is impassible, all but utterly untouched by
> matter, for it is in the nature of things separated from the body; its
> act is the act of Intellection or Intuition or True Knowing of real
> existences; it has its being in eternal contemplation of the Divine.
> Matter is without body; body is of earlier date [less distant from
> the divine] and merely includes Matter. Neither is Matter a spirit of
> a mind, it is not life, it is not reason, form or idea; it is not a limit;
> it might more nearly be described as a boundlessness; it is not a
> power or potentiality; it produces nothing and cannot come under
> the name of an existent; it is rather, not being; and it is not even
> this in the sense in which motion and rest can be called not being . . .
> it is merely a phantasm or shadow of space, an aspiration towards
> existence.[42]

If I had to name the text in Yeats's reading which most nearly corresponds to the climate of feeling of his poem, I should choose this of
Plotinus.

Having shown him the condition of the purified soul, Yeats's mentor
now takes him to see the workings of the purgatorial process:

> At midnight on the emperor's pavement flit
> Flames that no faggot feeds, nor steel has lit,
> Nor storm disturbs, flames begotten of flame.

These are obviously the purgatorial flames, well enough known from orthodox Christian symbolism; from Dante for example (and we should not forget the importance in Yeats's thought of Blake's illustrations), for Dante makes Arnaut Daniel expiate his past life by just such a means:

> Poi s'ascose nel foco che gli affina
> 'Then he stepped back into the fire which refines them.'[43]

Into these flames, at midnight (the hour of death) all 'blood-begotten spirits' pass, and they learn in the process to abandon 'all complexities of fury'; all those bitter and complex knots of remembered passion which have, in Yeats's system, to be unravelled during the Dreaming Back. These are the flames 'where you must move in measure, like a dancer',[44] and in Yeats the dance is one of sheer torment, though this is equivocally expressed: he calls it 'an agony of flame that cannot singe a sleeve'. His central source here was probably, as Henn points out, the Noh play *Motomezuka*,[45] whose plot he himself recounts. A young girl's sins during life are punished by torment through flame in the Buddhist purgatory, and the play ends with 'the dance of her agony', a scene which made a great impression on Yeats's mind:

> She had but to lay her hand upon a pillar to make it burst into flame; she was perpetually burning. The priest tells her that if she can but cease to believe in her punishments they will cease to exist. She listens in gratitude, but she cannot cease to believe, and while she is speaking they [her guilty scruples] come upon her and she rushes away enfolded in flames.[46]

This passage will explain why Yeats's flames 'cannot singe a sleeve'; they exist merely in the minds of the sufferers; if they can only overcome their remorse, jettison their past memories, their agony will cease to exist.

I will add a short note on the phrase 'flames begotten of flame', which is a Platonic reminiscence. Platonism distinguished, and medieval Platonic writers especially were concerned with, two forms of 'uncreated flame', called the higher and the lower fire and described by

Yeats as 'the bright and beautiful fire of inspiration and the holy spirit' and 'the dark fire of the fierce impersonal energy, or wrath, of God'.[47] The higher fire is thus the symbol of beatitude: it is 'God's holy fire' in which the sages of 'Sailing To Byzantium' stand. The lower fire, however, is the symbol of purgation, and as Agrippa is quoted by Yeats to say, 'the evil dead dream sometimes of being consumed by [this] flame'.[48] This, then, is why Yeats's flames, unlike those of an earthly martyrdom, need no faggot to feed them or steel to light them: they feed on their own dark energy, though they do so at the discretion of the emperor, whom I take therefore to be Yeats's symbol for God.[49]

When he has seen the sights both of heaven and purgatory, Yeats's spirit guide brings him where he can look down on a grand panorama of the city of the dead; he is shown the souls of men arriving there, and the great Platonic Sea of life, beating against the city walls:

> Astraddle on the dolphin's mire and blood,
> Spirit after spirit! The smithies break the flood,
> The golden smithies of the emperor!
> Marbles of the dancing floor
> Break bitter furies of complexity,
> Those images that yet
> Fresh images beget,
> That dolphin-torn, that gong-tormented sea.

Almost all this detail is Platonic, and most of it will be understood from my essay on 'News for the Delphic Oracle'; here are the dolphins, reminiscent of 'Raphael's dolphin carrying one of the holy innocents to heaven', and symbolic of the impulse which leads humanity to seek out its own perfection, symbolic also (its carnal aspect not forgotten) of the purifying power of love: here is the great sea, of time and space, of passion and remembered passion, opposed by the holy ('golden') smithies of the emperor, where the soul, in the later stages of its purification, is hammered into unity. All the 'complexity' of life is retrieved within these walls; to the Platonist, the complexity of life is its prime evil, all multiplicity being a fall from the One or Good.[50]

The punctuation of the final lines presents a problem; but I think it is readily soluble: Yeats has perhaps omitted more words than he was justified in doing, but I imagine his drift is as follows: 'The smithies break the flood [and, just as they do] marbles of the dancing floor break [in their own way] bitter furies of complexity. [The latter break] those images that yet fresh images beget [and the former break] that dolphin-torn, that gong-tormented sea'. The purgatorial marbles, that is, break or impose stillness upon the patterns made by the dancers' feet, which I take to symbolise the endless sequence of images which recur to the dreamer's mind during the process of the 'dreaming back'; and the smithies buttress the city against the prurient torrent of life itself. The 'images' which beget their kind can thus be read to refer to the hallucinations of Yeats's purgatory, which he compares to 'the imaginings of the dream condition', but there is here the possibility of an alternative interpretation; it may be syntactically permissible to take them as descriptive of the dancers themselves. We must not forget that the dreamer is himself all image now, in the sense of the Platonic *imago*, *eidolon* or ghost.

We are left with the poem's final line, where Yeats reverts to the description of his Platonic Sea. A first point here is the significance of the poem's ending as it does. Yeats's has been a disintegrating vision, as befits a man's glimpse of 'reality' through the mists of sickness: he has seen for a moment the purity of heaven, after which he has been led back, through purgatory, to the manifested world. It is therefore apt that his eyes should close upon the vision of the sea of life, for this is the condition to which, with consciousness, he will be restored. As for the meaning of the last line, with its wealth of symbolic detail, the preceding exegesis should make the interpretation clear. The sea is 'torn' by dolphins and reverberates with the echoes of St. Sophia's gong: the surface of man's life is split asunder by the passion of love and the desire for perfection, and it is endlessly tormented by the idea of death.

CHAPTER EIGHT

'CUCHULAIN COMFORTED'

No study of *The Death of Cuchulain* can seem complete which does not face up to Yeats's continuation of his theme in that strange companion-piece 'Cuchulain Comforted'.[1] Yeats first mentions the poem in a letter to Edith Shackleton Heald:

> I think my play is strange and the most moving I have written for some years. I am making a prose sketch for a poem—a kind of sequel —strange too, something new.[2]

The prose draft he mentions is preserved in Dorothy Wellesley's book on her friendship with him,[3] so that ample materials for exegesis exist.

'Cuchulain Comforted' depends for its full understanding on Yeats's theory of the daemon, which is perhaps his most significant departure from orthodox Platonic theory, and as such is best set out in some detail before we approach the text. Yeats's interest in the theory of the daemon (or guardian angel; though there are perverse daemons as well as good) originated, beyond theosophy, from Blake, who thought that all human achievement emanated from man's 'genius' 'which by the ancients was called an Angel and Spirit and Demon'.[4] Yeats's cardinal authority was Plutarch, who taught him that 'good spirits change always for the best', and are transformed in course of time into angels or daemons, 'and from Daemons, by degrees and in a long course of time, a few souls being refined and purified come to partake of the nature of the Divinity'.[5] Plutarch thought that it was the province of the daemon to care for and encourage humanity:

> Those souls, as Hesiod says, that are not to be put into another body, but are forced from all union with flesh, turn guardian Daemons, and preside over others; for as wrestlers, when old age makes them unfit for exercise, have some love for it still left, delight to see others wrestle, and encourage them; so souls that have passed all the stages of life, and by their virtue are exalted into Daemons, do not slight

the endeavours of man, but being kind to those that strive for the same attainments, and in some sort banding and siding with them, encourage and help them on, when they see them near their hope and ready to catch the desired prize.[6]

He taught that the daemon communicated with men 'in sleep', and sometimes in a waking trance condition, not as 'an apparition, but rather a sensible perception of a voice; as in a dream there is no real voice, yet we have fancies and apprehensions of words which make us imagine that we hear someone speak'.[7] Plutarch's theory was (I think) an influence upon medieval Christian angelology, which is well known in some respects to connect with Platonic teachings; and similar views on divine communication came to be expressed by Donne, who in 'Air and Angels' tells us how 'angels' often manifest 'in a voice'. Accepting all this as he did, Yeats had therefore ample precedent.

Where Yeats differed from Plutarch (and 'Cuchulain Comforted' cannot be understood apart from this) was in respect of the relation between man and his daemon. For Plutarch and Platonism generally, the daemon came to man as like to like, 'to those that strive for the same attainments'. But Yeats applied to Plutarch's thesis the theory of opposites of Heraclitus, and suggested that the daemon was never man's similar, always his opposite.

Plutarch's precepts . . . have it that a strange living man may win for Daemon an illustrious dead man; but now I add another thought: the Daemon comes not as like to like but seeking its own opposite, for man and Daemon feed the hunger in one another's hearts.[8]

As I have said, Yeats thought of the spiritual and the human as both opposite and complementary, each needing the other to attain to completeness; and he imagined that the daemon was irresistibly attracted to whatever man was possessed of the qualitie which, in life, it had itself lacked. Thus, man and daemon each completed the other's experience, and the daemon, from its own past knowledge, was able to lead the man on to his destiny: 'among things not impossible, whatever is most difficult'. Whatever seemed difficult to the man would be well within the guardian angel's reach.

All this is remembered in Yeats's poem, which is one of his most learned; and that the relation between man and daemon was much in his thoughts during his last years we can see from 'The Man And The Echo', which I think is connected with it:

O Rocky Voice,
Shall we in that great night rejoice?
What do we know but that we face
One another in this place?[9]

The arguments in favour of this poem's being about man's union with his daemon in the 'great night' of the life after death have been summarised by Vivienne Koch.[10]

If we now look at the prose draft of Yeats's poem, another chain of associations will at once suggest themselves, for the phrasing seems to me to make it virtually certain that he is remembering Dante. This is already suggested by the *terza rima* of the verse itself, one of whose functions is I think to help us to make the association with Dante Yeats requires, but the idiom and phrasing of the draft, particularly the conclusion, make the analogy more obvious. This is the prose version of the last few lines, whose inflection no lover of Dante could mistake:

> Then they [Yeats's 'convicted cowards'] began to sing, and they did not sing like men and women, but like linnets that had been stood on a perch and taught by a good singing master.[11]

Yeats may have pared down his allusions to Dante in a feeling that they were inessential to the understanding of his poem, but they do provide a short cut to the exegesis, and I do not see why we should not avail ourselves of it.

'Cuchulain Comforted', the draft tells us, is sited in 'a valley in the country of the dead', where Cuchulain, represented as a 'violent and famous' man, comes after death. In Dante, there is only one valley of the dead, the Valley of the Negligent Rulers in Purgatory, where 'kings and rulers who have neglected their higher functions for selfishness and selfish war' are consigned, 'dove la costa face di sè grembo', 'where the mountainside makes of itself a bosom'.[12] These spirits, it should be remembered, are outside the true purgatory; granted the ease they sought in life, their punishment is the desire they feel for active purgation. Now it is very clear that this valley is precisely the place in Purgatory to which Cuchulain's spirit might with propriety be consigned; he, if anyone, is in Dante's sense a negligent ruler, who has neglected his higher spiritual function for love and war, or as the poem puts it 'wounds and blood'. As for the likelihood of Yeats using Dante in his poems, I have already shown that it was sometimes his custom to use Dantesque symbolism for the different regions of Purgatory, as in 'News For The Delphic Oracle', with its set of allusions to Dante's limbo. It is also worth noting that Blake illustrated this valley in Dante; in his illustration we see Dante and Virgil, travelling as Yeats would have said in the spirit medium, dressed in long tenuous shroud-like garments much like the 'shrouds' which the spirits wear in Yeats's own poem. But what is perhaps most significant in the episode in Dante is that the spirits, at evening, and in a passage familiar through Eliot's parody in 'The Waste Land',[13] turn their faces to Paradise and offer up a hymn to God:

'Te lucis ante' sì devotamente
  le uscì di bocca, e con sì dolci note,
  che fece me a me uscir di mente.
E l'altre poi dolcemente e devote
  seguitar lei per tutto l'inno intero,
  avendo gli occhi alle superne rote.

'Te lucis ante' so devoutly proceeded from the leading spirit's mouth, and with such sweet music, that it rapt me from my sense of self.
    And the others then sweetly and devoutly accompanied it through the entire hymn, having their eyes fixed upon the eternal wheels.[14]

In Yeats's poem, the leading spirit similarly leads the others in a hymn:

'Now must we sing and sing the best we can.'

They sing in unison, seeming to have 'the throats of birds', Yeats's common symbol for the purified soul. The full significance of this reminiscence will be seen later.
    We are now in a position to look at the poem in full detail. Cuchulain is shown leaning against a tree in a valley of the dead, violent and turbulent in purgatory as in life, unwilling to reconcile himself to the new world around him, and continuing, in death, to 'meditate on wounds and blood'. Certain spirits come out from the trees to meet him; they are described as 'bird-like things', and are reminiscent, per-haps, of the bird-headed ghosts of Egyptian theurgy, where, before the *psychostasia*, souls also pass through a valley of the dead.[15] These spirits describe themselves in terms which make it clear that they are the 'great fighting man's' opposites:

'... first you must be told our character:
Convicted cowards all, by kindred slain
Or driven from home and left to die in fear.'

If we now apply the knowledge of Yeats's theory of the soul which we possess, it will be very clear that these spirits are Cuchulain's guardian angels or daemons, to whom he is in process of being united after death. Even so, and as we shall see, he still has need of their help.

Yeats offers us a wealth of incidental symbolism to underline the significance of his ghosts. We are told, for example, that they act always in unison:

'... all we do
All must together do'.

When they sing their hymn, again, all has to be done 'in common as before'. This detail takes us back to that passage in *A Vision* where Yeats calls up one of his instructors, who are his own guardian angels, for information as to the nature of life in the condition of the 'purification'; he asks if it is true that the soul loses all personal memory and preoccupation with the self. The spirit tells him that 'perfection is a shared purpose or ideal':

'We have no power except to purify our intention, of complexity. We do nothing singly. Every act is done by a number at the same time.'[16]

The image in 'Cuchulain Comforted' serves therefore to clarify that the 'bird-like things' are pure souls, who have escaped from the round of birth and death;* and parallel meaning is contained in the image of the needle's eye, which stands at the heart of the poem. The spirits are occupied in sewing 'shrouds', which I shall presently demonstrate to be a symbol for the celestial body, and they tell Cuchulain:

'We thread the needles' eyes, and all we do
All must together do.'

Yeats's image of the needle's eye as the gateway to paradise derives no doubt from the New Testament, and it is common in his poetry:

---

*I think the purgatorial dance in 'Byzantium' has something of the same significance: it symbolises the gradual subordination of individuality to a communal purpose. In both cases the underlying philosophical concept is of the merging of the individual *Purusha* (consciousness) in the universal self.

> All the stream that's roaring by
> Came out of a needle's eye . . .[17]

> The Father and his angelic hierarchy . . .
> Stood in the circuit of a needle's eye.[18]

The attraction of this image for Yeats lay no doubt in the fact, which has been noted, that he thought of eternity as something 'infinitely small' as well as 'infinitely great',[19] an argument he developed from Blake:

> Every Space larger than a red Globule of Man's blood
> Is visionary, and is created by the Hammer of Los.
> And every Space smaller than a Globule of Man's blood opens
> Into Eternity, of which the vegetable Earth is but a shadow.[20]

The symbol in 'Cuchulain Comforted' has, beyond the literal, the meaning that Yeats's spirits pass between the heavenly world and the physical at will, as it is the province of guardian angels to do.

The angels bring Cuchulain 'a bundle of linen' and advise him to make a shroud similar to those they themselves are wearing.

> 'Your life can grow much sweeter if you will
> Obey our ancient rule and make a shroud.'

The shroud is Yeats's symbol for the celestial body, though I had better say here that his theory does not necessarily commit him to literal belief. All is in one sense symbol, and the celestial body represents the pure way of life by which angels keep their spiritual integrity intact, just as the passionate body broadly symbolises the turbulent way of life of human beings while in the world. Cuchulain's predicament is made clear by a passage in *A Vision*: he is unwilling to renounce the turbulence of physical life, and this can only hinder him during the purgatorial process:

> If the passionate body does not disappear, the Spirit finds the celestial body only after long and perhaps painful dreams of the past.[21]

Cuchulain cannot bring himself to 'make his soul' of his own volition, and this is why he needs the help of his guardian angels.

The theory behind this passage is peculiarly remote. Yeats's prose symbolises the celestial body as 'the divine cloak lent to all', which 'falls away at the consummation',[22] or disappears at the moment of union with God, when the naked self stands revealed in all its purity; and he justifies himself from the Syriac Christian poem of Bardesan 'The Hymn Of The Soul'. I will quote his own paraphrase of this poem, from which the allegorical meaning will be apparent:

> A king's son asleep in Egypt (physical life) is sent a cloak . . . He sets out for his father's kingdom wrapped in that cloak.[23]

So in Yeats also, the soul sets out for heaven wrapped in a cloak, and the whole purgatorial process can be represented as the stitching of that cloak; the cloak itself is symbolised, in 'Byzantium', as 'mummy cloth', and here, by analogy and perhaps with a reminiscence of Blake's Dante illustrations, as a shroud. The stuff of which the celestial body is made, I should add, would be for a Platonist wisdom, for the nature of life in the heavenly world is wisdom, as I have quoted Plotinus to show.[24] This is why Yeats's spirits lay claim to omniscience:

> 'Mainly because of what we only know
> The rattle of those arms makes us afraid.'

Cuchulain's violent behaviour terrifies them, I think we must understand, because warfare is the symbol of the unreconciled opposites and thus of his kinship with the contaminated physical world.

When his daemons have persuaded Cuchulain to 'sew' his 'shroud', or make his soul, the argument of Yeats's weird and strangely moving poem is at an end, and it concludes with their Dantesque hymn of thanksgiving to God. They sing, but 'not in human tunes or words', for their music is the music of the angels.

This is all there is in the poem, but I may perhaps be permitted to add one speculation of my own. Though Yeats's primary source is Dante, his *terza rima* is hardly Dantesque in tone; yet its limpid, perfectly controlled flow is remarkably accomplished:

> A Shroud that seemed to have authority
> Among those bird-like things came, and let fall
> A bundle of linen.* Shrouds by two and three

---

*'Linen' because such is traditionally the fabric from which the raiment of angels is made (*v.* Revelation, xv, 6).

Came creeping up because the man was still.
And thereupon that linen-carrier said:
'Your life can grow much sweeter if you will

'Obey our ancient rule and make a shroud;
Mainly because of what we only know
The rattle of those arms makes us afraid.'

Since Yeats had had very little practice in the writing of *terza rima*
himself, this confident skill suggests that he was imitating some much-
loved master, and the source which commends itself to me is William
Morris's 'The Defence Of Guinevere'. Morris's subject-matter is of
course very different, but his terse, laconic style is similar to that of
Yeats. With this he manages to combine very great technical fluency;
here he stands closest to Yeats at the beginning of his poem, where
there is the same limpidity, the same tendency to overflow, the same
absence of punctuation within the line:

But knowing now that they would have her speak
She threw her wet hand backwards from her brow,
Her hand close to her mouth brushing her cheek

As if she had had there a painful blow . . .[25]

If Yeats had this text in mind, even subconsciously, the fact is remarkably interesting, for we have to remember that Morris's poem centres
about the curious episode of the choosing of the cloth.[26] This provides
an astonishingly close parallel with the central episode of 'Cuchulain
Comforted': Cuchulain's guardian angel bringing him the stuff from
which to make the celestial body. Here are the relevant lines in 'The
Defence Of Guinevere':

'Listen, suppose your time were come to die
And you were quite alone and very weak,
Yes, laid a-dying, while very mightily

'The wind was ruffling up the narrow streak
Of river through your broad lands running well.
Suppose a hush should come, then someone speak:

' "One of these cloths is heaven and one is hell.
Now choose one cloth for ever: which they be
I will not tell you, you must somehow tell

' "Of your own strength and mightiness; here, see!"
Yea, yea, my lord, and you to ope your eyes
At foot of your familiar bed to see

'A great God's angel standing.'

In Morris, one of these strange cloths which the angel holds 'within his hands' is 'blue, wavy and long' and one 'cut short and red', a fact which (if we suppose that the text was important to Yeats) may be relevant also to his own early exercise in the theory of the celestial body, 'The Cap And Bells'.[27] There the 'heart' and the 'soul' are dressed in red and blue cloths respectively, and the imagery may well be eclectic. It hardly matters what Morris himself knew of the tradition; Yeats wrote an essay to prove him an instinctive visionary,[28] and would have been in no doubt as to what lay behind these lines. As for the present context, I do not think we have to relate them to 'Cuchulain Comforted', but it is certainly a temptation to do so.

NOTES

Limitations of space have made it necessary to condense the notes which follow, and a number of abbreviations have been used. *C.P.* stands for *Collected Poems*, and *Plays* for *Collected Plays*; other abbreviations are formed in the same way, and are explained in the Bibliography. The full titles of works by Yeats's critics are also given in that place; I have used such short forms as 'Henn' for T. R. Henn's *The Lonely Tower*.

Unless an edition of a work is explicitly referred to in a given note, the edition on which I have drawn is that which the Bibliography lists.

If I had had more space, I should have expanded some of my rather laconic comments; but I think they will be found to be quite clear.

CHAPTER ONE

[1] *v.* 'Yeats: The Poet As Mythmaker' (reprinted from *Modern Poetry And The Tradition*); in *The Permanence Of Yeats*, p. 85.

[2] *v.* 'Yeats And His Symbols' (reprinted from *The Kenyon Review*); in *The Permanence Of Yeats*, p. 104.

[3] Neville Rogers: *Shelley At Work* (1956).

[4] Wilhelm Fränger, *The Millennium Of Hieronymus Bosch* (1942).

[5] Saurat, *Literature And Occult Tradition*, p. 6.

[6] *ibid.*

[7] *ibid.*, p. 9.

[8] *ibid.*, p. 56.

[9] 'Three Songs To The One Burden', *C.P.*, p. 372.

[10] C. G. Jung, *Psychology And Alchemy* (trans. R. F. C. Hull), 1953.

[11] *v.* Fränger, *op. cit.*, pp. 76, 78, 80–1, 91.

[12] Eliot, 'Burnt Norton', II.

[13] *ibid.*

[14] Von Hügel, *The Mystical Element Of Religion* (1908), II, pp. 283–4.

[15] This dream is recorded in *I.G.E.*, p. 29.

[16] For this dream, *v. P.A.S.L.*, p. 73.

[17] *1930 Diary*, pp. 46 ff. Yeats quotes the end of Shelley's 'The Sensitive Plant'.

[18] Eliot, 'Burnt Norton', III.

[19] *Essays 1931–6*, pp. 113–14.

[20] *C.P.*, p. 211.

[21] Hough, *The Last Romantics*, p. 229.

[22] Jung, *Psychology And Alchemy*, p. 463.

[23] Jung, *Psychology And Alchemy*, p. 15.

[24] *ibid.*, pp. 7–8.

[25] *ibid.*, p. 8.

[26] Bodkin, *Studies Of Type-Images*, preface.

[27] *ibid.*, p. 3.

[28] *ibid.*

[29] Bodkin, *Archetypal Patterns In Poetry*, p. 4.

[30] Eliot, 'The Waste Land', lines 403–4.

[31] Yet even Yeats's angelology is founded on Christian and Platonic convention, while the idea of a trans-sexual love in heaven is common to Kabbalistic, Platonic and Indian theology.

[32] *Letters To The New Island*, p. vii.

[33] May Daniels, *The French Drama Of The Unspoken*, p. 51.

[34] Arthur Symons, *Collected Works*, Vol. 8, p. 115.

[35] *ibid.*, p. 125.

[36] *T.C.T.*, p. 128.

[37] Yeats came to read D'Alviella's *The Migration Of Symbols* (1894) and Bayley's *The Lost Language Of Symbolism* (1912). Jung (*Psychology And Alchemy*, pp. 412 ff.) has much to say of the traditional descent of symbols, but the works of Ananda Coomaraswami, the Indian critic, comprise perhaps the thoroughest modern investigation. For a classic instance of inherited symbolism, *v.* Agrippa on the hawk-symbol—descending from Egypt to Greece and so to the middle ages—in *De Occulta Philosophia*, I, Cap. XXIII.

[38] *Kabbalah Unveiled* (1887).

[39] *ibid.*, pp. 5–6.

[40] *ibid.*, p. 21.

[41] The rituals are preserved in Regardie's *History Of The Golden Dawn*.

[42] *C.P.*, p. 375.

[43] *v.* W. Y. Evans-Wentz, *The Tibetan Book Of The Dead*, p. 7.

[44] Blavatsky, *The Secret Doctrine*, p. xlv.

[45] The Quaritch edition, edited by Yeats and Edwin Ellis, hereafter referred to as the Quaritch *Blake*.

[46] Preserved in early editions only.

[47] *The Wind Among The Reeds* (1900 edition), pp. 74–5.

[48] *Autos*, p. 329.

[49] *ibid.*

[50] *I.G.E.*, p. 46.

[51] *ibid.*, p. 79.

[52] *ibid.*, p. 41.

[53] *ibid.*, p. 43.

[54] *ibid.*, p. 175 (condensed).

[55] *C.O.A.*, p. 107.

[56] *I.G.E.*, p. 92 (condensed).

[57] *Autos*, p. 457.

[58] *ibid.*, p. 240.

[59] Preface to Tagore, *Gitanjali*, pp. xiv, xvi.

[60] *I.G.E.*, p. 201.

[61] *A Vision*, A, p. 202.

[62] *I.G.E.*, p. 176.

[63] *ibid.*, p. 158.

[64] *C.O.A.*, p. 33.

[65] Jung, *The Interpretation Of Nature And The Psyche* (trans. R. F. C. Hull), p. 32.

[66] In the mysteries we have the symbol of the bird as God laying the egg of the created universe, which is also a feature of Indian symbolism, as I show in Chapter Three. My essay on 'Byzantium' deals with Kabbalistic bird-symbolism. In Japanese legend, migrating wild geese symbolise the souls of the blessed, journeying to the Country of Perfection, but lamenting, as they go, their separation from their friends. *Cf.* that loveliest of Noh plays *Hagoromo*.

[67] This symbol is traced to source in Chapter Six. For Yeats's own explanation, *v. The Wind Among The Reeds*, p. 90. Occasionally he uses the ocean to represent Anima Mundi, and then the individual life becomes the foam on its surface.

[68] *Plays*, p. 145.

[69] *Cf. C.P.*, p. 535 (note); *I.G.E.*, pp. 83-8; and *T.C.T.*, pp. 10, 128, where Yeats reveals his source.

[70] *Cf. I.G.E.*, pp. 83-8 and *A Vision*, A, p. 202. Yeats was almost certainly right in supposing that Shelley knew Taylor's *Porphyry*, for Shelley's friend Peacock had a copy of the book.

[71] All these contentions are verified in Chapters Two and Six.

[72] Yeats knew Jowett's translation also and quotes it in *Irish Fairy And Folk Tales* (1894), p. xvi.

[73] Quoted from *I.G.E.*, p. 237.

[74] *P. and C.*, p. 216.

[75] *ibid.*, p. 122. Yeats has Ibsen as well as Maeterlinck in mind.

[76] Quoted from *I.G.E.*, p. 237.

[77] *Autos*, pp. 142, 143.

[78] *P. and C.*, p. 99.

[79] Coomaraswami, *The Mirror Of Gesture*, p. 7; *cf.* p. 9.

[80] *Plays For An Irish Theatre*, p. ix.

[81] *C.O.A.*, p. 6.

[82] The word is in fact Samuel Palmer's (*v.* Palmer's *Life And Letters*, ed. A. H. Palmer, p. 187); but Yeats uses it in *C.O.A.*, p. 33; *cf.* also *P. and C.*, p. 161, 'The end of art is peace.'

[83] *C.O.A.*, pp. 25-7.

[84] *ibid.*, p. 32.

[85] *Plays For An Irish Theatre*, preface, p. xii. This preface is an early form of the essay alluded to in my two previous notes.

[86] *C.O.A.*, p. 28.

[87] *Plays For An Irish Theatre*, preface, p. x.

[88] For the traditional basis of much of this symbolism, *v. I.G.E.*, p. 93.

[89] For the tradition here, *v.* Quaritch *Blake*, I, pp. 267, 273.

[90] *Plays*, p. 245.

[91] *W & B*, p. 103.

[92] *P. and C.*, p. 416.

[93] In that context Yeats shows his acquaintance with the drama of most modern European countries, and with the classical and even the Sanskrit theatre. *Cf.* pp. 71, 111, 120, 130, 150, 167–8; and *C.O.A.*, p. 119.

[94] *C.O.A.*, p. 2.

[95] 'Ideal beauty' is Miss Ishibashi's translation; 'mysterious calm' Ezra Pound's. *Cf.* Waley, *The No Plays Of Japan*, p. 44. This book, and the essays in Pound's *The Translations* (which reprint the material in his *No, or Accomplishment* [N.Y., 1917]), will be found to confirm all Yeats's statements as to the nature of the Noh theatre.

[96] The best reference here is to the discussion in *C.O.A.*, pp. 16–17.

[97] *P. and C.*, p. 416.

[98] *ibid.*, p. 417.

[99] *v.* Pound's *The Translations*, pp. 214 ff., 221.

[100] Quoted from *P. and C.*, p. 416.

[101] So Yeats says in *C.O.A.*, p. 1.

[102] Quoted from *P. and C.*, p. 208. This essay was written in the first flush of Yeats's enthusiasm for the Japanese drama, and the Noh theatre is implicitly under discussion throughout, as the context will show.

[103] *ibid.*

[104] *ibid.*, p. 213.

[105] *ibid.*, p. 212.

[106] *ibid.*, p. 207.

[107] *ibid.*, p. 213.

[108] This point is made in Miss Ishibashi's unpublished thesis (*v.* Bibliography).

[109] *C.O.A.*, p. 19.

[110] *ibid.*, p. 13.

[111] *P. and C.*, p. 213.

[112] *ibid.*

[113] *ibid.*, p. 458.

[114] *ibid.*

[115] Wade, *Letters*, p. 607.

[116] That Yeats connected the Japanese and Florentine cultures we have *P. and C.*, pp. 207–13 and p. 458, to show. Pound (*The Translations*, pp. 214, 244) preferred to associate medieval Japan with Provence; but this is hardly a distinction.

[117] MacNeice, p. 170.

[118] Ure, p. 90. It is maintained that the plays have no clearly defined symbolic

content, or that their symbolism is unimportant. They are 'merely the
embodiment of ritual in myth' (whatever this may mean).

[119] *K.O.G.C.T.* (Cuala edition), p. 19.
[120] *ibid.*
[121] *ibid.*, pp. 18–19.
[122] *ibid.*, p. 19.
[123] *v.* my second chapter. For Yeats's use of local colour, *cf.* Kermode's admirable '*The Dancer*'.
[124] *Autos*, p. 329.
[125] *K.O.G.C.T.*, p. 19.
[126] Wade, *Letters*, p. 840.
[127] This symbolism is explained in my sixth chapter.

CHAPTER TWO

[1] *Plays*, p. 631.
[2] *Plays*, p. 619.
[3] *A Full Moon In March* (1935 edition), preface.
[4] *Letters To D.W.*, p. 47.
[5] *K.O.G.C.T.* (Cuala edition), pp. 19–20.
[6] *ibid.*
[7] *ibid.*, p. 45.
[8] *ibid.*, p. 19.
[9] *A Full Moon In March*, preface.
[10] *Letters To Sturge Moore*, p. 8.
[11] *K.O.G.C.T.*, p. 20. In Heine ('Atta Troll', Kaput XIX), it is Herodias who is in love with the head. Had Yeats in mind some connection with the Jewish *Keraphim*, prophetic severed heads?
[12] Wade, *Letters*, p. 826.
[13] *C.P.*, p. 332.
[14] Blavatsky, *The Secret Doctrine*, I, p. 411.
[15] *ibid.*, I, p. 413.
[16] *ibid.*, II, p. 62.
[17] *ibid.*, I, p. 417.
[18] *ibid.*, II, p. 235.
[19] Blake, *The Marriage Of Heaven And Hell*, 6–7.
[20] Quaritch *Blake*, II, p. 63.
[21] *ibid.*
[22] *C.O.A.*, p. 67.
[23] Wade, *Letters*, p. 402.
[24] *v.* *The Birth Of Tragedy* (trans. W. Haussmann, 1909), pp. 25, 34.
[25] In *The Academy*, 30th August, 1902.
[26] *v.* *The Secret Doctrine*, I, p. 425.
[27] *T.C.T.*, p. 128; *I.G.E.*, pp. 83–8; *A Vision*, B, p. 19.
[28] Iamblichus, *Life Of Pythagoras*, trans. Thomas Taylor (1926 edition), p. 75.

[29] Taylor, *A Dissertation*, p. 7.
[30] *C.P.*, p. 280.
[31] *A Dissertation*, pp. 9–13. Plotinus, he says, took it over from Egyptian symbolism.
[32] *C.P.*, p. 536 (note). For Yeats's interpretation, *v.* Chapter Six.
[33] *A Dissertation*, p. 155. Yeats will also have read the note on p. 187 of Taylor's *Porphyry*. Mrs. Yeats points out that he knew Macrobius' essay.
[34] *A Dissertation*, p. 135.
[35] *ibid.*, p. 136.
[36] *ibid.*, p. 138.
[37] For these details *v. A Dissertation*, pp. 137, 139, 143.
[38] *ibid.*, p. 144.
[39] *ibid.*, p. 150.
[40] *ibid.*, p. 142.
[41] *v.* Myer, *The Oldest Books In The World*, p. 277. This book Yeats probably knew.
[42] *A Dissertation*, pp. 144, 150.
[43] *ibid.*, p. 151.
[44] *Plays*, p. 585.
[45] *ibid.*, p. 579.
[46] *C.P.*, p. 319.
[47] *ibid.*, p. 536 (note).
[48] *W & B*, p. 106.
[49] *Plays*, p. 577.
[50] *C.P.*, p. 211.
[51] *A Vision*, B, p. 245.
[52] Henn, p. 188.
[53] *A Vision*, B, p. 245.
[54] *ibid.*, B, p. 212.
[55] In Patmore, *Religio Poetae* (1893).
[56] *ibid.*, p. 11.
[57] *ibid.*, p. 12.
[58] *v. Leonardo da Vinci*, by Antonina Valentin, p. 554.
[59] Euripides, *Bacchae*, 1165.
[60] *v.* Taylor, *The Mystical Hymns Of Orpheus*, p. xlvi.
[61] *ibid.*, p. li. Proclus, whose work Yeats also knew, is Taylor's authority.
[62] 'Vacillation', p. 283.
[63] *The Works Of The Emperor Julian* (Loeb edition), I.
[64] *ibid.*, p. 461.
[65] *ibid.*, p. 463.
[66] *ibid.*, p. 467.
[67] *ibid.*, p. 473.
[68] *ibid.*, p. 499.
[69] *ibid.*, p. 440.
[70] *C.P.*, p. 283.

71 Julian, II, p. 31.

72 ibid., I, p. 473.

73 C.P., p. 283.

74 Ellmann, The Identity Of Yeats, p. 172.

75 The Secret Rose, p. 4 (in 1897 edition only).

76 ibid., p. 5. Mr. Henn points out that Yeats's tableau here probably derives from a memory of Rossetti's illustration to Morris's 'Tune Of Seven Towers'.

77 Also in C.P., p. 71.

78 The Four Zoas, II, 340. Yeats quotes these lines in I.G.E., p. 121.

79 C.P., p. 391.

80 'Ribh Denounces Patrick', C.P., p. 328.

81 Quaritch Blake, I, p. 247.

82 C.P., p. 328.

83 Plays, p. 677.

84 A Vision, A, p. 182; cf. pp. 133-4.

85 'Under The Round Tower', C.P., p. 154.

86 'The Four Ages Of Man', C.P., p. 332.

87 'Ribh Considers Christian Love Insufficient', C.P., p. 330.

88 C.P., p. 327.

89 ibid., p. 381.

90 Othello, III, iv, 86.

91 P.A.S.L., pp. 69-70.

92 Yeats saw a light blazing up from a ruined village which turned out to be a hallucination, and he wonders (Autos, p. 95) whether it may not have had some visionary significance.

93 W & B, pp. 37-8.

94 P.A.S.L., p. 11.

95 C.P., p. 257.

96 ibid., p. 294.

97 T.C.T., p. 92.

98 It is as though Christ were conversing with his own bitter and embittering crown of thorns. One must not forget the function of the thorn-tree in symbolism. For the 'dry tree' generally, v. I.G.E., pp. 52, 62; C.P., p. 54 ('The Two Trees'), and Myer, Qabbalah, pp. 431-6.

99 'The Delphic Oracle Upon Plotinus', C.P., p. 307.

100 v. C.P., p. 531 (note).

101 v. Plato, Republic, X, 617; for the fates in Greek religion, cf. Taylor, The Mystical Hymns Of Orpheus, pp. 121-2.

102 'His Bargain', C.P., p. 299.

103 Brihadaranyaka-Upanishad, quoted by Yeats in The Aphorisms Of Patanjali (introduction), p. 13.

104 v. Ellmann, The Identity Of Yeats, p. 314.

105 In The Wanderings Of Oisin (1892 edition), p. 56.

106 Plays, p. 702.

[107] *W & B*, p. 101.

[108] *A Dissertation*, p. 55.

[109] *T.C.T.*, p. 147. Yeats writes also of 'grass-green Avalon' (*C.P.*, p. 389).

[110] For the classical tradition here, *cf.* Tibullus, *Carmina*, I, 3.

[111] *C.P.*, p. 526 (note).

[112] *v. Republic*, X, 617.

[113] *Irish Fairy And Folk Tales*, edited by W. B. Yeats (1894), p. 200.

[114] In Wade, *Letters*, p. 817.

[115] *C.P.*, p. 327.

[116] *C.O.A.*, pp. 67–9.

[117] *v.* 'In A Myrtle Shade' where, as Kathleen Raine points out, the lover is compared to 'dung upon the ground'.

[118] Probably Erasmus, who says precisely this in the epilogue to *Moriae Encomium*. One might compare Erasmus' theory of the fool with Yeats's as I explain it in Chapter Three. I think there is an influence.

[119] *W & B*, p. 79.

[120] Yeats quotes Rabelais in the preface to *K.O.G.C.T.*

[121] *v.* 'The Phases Of The Moon', *C.P.*, p. 183.

[122] *A Vision*, B, p. 29.

[123] Von Hügel, *The Mystical Element Of Religion*, I, p. 223.

[124] *ibid.*

[125] *Essays 31–6*, p. 73.

[126] Taylor, *Porphyry*, p. 255. The Greek *hyle* means both 'matter' and 'a wood'. This is one of the symbols that Dante took over from the tradition, and Yeats knew it from his work also.

[127] *v. I.G.E.*, p. 94, for this distinction.

[128] *A Vision*, B, p. 271.

CHAPTER THREE

[1] *Plays*, p. 643.

[2] *Letters To D.W.*, p. 44.

[3] *ibid.*, p. 43.

[4] *v.* Yeats's introduction to her *Selected Poems*, printed in *Letters To D.W.*, pp. 25 ff.

[5] *ibid.*, p. 46.

[6] *The Ten Principal Upanishads*, translated by Shree Purohit Swami and W. B. Yeats.

[7] *W & B*, p. 139.

[8] *T.C.T.*, p. 108.

[9] *1930 Diary*, p. 19.

[10] *The Aphorisms Of Patanjali*, Yeats's introduction, p. 12.

[11] *A Vision*, B, p. 271.

[12] *The Aphorisms Of Patanjali*, introduction, p. 13.

[13] *ibid.*, p. 14.

[14] *C.P.*, p. 375.

[15] *Essays 31–6*, p. 113.
[16] 'He And She', *C.P.*, p. 331.
[17] *The Aphorisms Of Patanjali*, introduction, p. 15.
[18] ibid., p. 19.
[19] *v. K.O.G.C.T.* (Cuala edition), p. 44.
[20] *The Ten Principal Upanishads*, preface, p. 11.
[21] *Essays 31–6*, p. 80.
[22] ibid., p. 63.
[23] ibid., p. 62.
[24] ibid., p. 68.
[25] ibid., p. 73.
[26] ibid., p. 71.
[27] Ferguson, *Congal* (1872).
[28] *The Battle Of Magh Rath* (trans. John O'Donovan, 1842). The detail of the substitution of the eggs in Yeats's play suggests that he knew the book. In Ferguson there is no substitution and Congal rebels simply because he is served his egg in a wooden, not a golden, dish.
[29] *A Book Of Irish Verse:* introduction, p. xix.
[30] O'Donovan, *op. cit.*, pp. 1–29.
[31] Ferguson, *Congal*, preface, p. 9. This and the following quotation are taken from supplementary material given in the second edition only.
[32] ibid., p. 140.
[33] ibid. (1872 edition), p. 142.
[34] How little Yeats wished his heroine to be associated with Lafinda will be seen from the fact that he discarded Ferguson's name for her. Perhaps he had in mind St. Attracta, who lived in the fifth century at Boyle, Co. Roscommon.
[35] Melchiori, 'Leda And The Swan', p. 219.
[36] *Seraphita*, trans. Clara Bell (Dent, 1897).
[37] ibid., p. 40.
[38] *v.* Chapter 2, note 81.
[39] *Seraphita*, trans. Bell, p. 120.
[40] ibid., p. 41.
[41] ibid., p. 120.
[42] ibid., p. 29.
[43] ibid., p. 86.
[44] ibid., p. 57.
[45] Swedenborg, *Heaven And Hell* (1860 translation), p. 147.
[46] *The Ten Principal Upanishads*, p. 154.
[47] *Modern Philology*, 49, pp. 242 ff.
[48] Swedenborg, *Heaven And Hell*, p. 6.
[49] ibid., p. 7.
[50] ibid., p. 155.
[51] *Seraphita*, p. 148.
[52] *The Tibetan Book Of The Dead*, p. 68. The book was in Yeats's library.

[53] *The Poems Of William Blake* (1893), introduction, p. xxxiii.

[54] *A Vision*, B, p. 161.

[55] *The Holy Mountain*, pp. 103–4.

[56] *The Secret Doctrine*, I, p. 79.

[57] *ibid.*, I, p. 359.

[58] *ibid.*, I, p. 65. *Cf.* p. 333.

[59] *ibid.*, I, pp. 359 ff.

[60] *Isis Unveiled*, I, 56; *cf. The Secret Doctrine*, I, 65.

[61] *A Vision*, B, p. 268.

[62] *C.P.*, p. 281.

[63] *The Ten Principal Upanishads*, p. 142.

[64] *The Secret Rose*, pp. 212–14.

[65] *P. And C.*, p. 458.

[66] *Plays*, p. 449.

[67] *v. Essays 31–6*, p. 96.

[68] Quaritch *Blake*, I, p. 317.

[69] *V. And B.*, I, p. 272; *v.* also pp. 290–2.

[70] *A Vision*, B, p. 232.

[71] Plutarch, *Morals*, III, pp. 401–2.

[72] *Cf. V. And B.*, I, pp. 290–2.

[73] *Plays*, p. 704.

[74] Plutarch, *Morals*, III, pp. 401–2.

[75] *ibid.*

[76] *ibid.*, II, p. 224.

[77] *A Vision*, B, pp. 239–40.

[78] 'The Phases Of The Moon', *C.P.*, p. 269.

[79] 'Blood And The Moon', *C.P.*, p. 247.

[80] 'The Fool By The Roadside', *C.P.*, p. 247.

[81] *A Vision*, A, pp. 61–3.

[82] *ibid.*

[83] *ibid.*

[84] *Milton*, Book Second, 31.

[85] *The Four Zoas*, IX, 846–9.

[86] *Milton*, Book Second, 35.

[87] *C.P.*, p. 94.

[88] *The Secret Rose, etc.* (revised, 1913, edition), p. 52.

[89] *ibid.*, p. 69.

[90] *Where There Is Nothing* (1903), p. 44.

[91] *The Secret Rose, etc.* (1913), pp. 53 ff.

[92] *V. And B.*, II, 302.

[93] *v. Emanuel Swedenborg*, by Signe Toksvig, p. 356. *Cf. Conjugal Love*, p. 17 (1841 edition): 'Infernal love is opposite to heavenly love and consequently the delights of these two loves are in a state of discord and enmity, and, whenever they meet, they endeavour to destroy one another'. Infernal love is love of the Self.

94 *Heaven And Hell*, p. 155.

95 *The Wind Among The Reeds*, pp. 73–4.

96 For these terms, *v. Essays 31–6*, pp. 127–8.

97 It is interesting to find that the dog is used to symbolise man in the original Gaelic legend (O'Donovan, p. 9).

98 *1930 Diary*, p. 18.

99 *Cf.* the similar image in *Calvary: Plays*, p. 451.

100 *Cf.*, for instance, Rolleston's 'The Spell Struck', anthologised in Yeats's *A Book Of Irish Verse*, p. 198.

101 *The Ten Principal Upanishads*, p. 36.

102 *v. The Tibetan Book Of The Dead*, foreword, p. xxxiii.

103 *Cf. Where There Is Nothing*, p. 2.

104 *The Aphorisms Of Patanjali*, introduction, p. 17.

105 *Cf. C.P.*, pp. 385, 386, 390; *Plays*, p. 688; and, for the contrast, *C.P.*, pp. 376, 384, 389.

106 *Cf.* 'John Kinsella's Lament', *C.P.*, p. 384.

107 'The Spirit Medium', *C.P.*, p. 366.

108 *T.C.T.*, pp. 181–2.

109 *Cf. T.C.T.*, pp. 181–2.

110 *ibid.*

111 *A Vision*, A, p. 115.

112 *Plays*, p. 302.

113 *C.P.*, p. 129.

114 *With Mystics And Magicians In Tibet* (1931), pp. 35–6.

115 *The Ten Principal Upanishads*, p. 158. An explanation is given in Radhakrishnan, *The Principal Upanishads*, where the passage is translated on pp. 314–15.

116 *C.P.*, p. 256.

117 *v.* Radhakrishnan, *loc. cit.*

118 *The Tibetan Book of The Dead*, pp. 59–60.

119 *C.P.*, p. 358.

120 *ibid.*

CHAPTER FOUR

1 *Plays*, p. 679.

2 Wade, *Letters*, p. 907.

3 *ibid.*, p. 915.

4 *ibid.*, p. 913.

5 Quoted from 'My Descendants', *C.P.*, p. 229.

6 M. C. Stopes, *Plays Of Old Japan: The No*, p. 22.

7 Pound, *The Translations*, p. 286.

8 Trans. M. C. Stopes, *op. cit.*, p. 35. Since Yeats knew the play in 1917, when there was no other translation, he clearly knew the book. Ezra Pound had in fact at one time hoped that Dr. Stopes might collaborate with him in his own Noh translations.

⁹ 'The Philosophy Of Shelley's Poetry' (in *I.G.E.*) and 'Prometheus Unbound' (in *Essays 31-6*).

¹⁰ *A Vision*, A, pp. 220 ff; B, pp. 219 ff.

¹¹ *ibid.*, A, p. 227.

¹² *ibid.*, A, p. 229.

¹³ *ibid.*, B, p. 236.

¹⁴ He played for a time with the idea of the 'Vision Of Evil', but evil as such is hardly referred to in his philosophical writings.

¹⁵ *A Vision*, A, p. 230.

¹⁶ This I know from Kathleen Raine's unpublished essay 'The Lilly'.

¹⁷ Suzuki, *Introduction To Zen Buddhism*, p. 56.

¹⁸ MacKenna, II, p. 67.

¹⁹ *If I Were Four-and-twenty*, p. 6.

²⁰ *V. And B.*, II, 334.

²¹ *A Vision*, B, p. 220.

²² *W & B*, pp. 33-4.

²³ *A Vision*, B, p. 222.

²⁴ The Return is discussed in my sixth chapter. For the Plotinus reference, *v. A Vision*, B, p. 232.

²⁵ As Yeats hints in *A Vision*, B, p. 252.

²⁶ Blavatsky, *Isis Unveiled*, I, 432.

²⁷ For this, *v.* E. R. Dodds, Proclus: *The Elements Of Theology*, App. II.

²⁸ *V. And B.*, II, 328. Yeats knew Trismegistus in Mead's translation, Synesius (*On Providence*) and Proclus in Taylor's, and Philoponus as translated in Cudworth's *True Intellectual System* (iii, 512-30).

²⁹ *V. And B.*, II, 332. *Cf.* More, *A Collection Of Several Philosophical Writings* (1662), p. 119.

³⁰ *V. And B.*, II, 331.

³¹ *The Essays And Hymns Of Synesius*, trans. A. Fitzgerald, II, 335.

³² Taylor, *Porphyry*, p. 215.

³³ Mead, *Thrice Greatest Hermes*, II, p. 41.

³⁴ MacKenna, II, p. 74.

³⁵ *V. And B.*, II, p. 297.

³⁶ Pound, *The Translations*, p. 236.

³⁷ *V. And B.*, II, p. 309.

³⁸ *Arcana Coelestia*, 4633.

³⁹ *ibid.*, 695-6, 3224.

⁴⁰ *V. And B.*, II, 301.

⁴¹ Cudworth, *op. cit.*, iii, 513-15.

⁴² *V. And B.*, II, 318.

⁴³ *v.* More, *Theological Works* (1708), p. 21; *V. And B.*, II, 330. The book by More was in Yeats's library.

⁴⁴ For those three references *v. P.A.S.L.*, p. 89 and *W & B*, p. 34 (two places). *Cf. V. And B.*, II, 338.

⁴⁵ *W & B*, p. 35.

[46] *C.P.*, p. 280.

[47] These statements are made good in my essays on the poems (Chapters Six and Eight).

[48] *Isis Unveiled*, I, 5.

[49] Ceremonial magic (and de Flora himself, explicitly, in *The Tables Of The Law*) are Yeats's sources.

[50] *W & B*, p. 102.

[51] *A Vision*, B, p. 67.

[52] Plato, *Statesman*, 270 ff.

[53] *Cf.* Fränger, *op. cit.*, 80–1, 146 and *passim*.

[54] *Cf.* Fränger, p. 30. The one distinction is that while the Greek and Indian philosophers thought of history as an endless cyclic process, Swedenborg and de Flora believed that it would arrive at eventual consummation.

[55] *Hellas*, final chorus.

[56] Burnet, *Early Greek Philosophy*, p. 248; every cycle, that is, of the disintegrating, and so modern, kind.

[57] *C.P.*, p. 337.

[58] Plato, *Statesman*, 274.

[59] Mead's version is in *Thrice Greatest Hermes*, II, 351 ff. He explains that the passage connects with the 'Stoic tradition'.

[60] Taylor, *Select Works Of Plotinus* (1817 edition), pp. 550 ff.

[61] *ibid.*

[62] *C.P.*, p. 210.

[63] *W & B*, p. 18.

[64] *O.T.B.*, pp. 19–20.

[65] *ibid.*, p. 18.

[66] *Letters To D.W.*, p. 196.

[67] *O.T.B.*, p. 26.

[68] *ibid.*, pp. 27–9.

[69] *ibid.*, p. 26.

[70] Yeats had evidently read Tertullian's proof that 'pleasure and remorse' persist in the soul after death, as he could have done on pp. 40–1 of Vol. I of the anonymous translation (Tertullian, 3 vols., Clark, Edinburgh, 1869–95).

[71] *Eden Bower*, line 165. Yeats misquotes.

[72] *The Darkling Plain*, p. 205.

[73] For these two references, *v. C.P.*, pp. 230 and 276.

[74] *Cathleen Ni Houlihan*, *Plays*, p. 73; 'I Am Of Ireland', *C.P.*, p. 303.

[75] *Plays*, p. 245.

[76] *W & B*, p. 103.

[77] Waley, *The No Plays Of Japan*, p. 12.

[78] *C.O.A.*, p. 19.

[79] *Cf. Plays*, pp. 438, 445.

[80] For the *Raya Mehemna*, *v.* Scholem, *Major Trends In Jewish Mysticism*, pp. 180–92. *Cf.* also Ellmann, *The Identity Of Yeats*, p. 76; Myer, *Qabbalah*, pp. 431–6.

81 *I.G.E.*, pp. 52, 62.

82 *Plays*, p. 654.

83 *Essays* 31–6, pp. 63–4.

84 *C.P.*, p. 327.

85 *C.P.*, p. 350.

86 *v. King Lear*, IV, vii, 60: 'I am a very foolish, fond old man.'

87 Perhaps Yeats implies this in the Quaritch *Blake*, I, 238.

88 *Cf.*, for instance, *I.G.E.*, p. 169.

89 *Cf.*, perhaps, Lear's 'The little dogs and all . . .' (III, vi, 60).

90 *Cf.* the structure of *Sotoba Komachi*; in Waley, *op. cit.*, from p. 150.

CHAPTER FIVE

1 Wade, *Letters*, p. 917.

2 *ibid.*

3 *Plays*, p. 691.

4 *v.* Chapter 2, note 29.

5 *Cf.* (for instance) MacKenna, III, 41.

6 *The Ten Principal Upanishads*, p. 119.

7 'Vacillation', *C.P.*, p. 285.

8 *A Vision*, B, p. 211.

9 *Plays*, p. 649.

10 Taylor, *Select Works Of Plotinus*, p. lxxiii. MacKenna's version (IV, 77) is less easy to condense.

11 *C.P.*, p. 329.

12 *C.P.*, p. 328.

13 *Cf.* MacKenna IV, 80 ff.

14 Yeats's original source for his knowledge of this tablet was perhaps Blavatsky, *Isis Unveiled*, I, 35.

15 Taylor, *Select Works Of Plotinus*, p. 51.

16 'Old Tom Again', *C.P.*, p. 306.

17 'The Dancer At Cruachan And Cro-Patrick', *C.P.*, p. 304.

18 *C.P.*, pp. 327 ff. *Cf.* especially pp. 328, 330.

19 *v.* 'The Alternative Song', *Plays*, p. 641.

20 *C.P.*, p. 397.

21 *1930 Diary*, p. 18.

22 Plato, *Sophist*, 242 D,E.

23 For a directer statement of this theory, *v.* 'Rosa Alchemica', in *The Secret Rose* (1897); pp. 234–5.

24 *ibid.*, p. 245.

25 *v. C.P.*, pp. 397–8.

26 *v.* Plutarch, *Morals* IV, 14; and my essay on 'Cuchulain Comforted'.

27 The original myths on which Yeats based *The Only Jealousy Of Emer* (*Plays*, p. 279) and *The Green Helmet* (*Plays*, p. 221) may be found in Lady Gregory's *Cuchulain Of Muirthemne* (ch. IV, V, XIV).

28 *Cf.* 'The Morrigu appears to have a special interest in Cuchullin', Hull, *The Cuchullin Saga*, p. 102; and p. 105 (note).

29 *ibid.*, p. 105.

30 For title *v.* note 28. *Cf.* also the short note on Yeats's sources in Bjersby, p. 52.

31 Hull, *op. cit.*, p. 239.

32 *ibid.*, p. 240.

33 *ibid.*, p. 242.

34 *ibid.*, p. 243.

35 *ibid.*, p. 254.

36 *ibid.*, p. 263.

37 *ibid.*, p. 260.

38 *ibid.*

39 *ibid.*, p. 248.

40 *ibid.*

41 I learned this in conversation with Miss H. Ishibashi, the Japanese Yeats critic.

42 *C.P.*, p. 382.

43 Quoted in *C.O.A.*, p. 152.

44 *Cf.*, for instance, Yeats's discussion of the street song (*O.T.B.*, pp. 35–6); the poem 'Colonel Martin'; and Henn, p. 310.

45 In her thesis *W. B. Yeats And The Noh* (*v.* Bibliography). I cannot give pagination.

46 *ibid.*

47 *W & B*, p. 102.

48 *A Vision*, B, p. 263.

49 *W & B*, p. 103.

50 *v. W & B*, p. 103.

51 *Essays*, 31–6, p. 86.

52 Quoted from *W. B. Yeats And The Noh*.

53 Blake, 'The Everlasting Gospel'; text from Yeats's *Poems Of William Blake*, p. 118.

54 Blake, *Jerusalem*, 61.

55 *ibid.*, 57.

56 *The Adoration Of The Magi* (1904 edition), p. 52.

57 *The Secret Rose* (1897), p. 162.

58 *ibid.*

59 *Plays*, p. 385.

60 In 'Crazy Jane Reproved', *C.P.*, p. 291.

61 *v.*, for instance, Jung, *Psychology And Alchemy*, pp. 415 ff.

62 *Plays*, p. 325 (*v.* especially p. 337).

63 Regardie, *The Golden Dawn*, II, p. 118.

64 *Plays*, p. 679.

65 Quaritch *Blake*, I, pp. 292 ff., 302–4.

66 *ibid.*, p. 304.

[67] *The Adoration Of The Magi*, p. 52.

[68] *Cf.* Eugenie Strong, *Apotheosis And After-Life*, p. 215.

[69] Mead, *Thrice Greatest Hermes*, III, 161.

[70] There is, I believe, an anecdote in the *Journées* of a lover who writes letters to his mistress against another woman's back, and Yeats may perhaps have built upon it. His attitude towards de Sade will have been no more hostile than that of Blake, and in editing Blake he may well have glanced at de Sade's prose Mrs. Yeats confirms that this is likely.

[71] *Cf.* Melchiori 'Leda And The Swan', p. 167.

[72] I think, for instance, that he would have emended the irregular seventeenth line.

[73] *Plays*, pp. 295-6.

[74] *Cf.* Mead, *Thrice Greatest Hermes*, II, 97.

[75] *ibid.*

[76] *W & B*, p. 79.

[77] *O.T.B.*, p. 22.

[78] *Cf. O.T.B.*, pp. 16 ff.

[79] *C.P.*, p. 392.

[80] Hull, *op. cit.*, p. 239.

[81] *ibid.*, p. 243.

CHAPTER SIX

[1] I have already given authorities for all these symbols except those of cave and tomb. For the cave, *v.* Plato, *Republic*, 514. For the tomb—a symbol not used in the strict Platonic sense by Yeats—*v.* Taylor, *A Dissertation*, pp. 7-8.

[2] *C.P.*, p. 159.

[3] I imagine there may be some slight structural influence from Theocritus, whom Yeats had read.

[4] Quoted by Yeats in *Autos.* (1955 edition), p. 545.

[5] Taylor, *A Dissertation*, p. 138.

[6] *ibid.*

[7] Plato, *Statesman*, 270.

[8] Quoted from Thomas Taylor's *Plato*, IV, p. 123.

[9] *ibid.*

[10] Given in Taylor's *Plato*, IV, p. 120.

[11] '*Prometheus Unbound*', II, *v.* 99.

[12] *Essays* 31-6, pp. 55 ff.

[13] *V. and B.*, II, p. 303.

[14] Yeats later remembered this and quotes correctly in *Letters To Sturge Moore*, p. 114.

[15] *W & B*, p. 34.

[16] Quoted from Proclus' commentary; Taylor, *Plato*, IV, p. 120.

[17] *V. And B.*, II, p. 303.

[18] *ibid.*, p. 310.

19 'Under Ben Bulben', *C.P.*, p. 400.

20 Taylor, *Plato*, IV, p. 123.

21 Wade, *Letters*, p. 710. 'Chosen' is clearly the poem referred to.

22 Verse 2. Yeats of course admired Donne's poem, but that he wrote 'Chosen' in an opposite frame of mind we see from the end of his letter to Grierson (Wade, p. 711).

23 *C.P.*, p. 311.

24 At about the time he wrote 'Chosen', Yeats was reading MacKenna's *Plotinus*. The introduction to *The Tibetan Book Of The Dead*, which he was also reading, returned him to Plato's myth of Er, for Jowett's translation is quoted at length. 'His Bargain', in the same volume as 'Chosen', is founded on the myth.

25 *I.G.E.*, p. 159.

26 'His Bargain', *C.P.*, p. 299.

27 Plato, *Republic*, X, 619 (Jowett's translation). *v.* also Plotinus' commentary: MacKenna, II, p. 173.

28 *v. C.P.*, p. 270; *Letters To Sturge Moore*, p. 94.

29 MacKenna, *Plotinus*, II, p. 157.

30 *ibid.*

31 *v.* the translation in F. M. Cornford's *Plato And Parmenides* (1939).

32 *v. C.P.*, p. 519.

33 *C.P.*, p. 243.

34 Plato, *Symposium*, 190.

35 *C.P.*, p. 536 (note).

36 *v.* Chapter 2, note 33.

37 Taylor, *Porphyry*, p. 187.

38 *ibid.*

39 All the detail in this paragraph is taken from the source in Porphyry cited (pp. 186-93).

40 *C.P.*, p. 306.

41 W. Y. Tindall, in '*The Symbolism Of W. B. Yeats*; reprinted from *Accent* in *The Permanence Of Yeats*, p. 276.

42 In Taylor, *Porphyry*, p. 171.

43 *v. I.G.E.*, pp. 83-8; *A Vision*, A, p. 202.

44 Homer, *Odyssey*, XIII; for Homer's cave, *v.* XII, 92 *et seq.*

45 *v.* Taylor, *Porphyry*, pp. 241 ff.

46 *ibid.*, p. 183.

47 *ibid.*, p. 185; quoted in *I.G.E.*, p. 85.

48 *C.P.*, p. 535 (note).

49 *C.P.*, p. 230.

50 'Old Tom Again', *C.P.*, p. 306.

51 'Swift's Epitaph', *C.P.*, p. 277.

52 'Sailing To Byzantium', *C.P.*, p. 217.

53 In MacKenna, *Plotinus*, I, p. 22.

54 *A Collection Of Several Philosophical Writings Of Henry More* (1662), p. 181.

55 MacKenna, *op. cit.*, I, 24.

56 *ibid.*, p. 23.

57 *ibid.* But I use Taylor's wording of the translation.

58 More, *op. cit.*, p. 181.

59 MacKenna, I, p. 51.

60 'Crazy Jane On The Day Of Judgement', *C.P.*, p. 291.

61 W. E Houghton: 'Yeats And Crazy Jane'; reprinted from *Modern Philology* in *The Permanence Of Yeats*, p. 381.

62 *W & B*, p. 73.

63 MacKenna, I, p. 23.

64 Plato, *Gorgias*, 524.

65 For this point *v.* Ellmann, *The Identity Of Yeats*, p. 281; and *A Vision*, B, p. 203.

66 *C.P.*, p. 376.

67 *I.G.E.*, pp. 83-8.

68 *ibid.*, p. 67.

69 The explanation lies at the heart of 'The Philosophy Of Shelley's Poetry', in *I.G.E.*

70 *Letters To D.W.*, p. 173.

71 In Yeats's *A Book Of Irish Verse*, p. 6. 'Patrick Sheehan' is on p. 176; the 'Lament' on p. 242.

72 *W & B*, pp. 101-2.

73 In *O.T.B.*, p. 24.

74 Dante, 'Inferno', IV, 26.

75 *C.P.*, p. 49.

76 The wind moving upon the face of the waters is a Kabbalistic symbol for the heavenly union. *Cf. I.G.E.*, p. 166.

77 More, *op. cit.*, p. 184.

78 Mathers, *Kabbalah Unveiled*, p. 116. Myer, *Qabbalah*, p. 107.

79 In 'The Secret Rose', *C.P.*, p. 77.

80 *v.* A. H. Armstrong, *Plotinus*, p. 15; *cf.* MacKenna, I, p. 2.

81 *v.* *Plays*, p. 141, 'the white of leprosy'. *Cf.* 'The Ancient Mariner'.

82 *v.* *Plays*, p. 416; *C.P.*, p. 300.

83 *Letters to Sturge Moore*, p. 165.

84 *C.P.*, p. 281.

85 Yeats will have known the theosophical publication *Koré Kosmou* (1885) where the dolphin is discussed at p. 14.

86 Eugenie Strong, *Apotheosis And After-Life*, p. 215.

87 *v.* More, *op. cit.*, p. 125; quoted by Yeats in *P.A.S.L.*, p. 51.

88 *v.* Henn, pp. 235-6.

89 Taylor, *Porphyry*, p. 172.

90 Regardie, *The Golden Dawn*, II, 183.

91 Shelley, *The Witch Of Atlas*, IX.

92 Taylor, *Porphyry*, p. 178.

93 *C.P.*, p. 396.

94 Fragment 80 (my own translation). *Cf.* G. S. Kirk, *Heraclitus: The Cosmic Fragments*, p. 238.

95 *Cf.* Fragments 17, 35; p. 70 of W. E. Leonard's *The Fragments Of Empedocles*; and *A Vision*, B, p. 67.

96 MacKenna, II, pp. 16, 22, 28; 'all is war without rest, or truce.' *Cf.* the *Gita*. When Kathleen Raine's essay 'Luvah' is published, the archetypal nature of this battle-symbolism will be confirmed.

97 Taylor, *Five Books Of Plotinus*, p. 106. This passage, I learn from Kathleen Raine, is a probable source of Blake's own tower-symbolism.

98 *C.P.*, p. 270.

99 *The Fragments Of Empedocles*, trans. W. E. Leonard, p. 28.

100 *W & B*, p. 106.

101 *ibid.*, p. 101.

102 *ibid.*, p. 109.

103 *C.P.*, p. 359.

104 *v.* Plato, *Statesman*, 275.

105 *v.*, for instance, Tibullus, *Carmina*, I, iii, 35.

106 *Letters To D.W.*, p. 126.

107 *ibid.*

108 Jeffares, p. 297.

109 Shelley, *Laon And Cythna*, IV, 1.

110 *Secret Symbols Of The Rosicrucians* (1939 translation), p. 48.

111 In the preface he wrote to Finberg's translation of *Axel*, p. 7.

112 Yeats's last few poems mark the beginning of a new, meditative phase in his art (Wade, p. 921). He gave up, as far as possible, intellectual excogitation (Wade, p. 921) and the subject matter of his last poems was 'given' rather than sought for (Wade, p. 922). While we have little direct evidence as to how 'The Black Tower' was composed, one imagines the process to have been similar to that by which Yeats wrote the 'visionary' 'Cuchulain Comforted', for which *v.* Henn, p. 321.

113 *Cf.*, for instance, Ferguson, *Congal* (2nd edition), p. 140 (note).

114 *The Adoration Of The Magi*, p. 52.

115 *C.P.*, p. 78.

116 *C.P.*, p. 237.

117 Revelation, vii, 1; Daniel, vii, 2; Ezekiel, xiii, 11.

118 *C.P.*, p. 524 (note).

119 'Into The Twilight', *C.P.*, p. 66.

120 *Morte d'Arthur*, Book VII.

121 *C.P.*, p. 167.

CHAPTER SEVEN

1 *C.P.*, p. 280.

2 *C.P.*, p. 537 (note).

3 *C.P.*, p. 217.

4 *Letters To Sturge Moore*, p. 164.

[5] Quoted from an unpublished draft.

[6] For Yeats's comment on this symbol, *v. P.A.S.L.*, p. 85.

[7] *Essays*, 1931–6, p. 80.

[8] *Letters To Sturge Moore*, p. 164.

[9] 'The Four Ages Of Man', *C.P.*, p. 332.

[10] 'Ribh Considers Christian Love Insufficient', *C.P.*, p. 330.

[11] As such it is a traditional Celtic symbol. *v.* p. 84 above.

[12] Quoted from 'Her Dream', *C.P.*, p. 229.

[13] *Plays*, p. 565.

[14] *C.P.*, p. 265.

[15] *Cf.* Campbell, *The Mysteries*, p. 27. Yeats may or may not have known the text in Apollodorus cited.

[16] *C.P.*, p. 300.

[17] *W & B*, pp. 33–4.

[18] *The Ascent Of Mount Carmel* (trans. D. Lewis), pp. 94–7. Quoted in *The Mystical Element Of Religion*, II, 343.

[19] *v.* Chapter 2, note 29. The symbolism may be self-evident, but it is perfectly obvious that Yeats knew it to be traditional when he used it.

[20] Regardie, *The Golden Dawn*, IV, 17.

[21] *A Vision*, A, p. 252.

[22] Myer, *The Oldest Books In The World*, pp. 271–2.

[23] *W & B*, pp. 34–5. 'If spirits seem to stand before the bodily eyes . . . they are not present but their messengers.' *Cf. A Vision*, A, pp. 244–9.

[24] *The Witch Of Atlas*, LXX.

[25] Blake, *Jerusalem*, 77.

[26] *C.P.*, p. 256.

[27] *A Vision*, B, p. 232.

[28] Myer, *The Oldest Books In The World*, pp. 139, 275.

[29] *Cf.* the drift of *W & B*, pp. 34–5.

[30] *v.* Taylor, *A Dissertation* (p. 7), Yeats's source.

[31] *I.G.E.*, p. 40.

[32] He does so in the context referred to (*I.G.E.*, p. 40).

[33] Mathers, *Kabbalah Unveiled*, p. 104 (condensed).

[34] Regardie, *The Golden Dawn*, II, p. 135.

[35] *Cf. I.G.E.*, p. 94.

[36] *Cf.* especially *C.P.*, pp. 249, 250.

[37] *C.P.*, p. 273.

[38] *C.P.*, p. 265.

[39] Yeats relates the symbol to Dante in *V. And B.*, II, p. 338.

[40] Blake, *Jerusalem*, 91.

[41] *A Vision*, B., p. 232.

[42] MacKenna, II, pp. 67–8 (prefaced by a few words from I, p. 122). Yeats founded himself upon this passage in his long argument with Sturge Moore: *Letters To Sturge Moore*, pp. 92 ff.

[43] Dante, 'Purgatorio', Canto XXVI, 148.

[44] Quoted from Eliot, 'Little Gidding', II. Eliot is glossing the passage in Dante I have referred to.

[45] Trans. M. C. Stopes, *op. cit.*, p. 35.

[46] *V. And B.*, II, p. 334.

[47] In the Quaritch *Blake*, I, p. 254.

[48] *V. And B.*, II, p. 331. *Cf.* pp. 305–6.

[49] Kathleen Raine suggests that he is more precisely the Demiurge—the meaning of the Emperor card in the traditional Tarot symbolism. The Catalogue of the Reading University Yeats Exhibition (1957, pp. 26 ff.) gives details of the symbolic function of the Byzantine Emperor himself which would seem to support this interpretation. But I shall take up the issue in my next book.

One might add that the Reading Catalogue—though acknowledgement is made to myself—gives valuable additional material from which this essay may be supplemented.

[50] *Cf.* 'Ribh Denounces Patrick', *C.P.*, p. 328.

CHAPTER EIGHT

[1] *C.P.*, p. 395.

[2] Wade, *Letters*, p. 922.

[3] *Letters To D.W.*, pp. 212–13.

[4] Quoted by Yeats in the Quaritch *Blake*, I, p. 239.

[5] Plutarch, *Morals*, IV, 14.

[6] *ibid.*, II, 413.

[7] *ibid.*, II, 404.

[8] *P.A.S.L.*, p. 29.

[9] *C.P.*, p. 393.

[10] Koch, p. 100. She does not use the word 'daemon' but states that the dialogue is between man and his opposite or anti-self, which, if Yeats's theory is known, means precisely this. Shelley, as Oliver Edwards points out to me, also uses the traditional symbol of the 'echo' for the 'phantom' (in 'Epipsychidion').

[11] *Letters To D.W.*, p. 213.

[12] Dante, 'Purgatorio', VII, 68.

[13] Eliot, 'The Waste Land', lines 215 ff.

[14] Dante, 'Purgatorio', VIII, 13.

[15] Myer, *The Oldest Books In The World*, p. 271.

[16] *A Vision*, B, p. 233.

[17] 'A Needle's Eye', *C.P.*, p. 333.

[18] 'Veronica's Napkin', *C.P.*, p. 270.

[19] Hone, p. 327.

[20] Blake, *Milton*, 28.

[21] *A Vision*, B, p. 224.

[22] *A Vision*, B, p. 232. Yeats's adoption of the 'shroud' to symbolise the

'divine cloak' is a usage which a more purely Platonic poet, Shelley for instance, would not have permitted himself. The Egyptian mummy-symbolism did not persist; there was divergence in the tradition; and graveclothes, for Plato, symbolise the mortal body, in the tomb of the world. In 'Cuchulain Comforted', however, the 'shrouds' are explicitly 'the dead'.

23 *A Vision*, B, p. 232.

24 'The life there is wisdom' (Plotinus). *v.* p. 163 above.

25 'The Defence of Guinevere', verses 1–2.

26 *ibid.*, verses 6–14.

27 *C.P.*, p. 71.

28 *v.* 'The Happiest Of The Poets', in *I.G.E.*, p. 50.

BIBLIOGRAPHY

The following are the works to which I have referred. Any abbreviations I may have used are given in parentheses.

(a) Texts.

Collected Poems Of W. B. Yeats (C.P.). London, 1950.

Collected Plays Of W. B. Yeats (Plays). London, 1952.

Autobiographies (Autos). London, 1926.

The Celtic Twilight (T.C.T.). London, 1912.

The Cutting Of An Agate (C.O.A.). London, 1919.

Essays, 1931 to 1936 (Essays 31–6). Cuala Press, Dublin, 1937.

A Full Moon In March. London, 1935.

Ideas Of Good And Evil (I.G.E.). London, 1914 edition.

If I Were Four-and-twenty. Cuala Press, Dublin, 1940.

The King Of The Great Clock Tower (K.O.G.C.T.). Cuala Press, Dublin, 1934.

Letters, ed. Allan Wade. London, 1954.

Letters On Poetry To Dorothy Wellesley (Letters to D.W.). London, 1940.

Letters To The New Island. Cambridge, Mass., 1934.

On The Boiler (O.T.B.). Cuala Press, Dublin, 1939.

Pages From A Diary Written In 1930 (1930 Diary). Cuala Press, Dublin, 1944.

Per Amica Silentia Lunae (P.A.S.L.). London, 1918.

Plays And Controversies (P. and C.). London, 1923.

Plays For An Irish Theatre. London, 1911.

The Secret Rose. London, 1897 edition.

The Tables Of The Law and The Adoration Of The Magi. London, 1905.

A Vision, first edition (*A Vision,* A). London, 1925.

A Vision, revised and amplified edition (*A Vision,* B). London, 1937.

The Wanderings Of Oisin. London, 1892.

Wheels And Butterflies (W & B). London, 1934.

Where There Is Nothing. London, 1903.

The Wind Among The Reeds. London, 1900.

W. B. Yeats And T. Sturge Moore: Their Correspondence (Letters To Sturge Moore). London, 1953.

(b) Works edited, translated or introduced by Yeats.

The Poems Of William Blake, edited by W. B. Yeats. London, 1893.

Blake. Works. Edited by E. J. Ellis and W. B. Yeats, 3 volumes (Quaritch *Blake*). London, 1893.

Irish Fairy And Folk Tales, edited by W. B. Yeats. London, 1893.

A Book Of Irish Verse, selected by W. B. Yeats. London, 1895.

Gitanjali, by Rabindranath Tagore; Introd. by W. B. Yeats. London, 1913.

Axel, trans. by H. P. R. Finberg; Preface by W. B. Yeats. London, 1925.

An Indian Monk by Purohit Swami; Introd. by W. B. Yeats. London, 1932.

The Ten Principal Upanishads, trans. Shree Purohit Swami and W. B. Yeats. London, 1937.

The Aphorisms Of Patanjali. Introduction by W. B. Yeats. London, 1938.

Selections From The Poems Of Dorothy Wellesley; Introduction by W. B. Yeats. London, 1936.

Visions And Beliefs In The West Of Ireland, by Lady Gregory, 2 volumes (V. and B.), with essays by W. B. Yeats. London, 1920.

(*c*) Criticism, Biography, etc.

Adams, Hazard:	*Blake And Yeats: The Contrary Vision*; New York, 1955.
Bjersby, Birgit:	*The Cuchulain Legend In The Works Of W. B. Yeats*; Upsala, 1951.
Ellmann, Richard:	*Yeats: The Man And The Masks*; New York, 1948.
	The Identity Of Yeats; London, 1954.
Heath-Stubbs, John:	*The Darkling Plain*; London, 1950.
Henn, T. R.:	*The Lonely Tower*; London, 1950.
Hone, J. M.:	*W. B. Yeats*; London, 1942.
Hough, Graham:	*The Last Romantics*; London, 1949.
Jeffares, A. N.:	*W. B. Yeats, Man And Poet*; London, 1949.
Kermode, Frank:	*Romantic Image*; London, 1957.
Koch, Vivienne:	*W. B. Yeats: The Tragic Phase*; London, 1951.
MacNeice, Louis:	*The Poetry Of W. B. Yeats*; London, 1941.
Moore, Virginia:	*The Unicorn: William Butler Yeats' Search For Reality*; New York, 1954.
Parkinson, Thomas:	*W. B. Yeats: Self-Critic*; Calif., 1951.
Rudd, Margaret:	*Divided Image*; London, 1953.
Ure, Peter:	*Towards A Mythology*; London, 1946.

The Permanence Of Yeats, Selected Criticism, edited by James Hall and Martin Steinmann, New York, 1950.

(*d*) General.

d'Alviella, Count Goblet:	*The Migration Of Symbols*; London, 1894.
Armstrong, A. H.:	*Plotinus*; London, 1953.
Bayley, Harold:	*The Lost Language Of Symbolism*; London, 1912.
Blavatsky, H. P.:	*Isis Unveiled*; London, 1910.
	The Secret Doctrine; Point Loma, 1909.

Bodkin, Maud: *Archetypal Patterns In Poetry*; London, 1934.

Studies Of Type Images; London, 1951.

Campbell, Joseph: *The Hero With A Thousand Faces*; New York, 1949.

(editor):   *The Mysteries*; London, 1955.

Coomaraswami, Ananda: *The Mirror Of Gesture*; Cambridge, Mass., 1917.

Cornford, F. M.:   *Plato And Parmenides*; London, 1939.

Cudworth: *The True Intellectual System Of The Universe*; 1820 edition.

Daniels, May: *The French Drama Of The Unspoken*; Edinburgh, 1953.

David-Neel, Alexandra: *With Mystics And Magicians In Tibet*; London, 1931.

Dodds, E. R.:   *Proclus, The Elements Of Theology*; Oxford, 1933.

Evans Wentz, W. Y. (editor):   *The Tibetan Book Of The Dead*; Oxford, 1927.

Ferguson, Samuel: *Congal*; London, 1872.

Fitzgerald, A.:   *The Essays And Hymns Of Synesius*, 2 volumes; London, 1930.

Fränger, Wilhelm: *The Millennium Of Hieronymus Bosch*; London, 1942.

Gregory, Lady Augusta: *Cuchulain Of Muirthemne*; London, 1902.

Hearn, Lafcadio (translator):   *The Temptation Of St. Anthony*; London, 1911.

Von Hügel, Baron: *The Mystical Element Of Religion*; London, 1908.

Hull, Eleanor: *The Cuchullin Saga*; London, 1898.

Jowett, B.:   *The Translations Of Plato*, 5 volumes; 1892 edition.

The Works Of The Emperor Julian, 3 volumes, with a translation by W. C. Wright. London, 1913.

Jung, C. G.:   *Psychology And Alchemy* (trans. R. F. C. Hull); London, 1953.

The Interpretation Of Nature And The Psyche (trans. R. F. C. Hull); London, 1955.

Kirk, G. S. (editor):   *Heraclitus: The Cosmic Fragments*; Cambridge, 1954.

Koré Kosmou, trans. Anna Kingsford and Edward Maitland, Madras, 1885.

Leonard, W. E. (translator):   *The Fragments Of Empedocles*; Chicago, 1908.

Lewis, David (translator):   *The Ascent Of Mount Carmel*; London, 1889.

MacKenna, Stephen (translator):   *Plotinus*, 5 volumes. London, 1917–30.

Mathers, Macgregor: *Kabbalah Unveiled*; London, 1887.

Mead, G. R. S.:   *Thrice Greatest Hermes*; London, 1906.

More, Henry: *A Collection Of Several Philosophical Writings Of Dr. Henry More* (1662). *Theological Works* (1708).

Myer, Isaac: *The Oldest Books In The World*; London, 1900.
                                  Qabbalah; Philadelphia, 1888.

Nietzsche: *The Birth Of Tragedy*, trans. W. Haussmann; London, 1909.

O'Donovan, J. (translator):   *The Battle Of Magh Rath*; Dublin, 1842.

Palmer, Samuel: *Life And Letters*, edited by A. H. Palmer; London, 1892.

Patmore, Coventry: *Religio Poetae*; London, 1893.

Plutarch: *Morals*, translated by several hands, 5 volumes; London, 1870.

Pound, Ezra: *'No', or Accomplishment*; New York, 1917. *The Translations*; London, 1951.

Radhakrishnan, Sir S.:   *The Principal Upanishads*; London, 1953.

Regardie, Israel: *The History Of The Golden Dawn*; Chicago, 1936.

Rhys, Sir J.:   *Lectures On The Origin And Growth Of Religion As Illustrated By Celtic Heathendom*; London, 1888.

Rogers, Neville: *Shelley At Work*; Oxford, 1956.

Secret Symbols Of The Rosicrucians; London, 1939 translation.

Saurat, Denis: *Literature And Occult Tradition*; London, 1930.

Scholem, G. G.:   *Major Trends In Jewish Mysticism*; New York, 1946.

Stopes, M. C.:   *Plays Of Old Japan: The No*; London, 1912.

Strong, Eugenie: *Apotheosis And After-Life*; London, 1915.

Suzuki, D. T.:   *Introduction To Zen Buddhism*; London, 1949 edition.

Swedenborg: *Arcana Coelestia* (1857–60 translation); *Conjugal Love* (1841); *Heaven And Hell* (1860).

Symons, Arthur: *Collected Works*; London, 1924.

Taylor, Thomas: *A Dissertation*; Amsterdam, 1790. *Iamblichus: Life Of Pythagoras*; London, 1926 edition.

	Iamblichus: On The Mysteries; London, 1895 edition.
	The Mystical Hymns Of Orpheus; London, 1896 edition.
	Plato, 5 volumes; London, 1804.
	Five Books Of Plotinus; London, 1794.
	Select Works Of Plotinus (with Synesius, 'On Providence'); London, 1895 edition.
	Porphyrius: Select Works; London, 1823.
	Proclus, 2 volumes; London, 1816.
Tertullian:	*Works* (in English translation), 3 volumes; Edinburgh, 1869–95.
Toksvig, Signe:	*Emanuel Swedenborg*; London, 1949.
Valentin, Antonina:	*Leonardo da Vinci*; London, 1939.
Waley, Arthur:	*The Nō Plays Of Japan*; London, 1921.

(*e*) Theses.

H. Bachchan:	*W. B. Yeats And Occultism* (Cambridge, 1953).
Marilyn Denton:	*The Versification Of W. B. Yeats* (University Of Wisconsin, 1957).
Hiro Ishibashi:	*W. B. Yeats And The Noh* (Keio University, Japan, 1956).

(*f*) Articles, etc.

Carl Benson, 'Yeats and Balzac's *Louis Lambert*', *Modern Philology*, 49.
Giorgio Melchiori, 'Leda And The Swan', in *English Miscellany* 7, Rome, 1956.
Arthur Symons, 'The Cult Of Dionysus', in *The Academy*, 30th August, 1902.
The Catalogue Of The Reading University Yeats Exhibition (1957).

INDEX